Creative Cross Stitch

Creative Cross Stitch

Trafalgar Square Publishing
NORTH POMFRET, VERMONT

Contents

6 **Introduction**

PART I
CROSS STITCH FOR THE HOME

10 **Going Greek** Greek key napkin rings

12 **Turkish delight** Napkin motif

14 **Modern mosaic** Set of table mats

16 **Shades of lavender** Floral tablecloth

20 **Scandinavian tulips** Table runner

22 **Traditional prettiness** Flowered guest towel

24 **Bold and bright** Vivid cushion covers

PART II
GIFT IDEAS

28 **Bright comforter** Embroidered baby quilt

30 **Welcome to the world** Baby greeting card

34 **Sun flowers** Blossoms for a sundress

36 **Flying high** Kite motif

38 **3D dazzler** Cross stitch mobile

42 **Colonial Charmer** Sampler

44 **Designing a sampler**

48 **For quiet times** Bookmark and spectacles case

50 **Easy as ABC** Useful alphabets

54 **Under glass** Paperweight

56 **Shy violets** Dress pocket motif

58 **Luxurious lingerie** Embroidered lingerie

First published in the
United States of America in 1994 by
Trafalgar Square Publishing,
North Pomfret, Vermont 05053

First published in Great Britain in 1994
by Anaya Publishers Ltd, Strode House,
44–50 Osnaburgh Street, London NW1 3ND

With thanks to Gail Lawther, Julia Jones and Barbara Deer for providing the designs in this book. The designs on the front cover are by Melinda Coss, taken from *Floral Cross Stitch*, also published by Trafalgar Square Publishing.

ISBN 1-57076-007-1

Library of Congress Catalog Card Number:
94-60192

Printed in Hong Kong

60 **Oriental splendour** Fan-shaped clutch purse

64 **Midnight blues** Cat card

66 **Cat picture**

68 **Happy ever after** Wedding photo frame

72 **Glittering beauty** Trinket box

74 **Baubles, bangles and beads** Cross stitched jewellery

76 **Plains Indian belt** Fashion belt

PART III
SPECIAL OCCASIONS

80 **Deck the tree** Christmas tree ornaments

82 **Presents galore** Tree cloth

84 **Seasonal design** Buffet cloth

86 **Season's greetings** Christmas cards

PART IV
CROSS STITCH PICTURES

92 **Country fruits**

94 **Tiger lilies**

96 **Sweet violets**

98 **A sprig of roses**

100 **A pot of geraniums**

102 **Strawberry circlet**

104 **Summer nosegay**

106 **Blue vase**

110 **Butterfly and flowers**

112 **March hare**

114 **Parrot**

116 **A flock of birds**

120 **Bear with balloons**

123 **Tiger bright**

126 **Tabby cat**

128 **Summer's bounty**

PART V
ROMANTIC KEEPSAKES

134 **Valentine hearts**

138 **Two hearts as one**

140 **Hearts and roses**

142 **Loving thoughts**

PART VI
SAMPLERS AND GREETINGS

146 **Alphabet sampler**

150 **Decorative borders**

152 **Horseshoes and roses**

155 **Christmas sampler**

158 **Christmas cards**

160 **Welcome to baby**

162 **Gardener's sampler**

164 **Home, sweet home**

166 **Greetings for a special friend**

168 **Clown picture**

170 **Motif medley**

174 **Better embroidery**

190 **Useful addresses**

191 **Threads and yarns conversion chart**

Introduction

The revival of cross stitch combines an ancient embroidery technique with modern fabrics and threads, producing items that are practical enough for everyday use but pretty enough to become heirlooms.

Cross stitching was probably the first effective method of lacing animal skins together to make body coverings and sleeping covers. Gradually, with the development of hand-woven fabrics, cross stitch evolved into a stitch which was decorative as well as functional.

No-one knows exactly where cross stitch originated. The Crusaders brought embroidered textiles back to the west after the Crusades and cross stitch would have been on the textiles. Embroidery craftsmen worked the trade routes across the middle east and Europe, taking the skills wherever they settled and this must have helped to familiarize westerners with eastern embroidery stitches.

However, if you spend a little time studying international embroidery designs you will be fascinated to see similar cross stitch motifs occurring in embroideries of countries as far apart as Mexico and Greece, Hungary and Thailand.

In sixteenth-century Europe, all forms of embroidery, including cross stitch, were exceedingly popular. Embroidery was worked for pleasure by ladies and noblewomen of the royal courts. Professional designers travelled the country, making patterns for use on bed-hangings, linens, clothing and accessories for adornment.

Skill with a needle was also considered to be of prime importance in the education of young girls and, together with music and painting, was a great asset for a prospective wife.

Origins of samplers

The samplers of this time, worked on linen cloth, were very charming in design although sometimes naive in concept. Early examples were known as 'random' or 'spot' samplers and designs were scattered over the fabric with no attempt at symmetry. Some of these strips of fabric, covered with motifs and blocks of stitches, are up to 24in (60cm) long.

By the 17th century, the random method of working samplers had disappeared, replaced by designs of alphabets and numbers, flowers and figures.

The sampler as we know it today came into being in the 18th century, with cross stitch as the predominant stitch. It continued in popularity until, by the 19th century, rows of numbers and alphabets began to be replaced by religious and uplifting texts.

Luckily, today's needleworkers are able to enjoy cross stitch – and making samplers – as a relaxing and highly enjoyable leisure occupation.

Quick to learn

Cross stitch is extremely easy to do and most people, men and women and children too, usually master it in about an hour. It is possible for someone who has never before worked an embroidery stitch to produce a piece of cross stitching that looks as good as that produced by an expert. Because it is so easy, and so relaxing to do, cross stitch is now becoming the most popular needlecraft in the western world. Most people begin with a small motif or a picture that they can complete in one evening. Later, they go on to work bigger pieces.

Something for everyone

This book has something for everyone to enjoy, not just experienced needleworkers but also those thousands of people who would love to do embroidery if only they knew how. If you are one of these then this is where you start doing probably the most fascinating and absorbing needlecraft in the world, with projects so simple they can be finished in an evening. More experienced needleworkers will find this compendium rich in patterns and projects and will also discover a useful source of tips and techniques to help them to develop their creativity.

In the section Cross Stitch for the Home you will find designs for making attractive furnishings and accessories, such as table linens, towels, runners and cushions. These are complemented by a collection of cross stitched samplers for every occasion, together with a library of useful alphabets and motifs.

Gifts and Greetings

Gift Ideas has designs for children and babies – a simple bedcover, a nursery mobile and motifs for decorating playclothes. And, if you are looking for other gift ideas, there is a simple bookmark, a charming needlecase, a smart wool-embroidered purse and a trinket box. For an engagement or wedding gift, a beribboned photo frame will be treasured for ever. And why not complete the gift with an embroidered card? Cross-stitched greeting cards are fun to do and there is a good choice of designs here including a selection for the Christmas holiday season.

Finally, in Better Embroidery, you'll find some of the secrets for working successful embroidery to help you to achieve perfect stitchery every time.

Happy cross stitching!

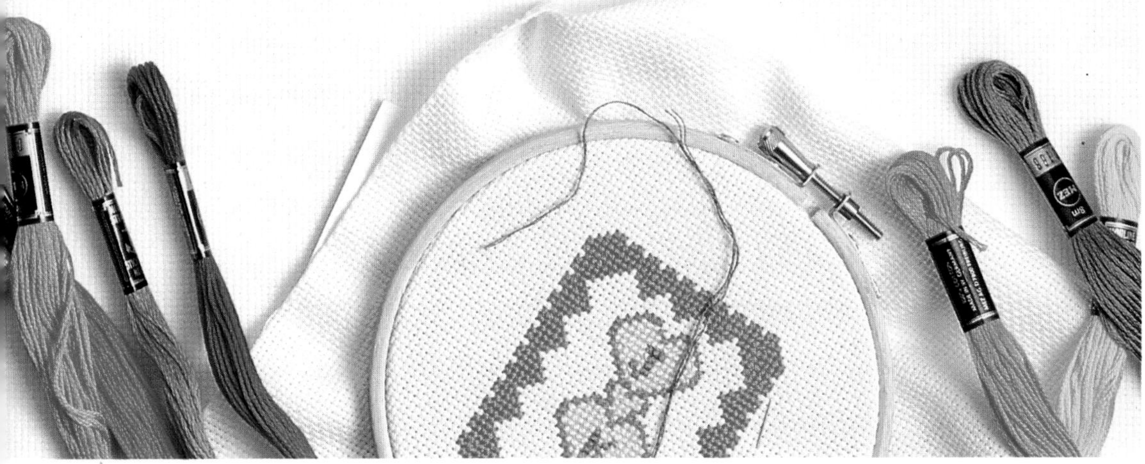

Cross Stitch for the Home

Going Greek

The ancient Greek key pattern, sometimes called the Meander Pattern, is used for these smart napkin rings. They could be worked to tone with the table mats on page 14, or embroider the rings in different colour schemes for each member of the family.

Materials (for six rings)
Six pieces of cream Aida cloth 8×3in (20×7.5cm), 11 threads to 1in (2.5cm)
DMC stranded cottons as follows: five skeins of 727 pale yellow, six skeins of 742 dark yellow, two skeins of 740 pale orange, two skeins of 606 dark orange
Cardboard tube 1$\frac{1}{2}$in (37mm) diameter (or stiff card and sticky tape; see this page)
Clear adhesive
Yellow fabric (or paper) for lining.

Preparation
1 Measure and mark the middle of the fabric both vertically and horizontally with basting stitches.

Working the embroidery
2 The centre of the chart for the Greek key pattern is indicated by arrows at the edges and these coincide with your basted stitches. Following the chart and the key, begin embroidery in the middle of the design, using 4 strands of thread together. Work the area shown on the chart.

Finishing
3 Press the finished embroidery on the wrong side lightly. Measure to check that the embroidery is square. If it has distorted in working, lightly spray the wrong side of the embroidery with water, gently pull into shape, pin down at corners and leave to dry. Trim excess fabric back to within $\frac{1}{2}$in (1cm) of the embroidery.

Making the napkin rings
4 Using a sharp crafts knife, cut rings from the cardboard tube, 1$\frac{1}{2}$in (37mm) thick.

5 Spread glue thinly on the back of the embroidery. Smooth the fabric onto the cardboard ring, overlapping the short ends and glueing down. Fold and glue the long edges of the fabric to the inside of the ring.

6 Cut strips of yellow fabric (or paper) to line the ring. Spread glue thinly on the back and press to the inside of the ring. Leave to dry. Make five more rings in the same way.

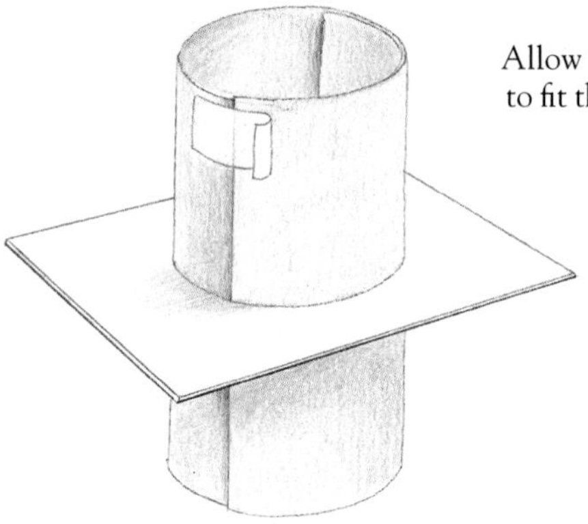

Allow tube to open to fit the hole, tape

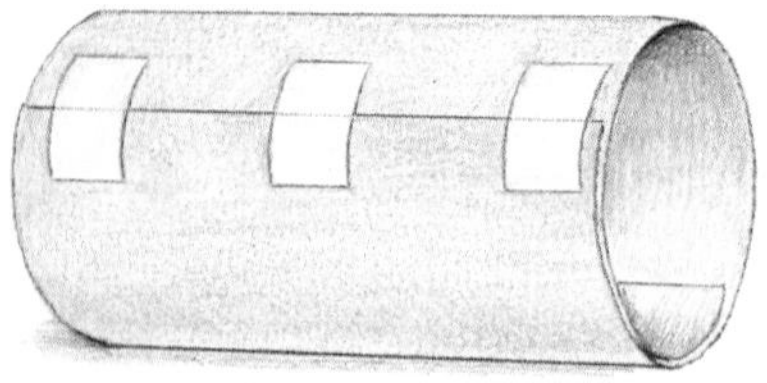

Tape the tube, cut as required

Making cardboard rings
Using a pair of compasses, draw a 1$\frac{1}{2}$in (37mm) diameter circle on thin, stiff card. Cut another piece of card 4$\frac{1}{2}$in (11cm) long by 1$\frac{1}{2}$in (37mm). Roll up, insert in the hole, allow to open. Tape the join and remove. Cut rings as required.

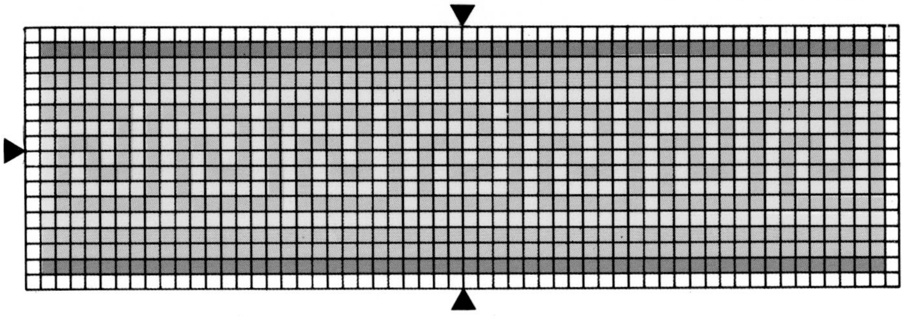

KEY
- 727
- 742
- 740
- 606

Turkish delight

Go for the classical look with these table napkins, embroidered with a traditional motif taken from Turkish rugs. To complete the classical effect, team them with the Greek key napkin rings (page 10) and the Roman mosaic table mats (page 14), using toning colours – or work them in a different scheme to match your dinner service.

Materials
Six linen napkins
DMC stranded cottons as follows: one skein of 400 brown, two skeins of 666 red
Bronze metallic thread.

Preparation
1 First, check the weave of the napkin in both directions. Some linen fabrics have more threads in one direction than the other; lay a ruler horizontally over the threads and count how many there are to an inch (or centimetre), then lay the ruler the other way and count how many threads there are in the other direction.

2 If the napkins have more threads in one direction than the other, work with the tightly-spaced threads running horizontally; this will mean that the design will come out square, as in the picture. If your napkins have the same number of threads to the inch (or centimetre) in both directions, the design will come out rectangular, as in the chart.

Working the embroidery
3 Using three strands of red thread together, begin working the design 1$\frac{1}{2}$in (37mm) in from the right and bottom edges of the napkin.

4 Using three strands of metallic thread together, work the bronze border inside the red border. Complete the motif, using three strands of red and three strands of brown thread.

KEY
■ 666
■ 400
■ Bronze metallic

5 Embroider the remaining five napkins in the same way. (If you prefer to make your own napkins, use a coloured, evenweave embroidery linen and finish the edges as for the mats on page 14).

Finishing
6 Use a cool iron to press the embroidery on the wrong side. Place a piece of tissue paper between embroidery and iron. Take care not to use an iron that is too hot or the metallic threads may melt.

> If you find it difficult to buy the metallic thread, substitute DMC shade 921 instead; you will need one skein.

Modern mosaic

Shaded Roman mosaic patterns provided the inspiration for this simple repeat design; work it on a set of table mats and, if you're feeling inspired, you could repeat it round the hem of a matching tablecloth.

Materials (for six mats)
Six pieces of orange hessian 21 × 15in (53 × 38cm), 16 threads to 1in (2.5cm)
Orange sewing thread
DMC tapisserie wools as follows: two skeins each of 7740 pale orange, 7947 mid-orange, 7606 dark orange, 7106 light red, 7849 rich red.

Preparation
1 Work a line of narrow machine zigzag stitches $1\frac{1}{2}$in (37mm) from the edges on the pieces of hessian.

Working the embroidery
2 Following the chart and starting at A, begin working the pattern over two threads of the fabric, $1\frac{1}{2}$in (37mm) up from the bottom edge of the fabric and 2in (5cm) in from the left-hand edge.

3 Fit in as many complete repeats of the pattern (A–B) as you can, to within $1\frac{1}{2}$in (37mm) of the top edge (19 or 20 repeats).

4 Work the embroidery on the remaining mats in the same way.

5 Press the embroidered mats on the wrong side using a warm iron, making sure that vertical and horizontal threads are running square.

Finishing
6 Fringe the mats by snipping into the fabric edges, at 1in (2.5cm) intervals, almost up to the stitching line. Pull out threads. For a different finish turn under a single hem and stitch with wide zigzag of machine-stitching, using matching or contrasting thread. Alternatively, bind the edges with orange bias binding.

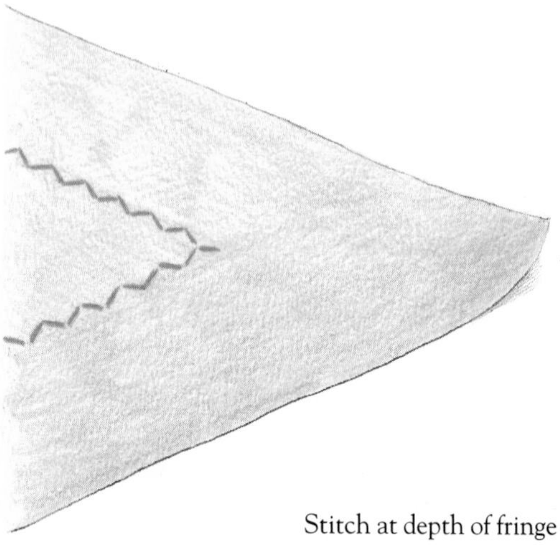

Stitch at depth of fringe

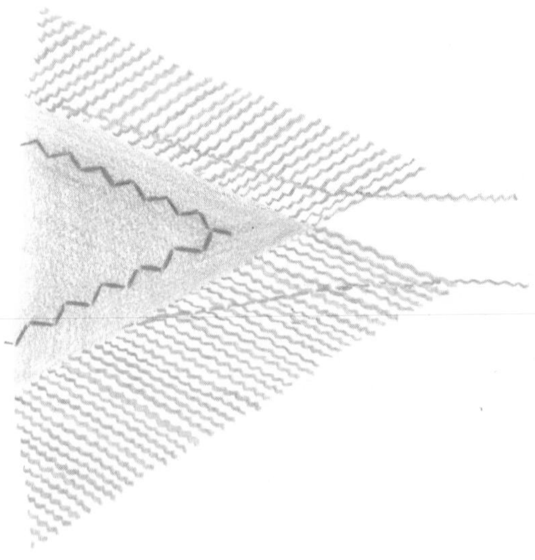

Pull out threads

The mosaic pattern is also suitable for working matching napkin rings. The depth of the pattern can be extended as you desire. You might use some bronze-coloured metallic thread to oversew the edges.

B
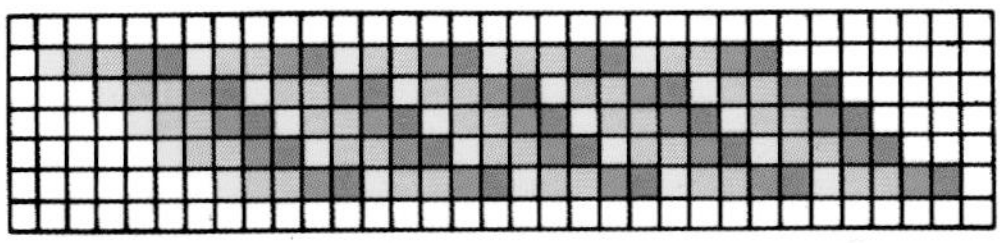
A

KEY
- 7740
- 7947
- 7606
- 7106
- 7849

Shades of lavender

If the idea of embroidering an entire tablecloth seems a little daunting, cheat a little by painting designs with fabric paints then embellish with cross stitches to give texture to the design.

Materials

Circular tablecloth approximately 70in (175cm) diameter
Squared dressmaker's pattern paper, one square = 1in (2.5cm)
Dressmaker's carbon paper
Fabric paints or fabric painting crayons in green, purple, white
Paintbrushes of different sizes
DMC stranded cottons as follows: one skein each of purple 208, 210, 553, 3609 and 211.

Preparation

1 Trace the lavender sprays on page 18. Fold the tablecloth in half, then quarters. Using dressmaker's carbon paper, transfer the lavender sprays to the cloth, stems $1\frac{1}{2}$in (37mm) from the hem and heads towards the centre. Space them as desired. Unfold the cloth and transfer the design to the second quarter. Complete the rest of the tablecloth, so that there are lavender sprays all round. (If you prefer, you can draw the lavender sprays directly on to the cloth.)

2 Spread the tablecloth on several layers of clean newspaper on a flat surface. Mix the green paint, brush in the stems and leaves, working one quarter of the cloth at a time. Leave to dry before working the next quarter. Next, paint in the lavender heads using the brush almost dry and with free strokes.

3 When painting is completed and the paint quite dry, fix the paint following the manufacturer's instructions.

Working the embroidery

4 Using six strands of thread together, work random cross stitches over the lavender heads, using all five shades, keeping the darker colours near to the bottom of the heads and the lighter near the top.

5 If you wish, you could also work a few straight stitches on the leaves using closely related green tones, such as the range in DMC colours 369, 368 and 320.

The fabric painting technique can be used on other projects in this book. For instance, try painting some of the motifs for the sampler on page 47, adding a few cross stitches afterwards for texture and additional colour.

Trace these two sprays of lavender and transfer to the table cloth, or copy them and draw them in place using an embroidery pencil

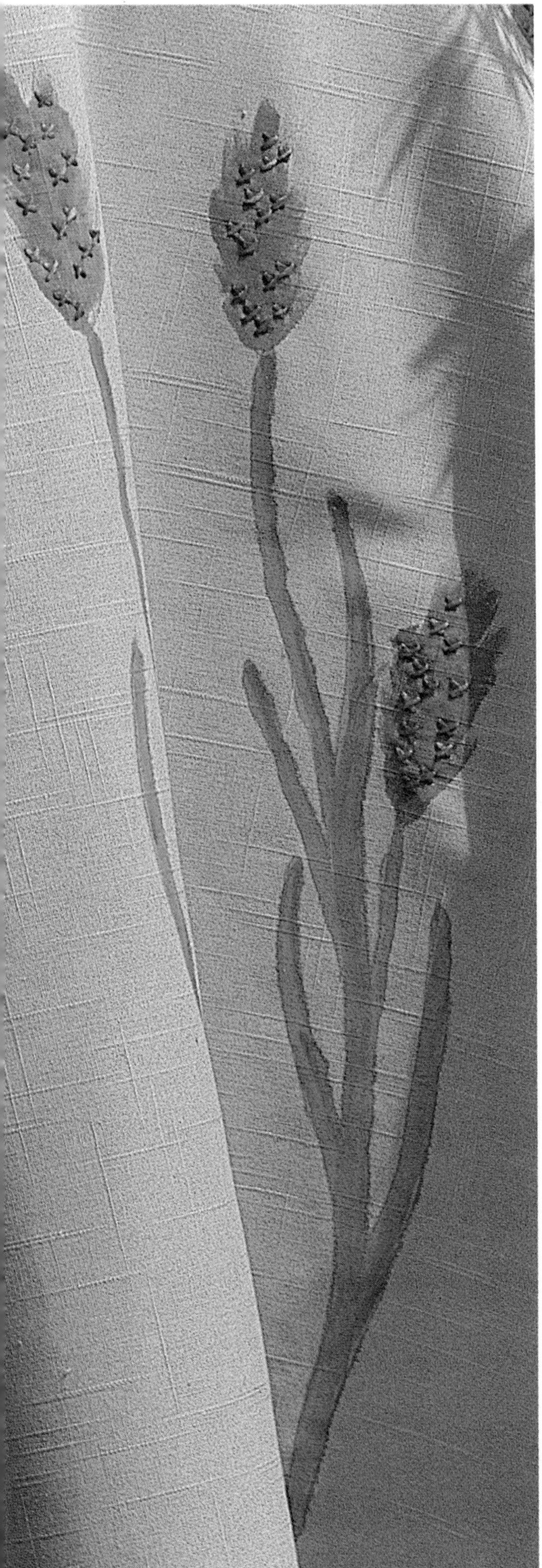

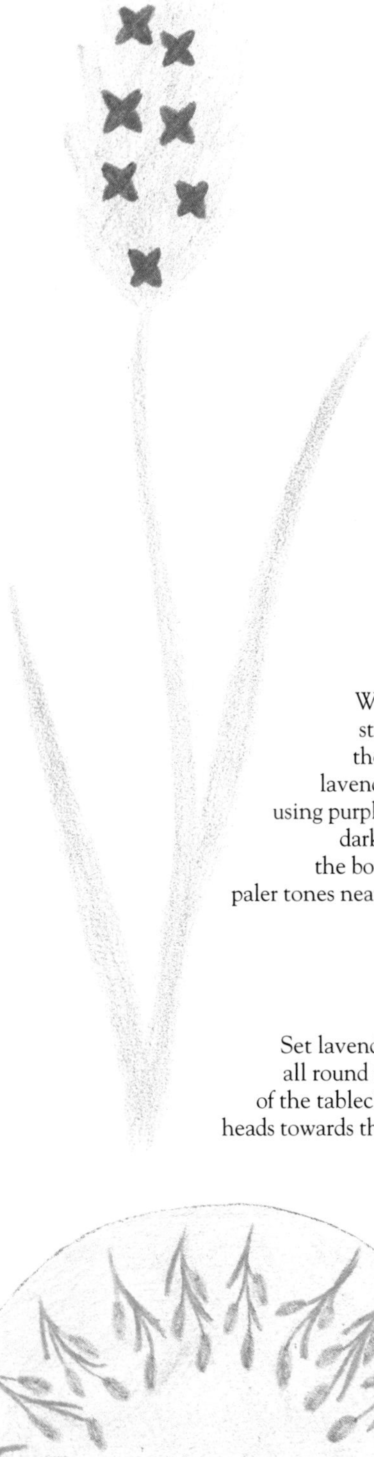

Work cross
stitches on
the painted
lavender heads
using purple shades,
dark tones at
the bottom and
paler tones near the top.

Set lavender sprays
all round the edges
of the tablecloth with
heads towards the centre.

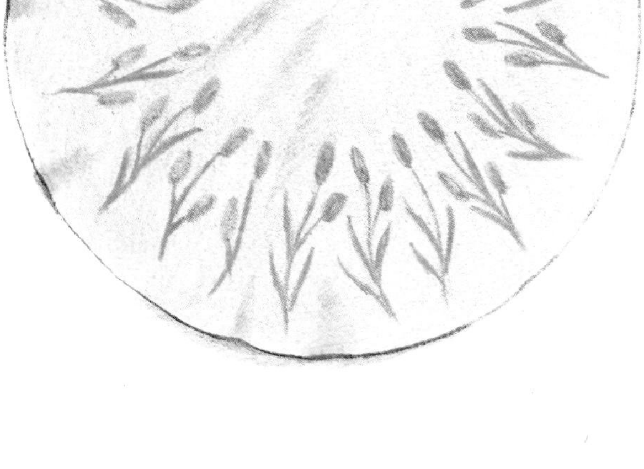

Scandinavian tulips

Embroider a table runner to display your ornaments, or to make a dressing table even prettier. Tulips often feature in painted and embroidered designs from Norway, Sweden and Denmark; this one is worked in subtle shades of pink and grey-green, but you could also use a different bright colour for each pair of tulips, yellow, red and blue or turquoise to make the design even more eye-catching.

Materials
Piece of white evenweave fabric 24×14in (60×35cm), 28–30 threads to 1in (2.5cm)
DMC stranded cottons as follows: two skeins each of 3706 pink, 320 green.

Preparation
1 Work a line of narrow machine-zigzag stitches 1in (2.5cm) from the edge all round (see page 14).

Working the embroidery
2 Following the chart and starting at A, begin the embroidery 3in (7.5cm) up from the long edge and from the left-hand edge. Use four strands of thread together throughout and work stitches over four threads of fabric.

3 Repeat the design along the other long edge, making sure that the stems are still on the outside edge of the runner with the flowers towards the centre.

Finishing
4 When the embroidery is completed, press on the wrong side with a warm iron. Fringe the edges as described for the table mats on page 14.

> This motif is ideal for working on cross stitch border tape. Stitch the tape to fabric for a shelf edging

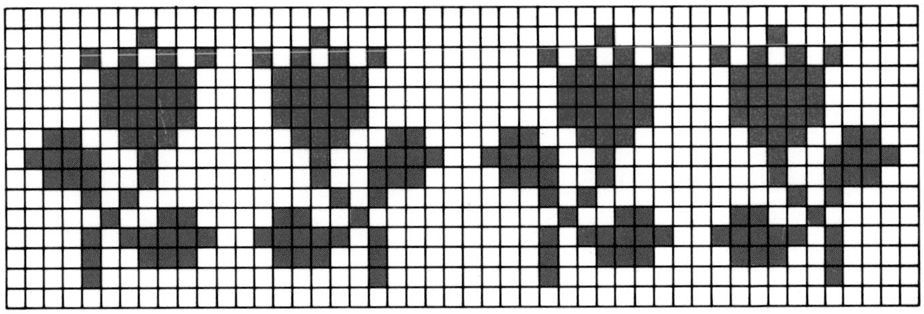

A

- 3706
- 320

Traditional prettiness

Welcome guests by putting out a hand-embroidered fingertip towel for their use. This one is decorated with a delicate design of pinks and forget-me-not flowers which you can work to the colour scheme given, or choose one of your own.

Materials

White fingertip towel with border 32 threads wide

DMC pearl cottons as follows: one skein each of 956 dark pink, 957 light pink, 369 green, 726 yellow, 793 blue.

Note: If a suitable towel cannot be purchased, work the design on white evenweave embroidery fabric, turn under the edges about ¼ in (6mm) all round and sew or machine-stitch the strip to the towel when the embroidery is completed. This type of decoration is ideal for making a set of towels for a new bride, or for a girl setting up in her own home.

Working the embroidery

Following the chart and key begin working the design on the left-hand bottom edge of the border. Work each cross stitch over two fabric threads. Repeat the section of the design as indicated on the chart.

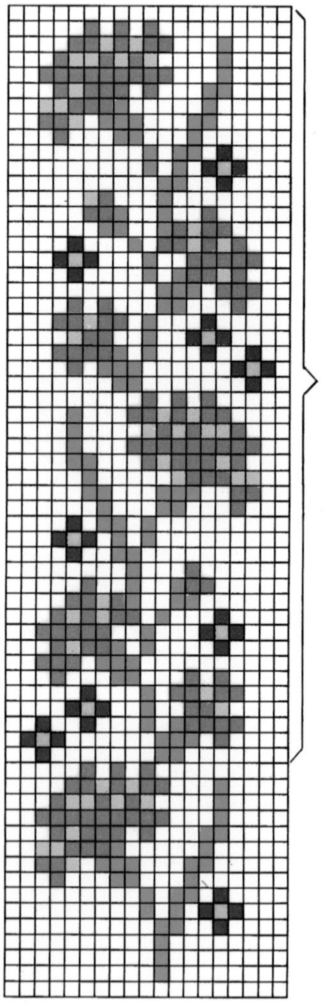

KEY

- 956
- 957
- 369
- 726
- 793

Cross-stitch tape (see page 34) could also be used for a towel, or the waste canvas method described on page 36 could be used. This border design has other uses in embroidery of household linens. It would look pretty on a white hessian tablecloth with matching napkins, or on a set of table mats. Or you might work the border on pillowcases, using white cotton on white, or matching a pastel colour to the fabric on coloured linens.

Bold and bright

African beadwork designs have been translated here into two colourful cushion covers that will brighten up your living room.

Materials (for two cushions)
2 pieces of Binca fabric 15in (38cm) square, 6 threads to 1in (2.5cm)
4 pieces of backing fabric 15×10in (38×25.5cm)
Double knitting yarn as follows: 1 ball each of purple, dark blue, light blue, green, red, aqua and yellow.

Note: Double knitting wools vary slightly in thickness, so experiment first to make sure that the stitches cover the fabric. On a waste piece of Binca, work two or three cross stitches using four strands of wool across two holes. If the wool covers the background so that no canvas can be seen behind, work the designs with four strands of wool throughout. If the work looks a little 'gappy', use five strands.

Working the embroidery
1 Work the designs on the Binca over two holes, following the charts and starting at A.

2 When the embroidery is completed, press the work lightly on the wrong side with a warm iron, pulling gently into shape so that the fabric is square.

Making the cushion
3 Turn under, press and machine-stitch one long edge on each piece of backing fabric.

4 Trim the embroidered pieces back to within $\frac{3}{4}$in (2cm) of the stitches.

5 Pin and baste the backing pieces together, overlapping the neatened edges, so that the back is the same size as the embroidery.

6 Machine-stitch all round, stitching on the edge of the embroidery. Stitch over the same line again for extra strength.

7 Trim the seams to within $\frac{1}{2}$in (12mm) of the stitching, and clip the corners. Turn right side out and press.

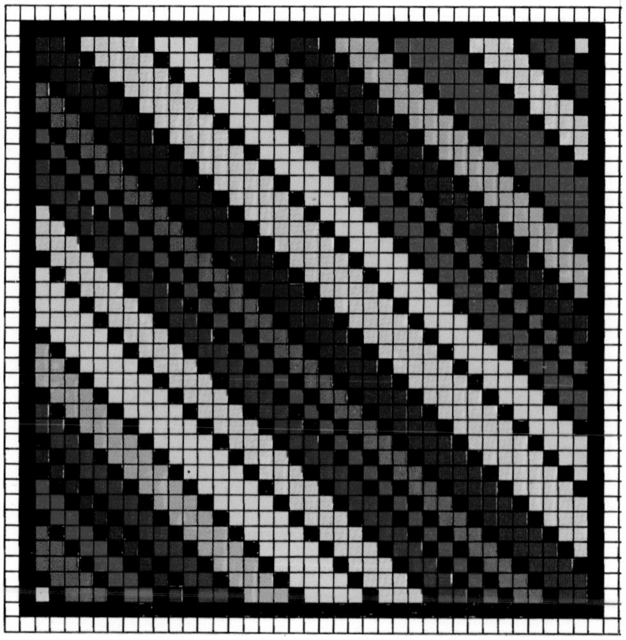

A

Colours on the charts are those listed in materials – purple, dark blue, light blue, black, green, red, aqua and yellow

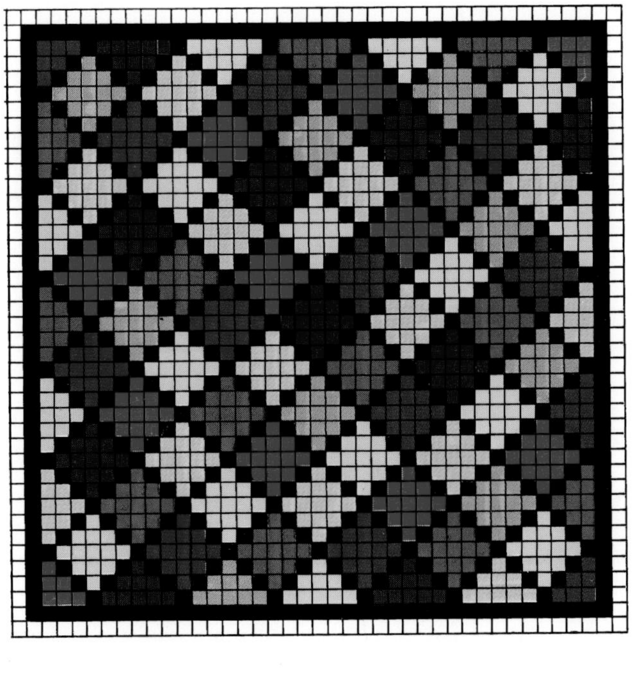

Gift Ideas

Bright comforter

Cotton gingham is ideal for making cot quilts because it washes so easily and you can use the pattern for placing cross stitches in decorative patterns. Work the embroidery through the fabric, wadding and muslin backing to achieve a quilted effect.

Materials

Piece of gingham with ¼in (6mm) checks, 44×28in (112×72cm) wide
Piece of medium-weight washable polyester wadding the same size
Piece of muslin the same size
Piece of matching, plain fabric for backing the quilt, 50×33in (128×84cm)
DMC stranded cottons as follows: two skeins each of 3607 red, 209 mauve.

Preparation

1 Baste the gingham, wadding and muslin together round the edges and then across vertically and horizontally, thus marking the middle.

Working the embroidery

2 The middle of the chart 1 is indicated by arrows which correspond with the middle of the fabric marked with basting. Using three strands of mauve and three strands of red, work the design in double cross stitch (see diagram), starting in the middle, and working on white squares.

3 Work chart 2 design, using three strands of red thread, 13 check squares in from the edges at each corner, working double cross stitches on white squares.

Finishing

4 Remove the horizontal and vertical basting threads. Pin and baste the quilt right side up on the plain backing fabric, wrong sides together.

5 Turn the backing fabric edges onto the quilt with a narrow hem and work hemming stitches all round or, if you prefer, machine-stitch the hem. Fold the corners neatly. Remove any basting threads that still show.

Chart 1

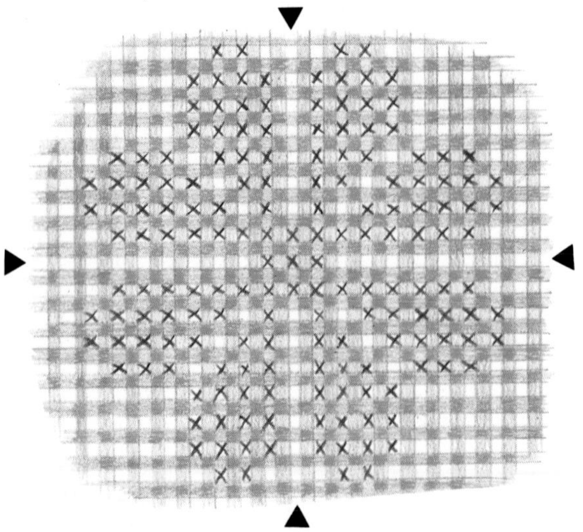

Chart 2

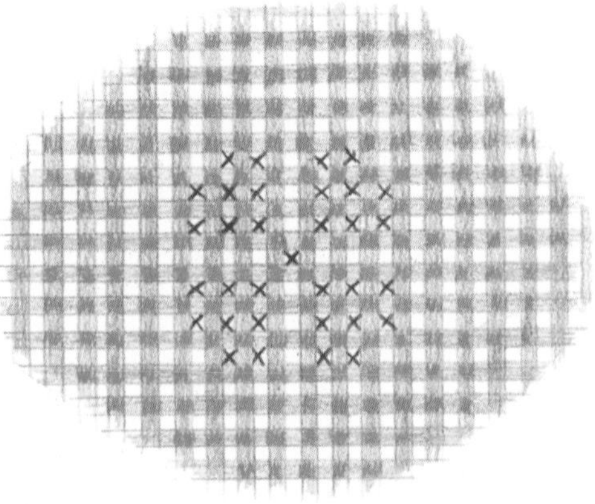

Welcome to the world

Combine a greeting and a delightful gift with one of these made-to-keep birth congratulation cards. The cards may be framed afterwards for nursery pictures. Adapt the ABC card to carry the baby's initials, and the date of birth, worked from the alphabet chart overleaf.

Materials

Teddy bear

Piece of white Aida fabric 4×5in (10×12.5cm), 14 threads to 1 in (2.5cm)
DMC stranded cottons as follows: one skein each of 310 black, 606 red, 739 pale beige, 778 beige, 563 green, 801 brown
Cream oval-window card blank.

ABC card

Piece of white Aida fabric 4×5in (10×12.5cm), 14 threads to 1in (2.5cm)
DMC stranded cottons as follows; one skein each of 3753 blue, 761 pink, 745 yellow, 993 green
White round-window card blank.

Bootee card

Piece of white Aida fabric 4×5in) (10×12.5cm), 11 threads to 1in (2.5cm)
DMC stranded cottons as follows: one skein each of 827 blue (or 761 pink), white
12in (30cm) piece of white satin ribbon ¼in (6mm)-wide
Blue round-window card blank.

Preparation

1 Measure and mark the middle of the fabric with lines of basting stitches, vertically and horizontally.

Working and embroidery

2 The middle of charts is indicated by arrows on the edges. This corresponds with the middle of your fabric, marked with basting.

Teddy bear

3 Work the design from chart 1 following the key and starting in the middle. Use three strands of thread together. Work the balloon string in back stitch using one strand of black thread.

ABC card

4 Work the design from chart 2, following the key and using four strands of thread together for cross stitches. If initials are required, work from selected letters in chart 4. Use three strands of green thread to work the child's date of birth, if desired, following chart 4.

Bootee card

5 Work the design from chart 3, following the key and using four strands of thread together for cross stitches. Use one strand of thread for back stitches where marked on the chart. Work a single diagonal stitch or half a cross stitch where indicated on the chart.

Finishing

6 Cut the ribbon in half and thread one piece through from the back of the embroidery so that the ends emerge at each side of one bootee. Tie in a neat bow. Repeat with the second piece of ribbon on the second bootee.

Mounting the embroidery

7 Trim the fabric so that it fits behind the window of the card. Spread glue thinly around the inside of the window, place the embroidery in position and press down firmly. Spread glue on the back of the third fold, fold and press down onto the back of the embroidery.

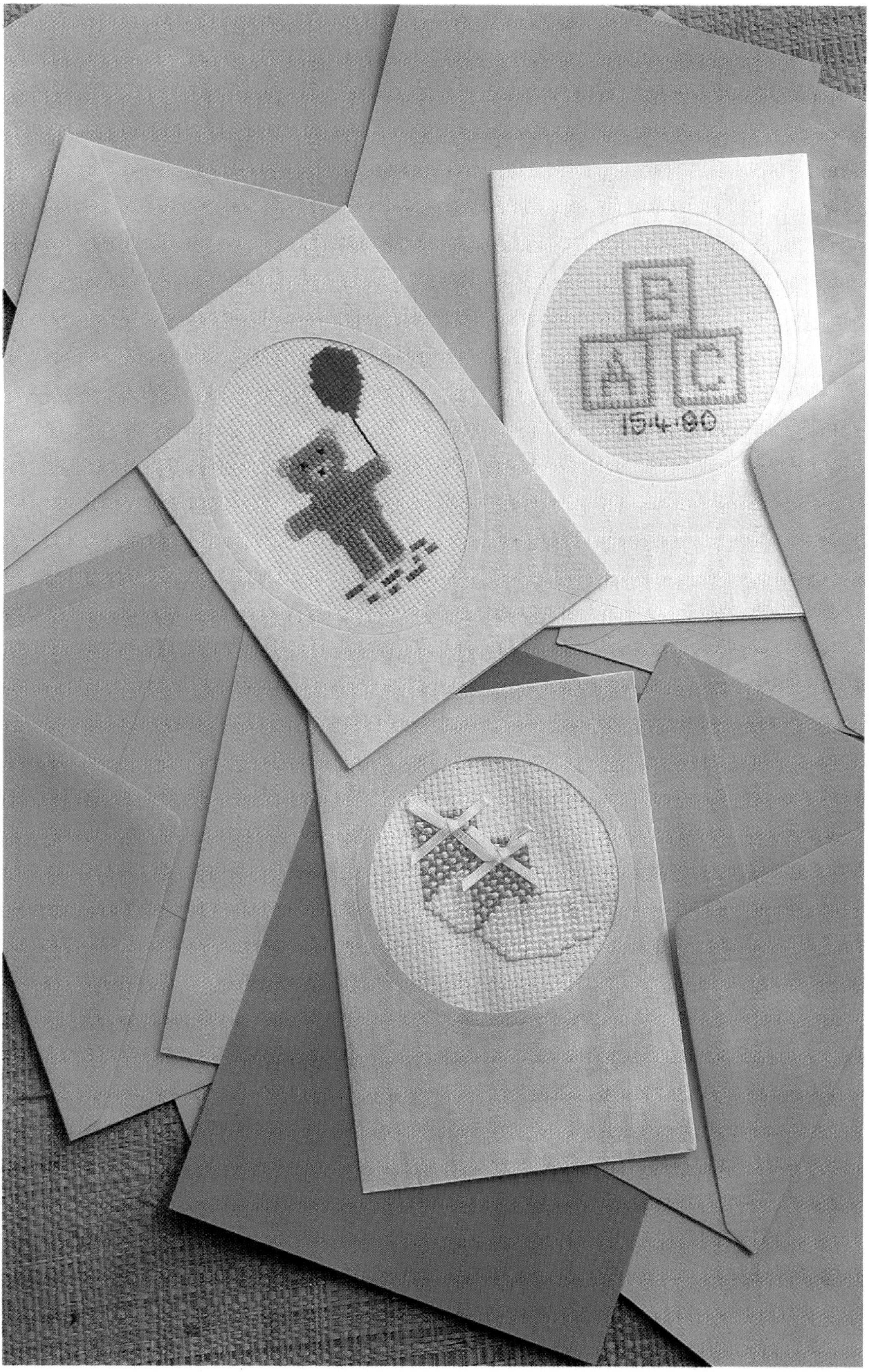
B
A
C
15·4·90

Chart 4

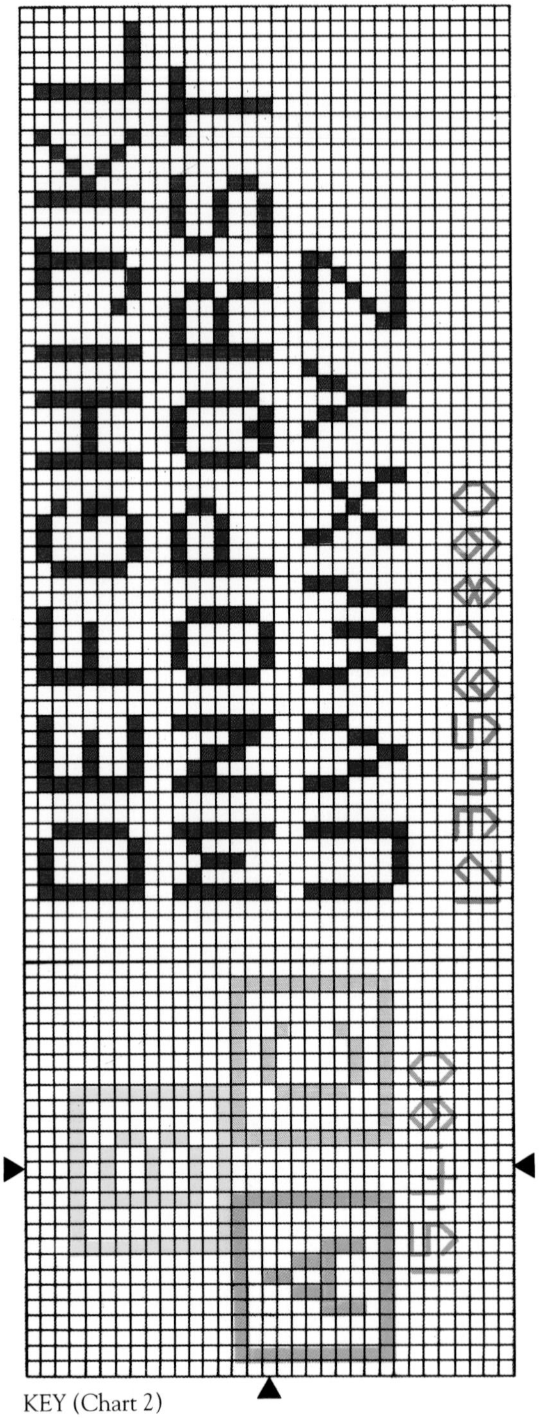

KEY (Chart 1)

- 310
- 606
- 739
- 778
- 563
- 801

KEY (Chart 2)

- 3753
- 761
- 745
- 993

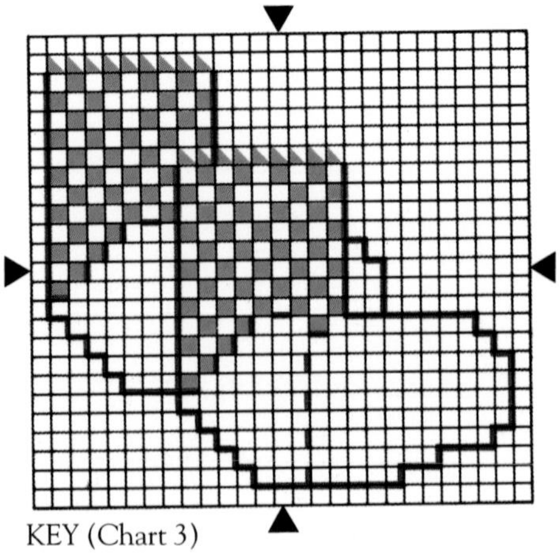

KEY (Chart 3)

- 827 (or 761)
- White
- Back stitches

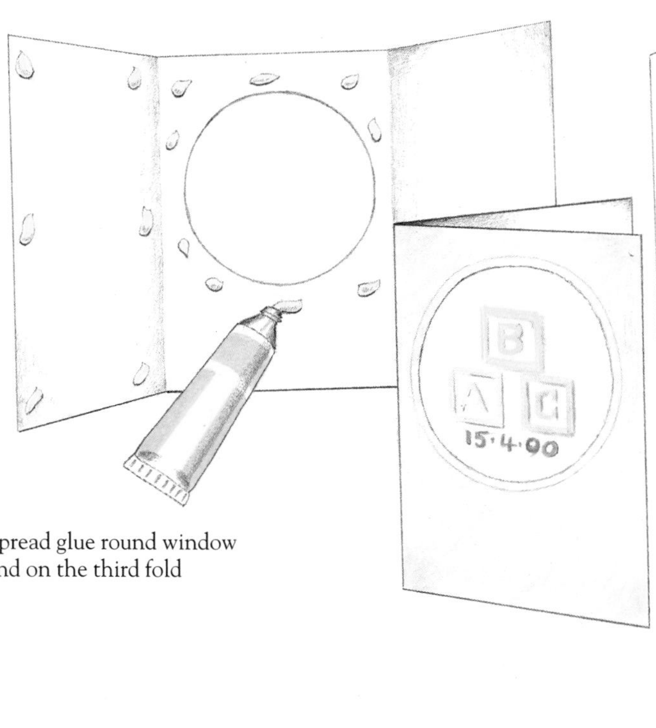

Spread glue round window and on the third fold

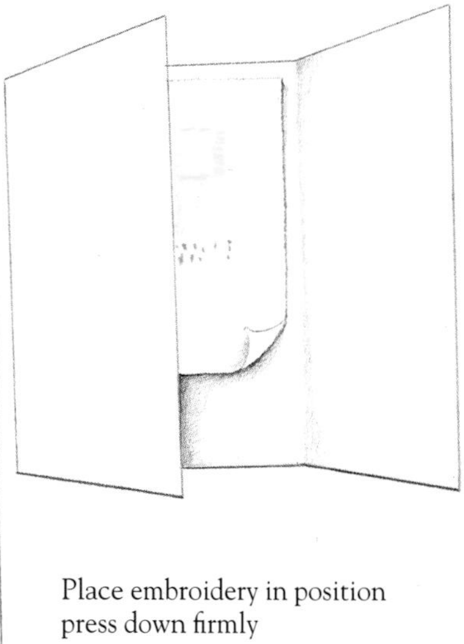

Place embroidery in position press down firmly

Sun flowers

A simple sundress can be made into something special by adding borders of cross stitch flowers to the hem and waist. A matching hairband would make an outfit pretty enough for a party.

Materials
Sundress to fit ages 3–4
White cross stitch border tape with blue edging, 14 threads to 1in (2.5cm)
DMC stranded cottons as follows: 8 skeins of 809 blue, 1 skein of 956 dark pink, 4 skeins of 3706 light pink
Small piece of $\frac{1}{4}$in (6mm)-wide elastic for hairband.

Note: To estimate tape quantities measure round the dress at the waist and hem, add 2in (5cm) for seam allowance on each piece. Allow 14in (36cm) for a hairband.

Preparation
1 Measure and mark the centre of each piece of tape.

Working the embroidery
2 Following the chart and key (the centre of the design is indicated by arrows), begin embroidery in the centre of the tape and work towards the ends. Use six strands of thread together, and work each stitch across two threads of fabric.

Finishing
3 Turn under the short ends of the embroidered tapes for the sundress, and appliqué them in position on the dress by hand (using hemming) or machine-stitching.

Alternatively, a better finish is achieved by opening the dress side-seams where the tape is to be applied. Apply the tape flat to front and back, then re-stitch the seams.

Hairband
4 Turn and sew the short edges of the hairband to neaten, cut and pin on a piece of elastic so that the hairband will fit the child's head. Sew the elastic into place.

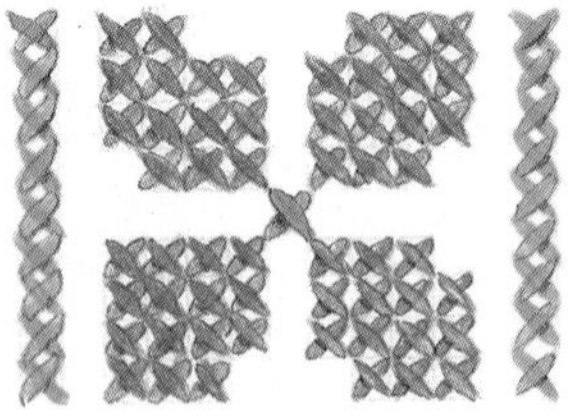

Stitch the embroidered tape to the skirt pieces

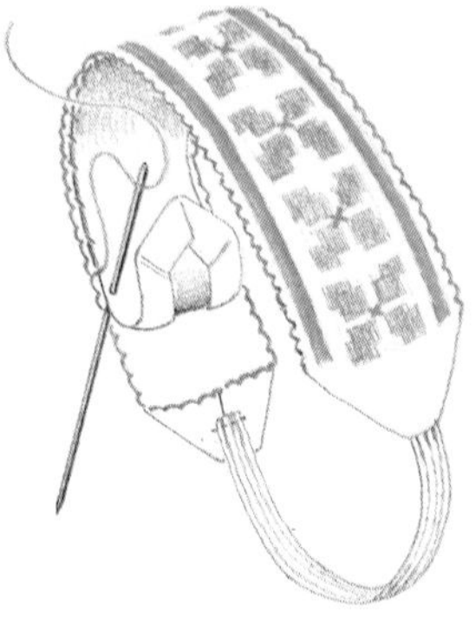

Make a matching hairband for a party outfit

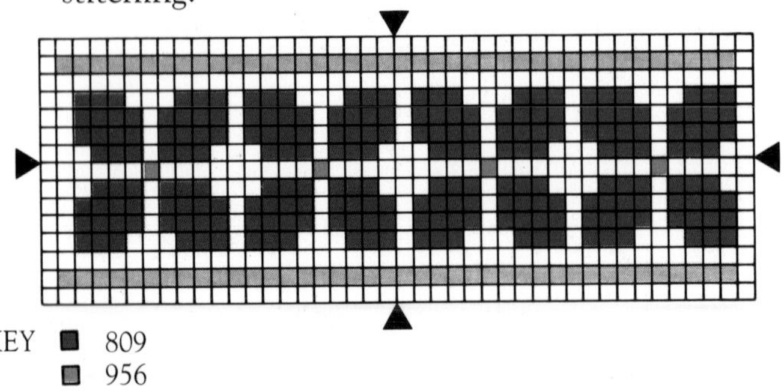

KEY
- ■ 809
- ■ 956
- ■ 3706

Flying high

Cross stitch doesn't always have to be done on canvas or on evenweave fabric; use the waste canvas method to embroider pretty designs – such as this kite – on ready-made children's clothes.

Materials

Pair of child's dungarees with a plain bib measuring at least 4in (10cm) square

DMC stranded cottons as follows: one skein each of 209 mauve, 996 blue, 701 green, 3608 pink, 444 yellow, 3746 purple

Piece of waste canvas, 5in (12.5cm) square, 11 threads to 1in (2.5cm).

Preparation

1 Baste the waste canvas to the dungarees over the area where the motif is to be worked. Mark the middle with horizontal and vertical lines of basting stitches.

Working the embroidery

2 The middle of the design on the chart is indicated by arrows. This corresponds with the middle of your fabric, marked with basting threads.

3 Using four strands of thread together, embroider the design through the canvas and the fabric, following the chart and the key and starting in the middle.

Finishing

4 When the embroidery is completed, remove the basting threads and dampen the canvas; this dissolves the glue holding the canvas together.

5 Pull the vertical and horizontal strands of the canvas out from under the cross stitches, until only the embroidery remains on the dungarees.

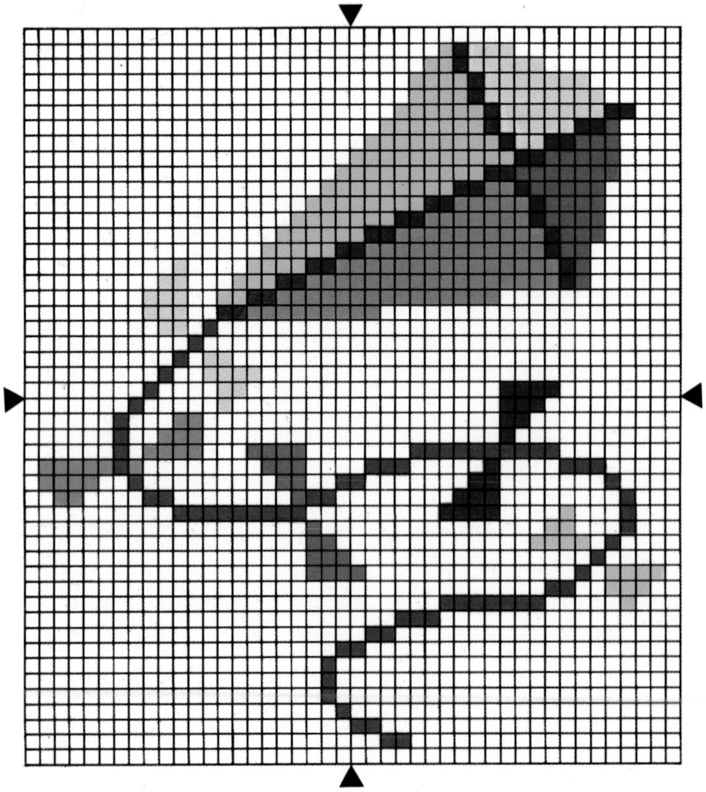

KEY
209
996
701
3608
444
3746

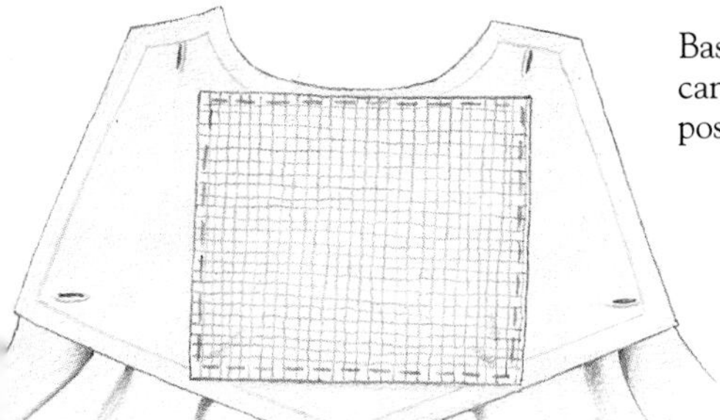

Baste the waste canvas in position

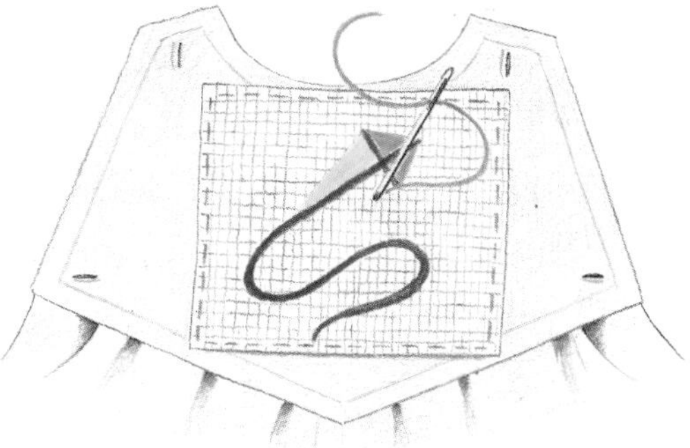

Embroider the design on the canvas

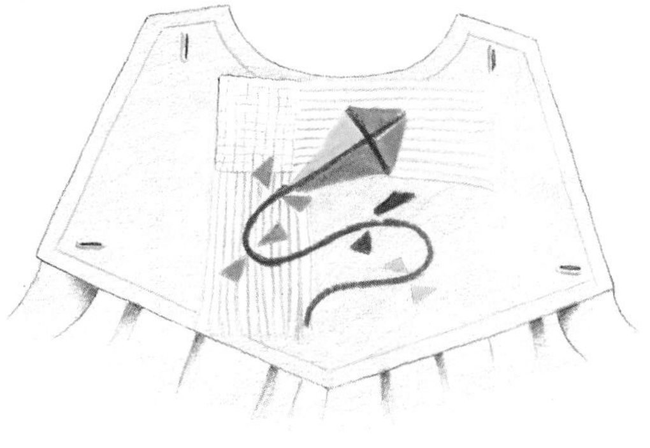

Dampen, then withdraw the canvas threads

3D dazzler

Babies love watching bright colours; dangle this cross-stitch mobile over a cot to provide visual stimulation. It's worked on cross-stitch paper, so it isn't robust enough to play with; hang it out of reach but where the bright colours will catch the light.

Materials

Sheets of cross stitch paper in white, red, green and gold

DMC stranded cottons as follows: one skein each of 996 blue, 444 yellow, 3746 purple, 3608 pink

Transparent plastic thread (for stringing the mobile)

Crafts knife

White card

Coloured papers in blue, red, green and pink

Clear glue.

Preparation

1 Cut squares from the cross stitch paper to the following sizes (dimensions are for complete holes so, if the square is 81 holes along each edge, cut the paper on the 82nd hole):

White – 1 square 81 × 81 holes

Red – 1 square 61 × 61 holes

Green – 1 square 41 × 41 holes

Gold – 1 square 21 × 21 holes.

2 Use the crafts knife to cut out the centre of each square, leaving a frame of five complete holes wide.

Working the embroidery

3 Using six strands of thread together and following the chart on pages 40–41 for colours, work cross stitches over two holes round the frames. (Note that the chart is in two pieces and is joined where indicated with arrows.)

Finishing

4 Brush glue sparingly on to the back of each embroidered frame and stick onto the white card. Press down firmly.

5 When the glue is dry, cut out the four mounted, embroidered frames.

6 Glue each frame to coloured paper, cut out when dry.

7 Thread a sharp, strong needle with the transparent thread and string the mobile sections together, the largest at the top.

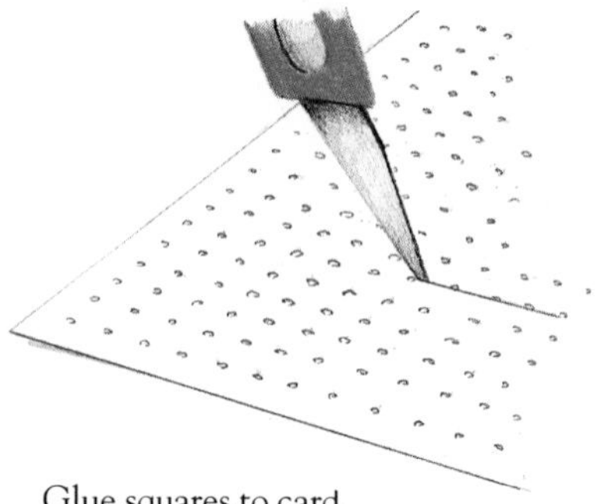

Cut the centre from the squares

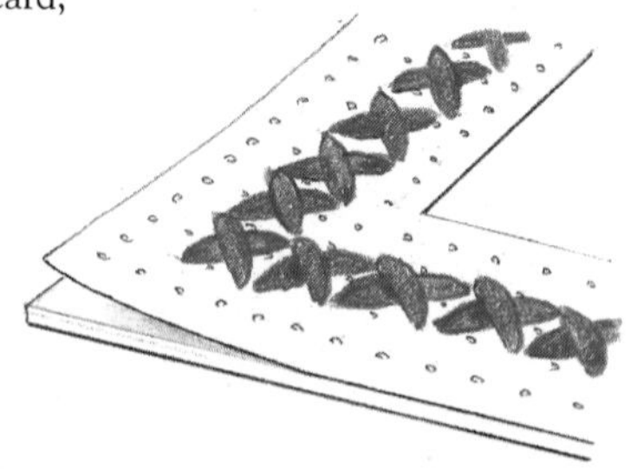

Glue squares to card, then cut out

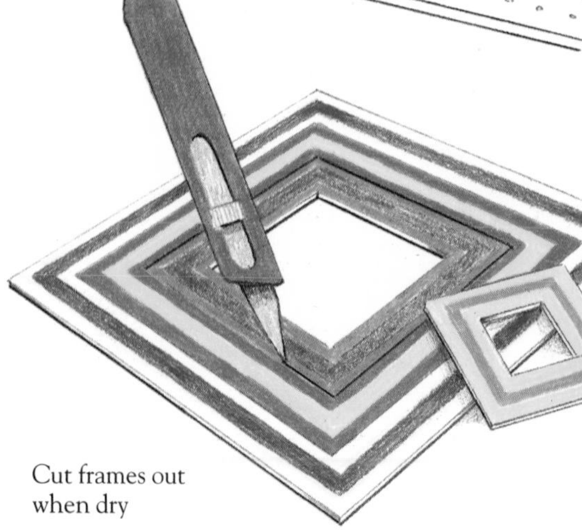

Cut frames out when dry

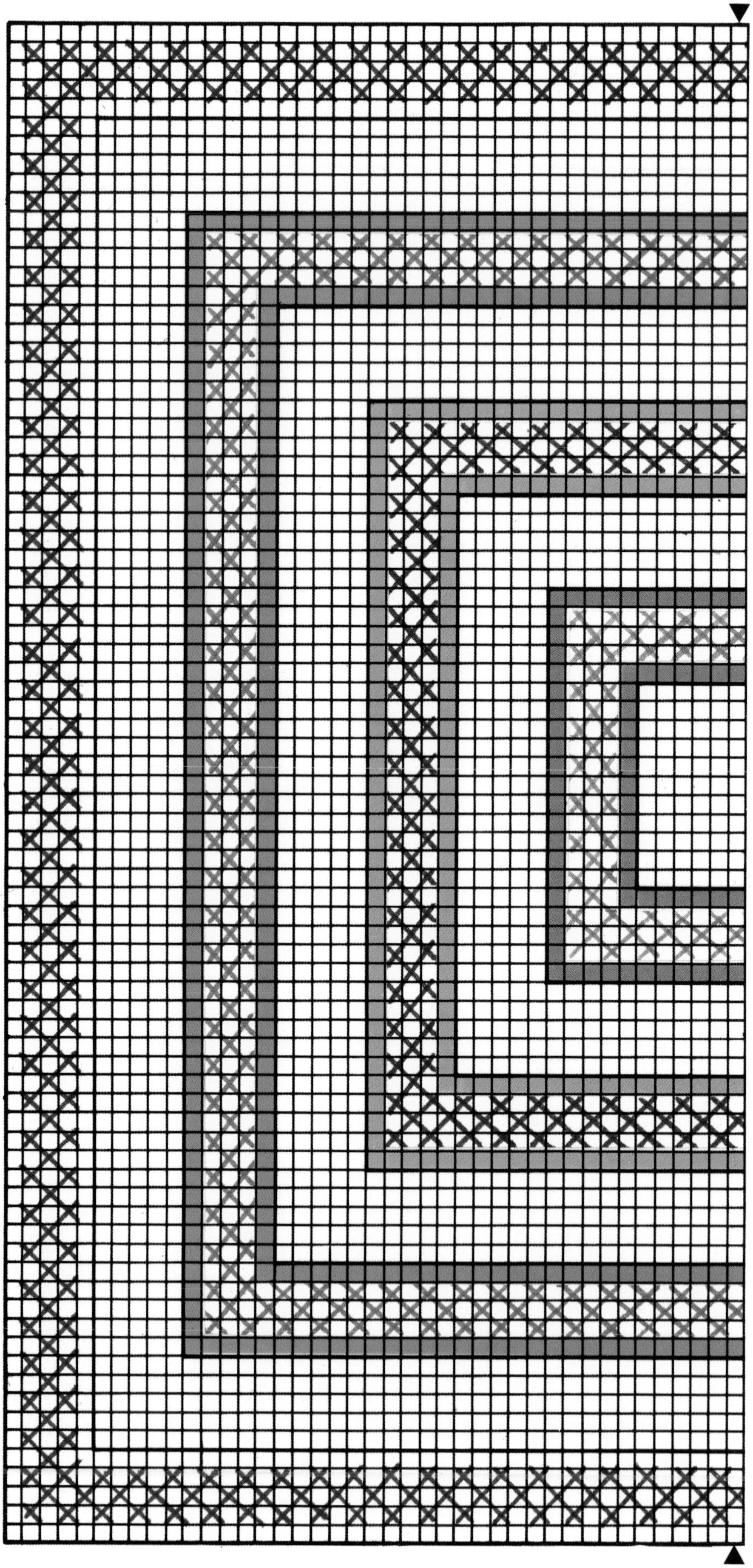

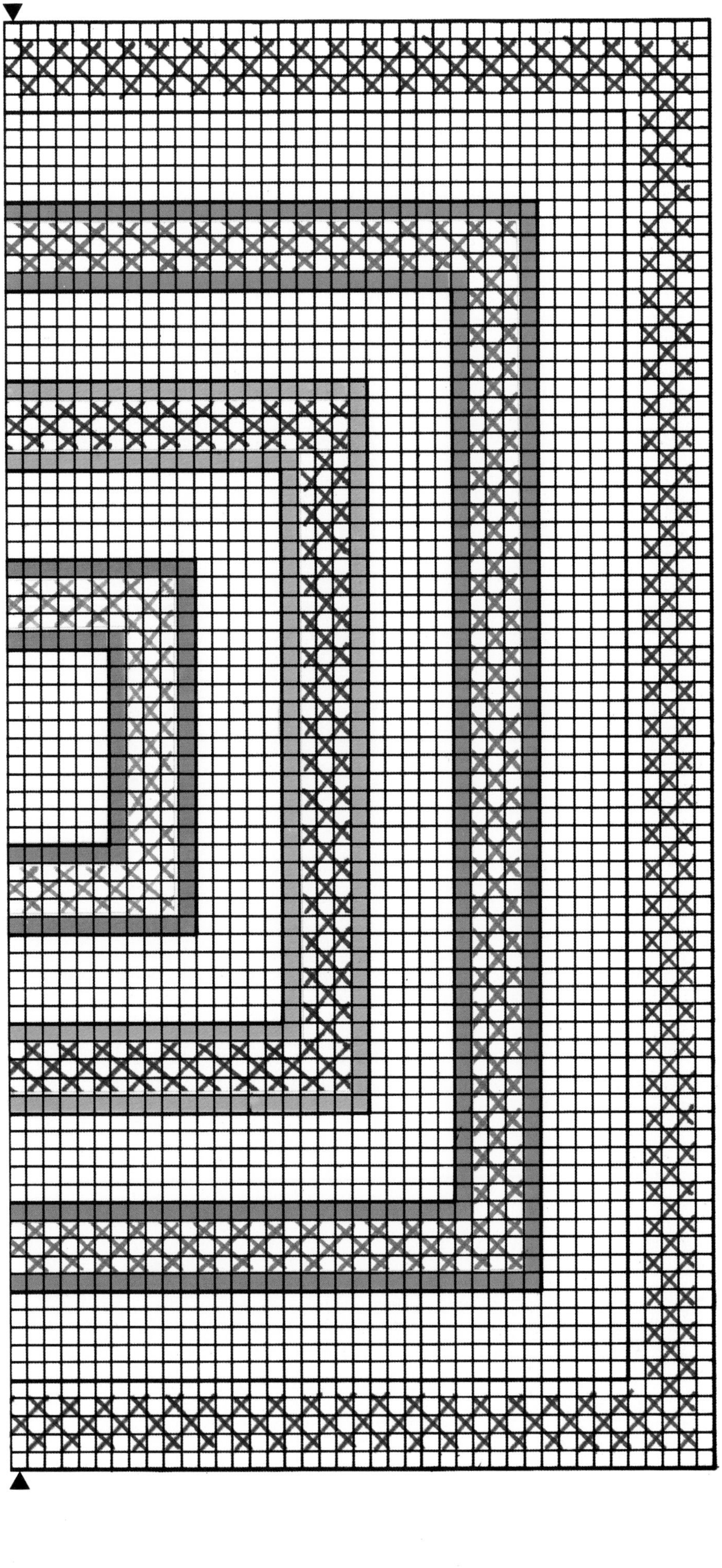

Chart for 3-D dazzler

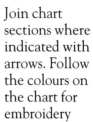

Join chart sections where indicated with arrows. Follow the colours on the chart for embroidery

Colonial charmer

Samplers are always favourite cross-stitch designs, and this one is based on some of the many American Colonial patterns. Stitch one for a special friend or a young child, or indulge yourself with one to decorate your own home.

Materials
Piece of pale green Aida cloth, 14 × 18in (35 × 45cm), 14 threads to 1in (2.5cm)
DMC stranded cottons as follows: one skein each of 993 pale green, 726 dark yellow; two skeins each of 104 variegated yellow, 699 dark green, 910 mid-green
Piece of press-on adhesive board to fit your chosen picture frame
Masking tape.

Preparation
1 Measure and mark the middle of the fabric with lines of basting stitches, vertically and horizontally.

Working the embroidery
2 The middle of the sampler chart is indicated by arrows on the edges. This corresponds with the middle of your fabric, marked with basting.

3 Using six strands of thread together, and working across two threads of the canvas each way, work the design, following the chart and key. Work the border first, then complete the design, counting threads to position the motifs and letters.

Finishing
4 When the embroidery is completed, press lightly on the wrong side.

Mounting the sampler
5 Peel the protective covering from the press-on board, and position the embroidery on top. Smooth the fabric onto the sticky surface, from the centre outwards.

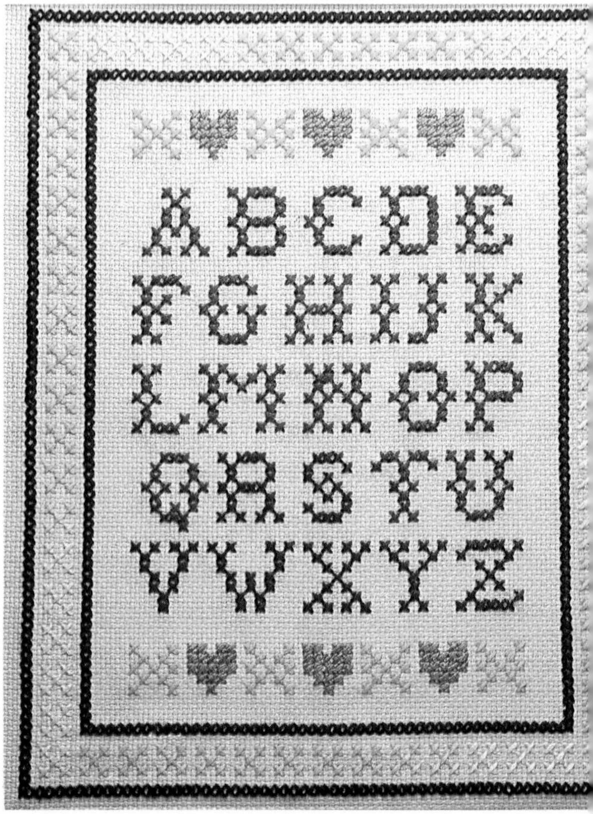

6 Turn the excess fabric onto the back of the board, secure with masking tape. The sampler is now ready for framing.

The finished size of this sampler is approximately 12 x 10in (30 x 25cm) but you could enlarge it on a bigger piece of fabric by working the border sides longer. You might also add one or two of the motifs from page 43. The row of houses could go across the bottom under the hearts and flowers.

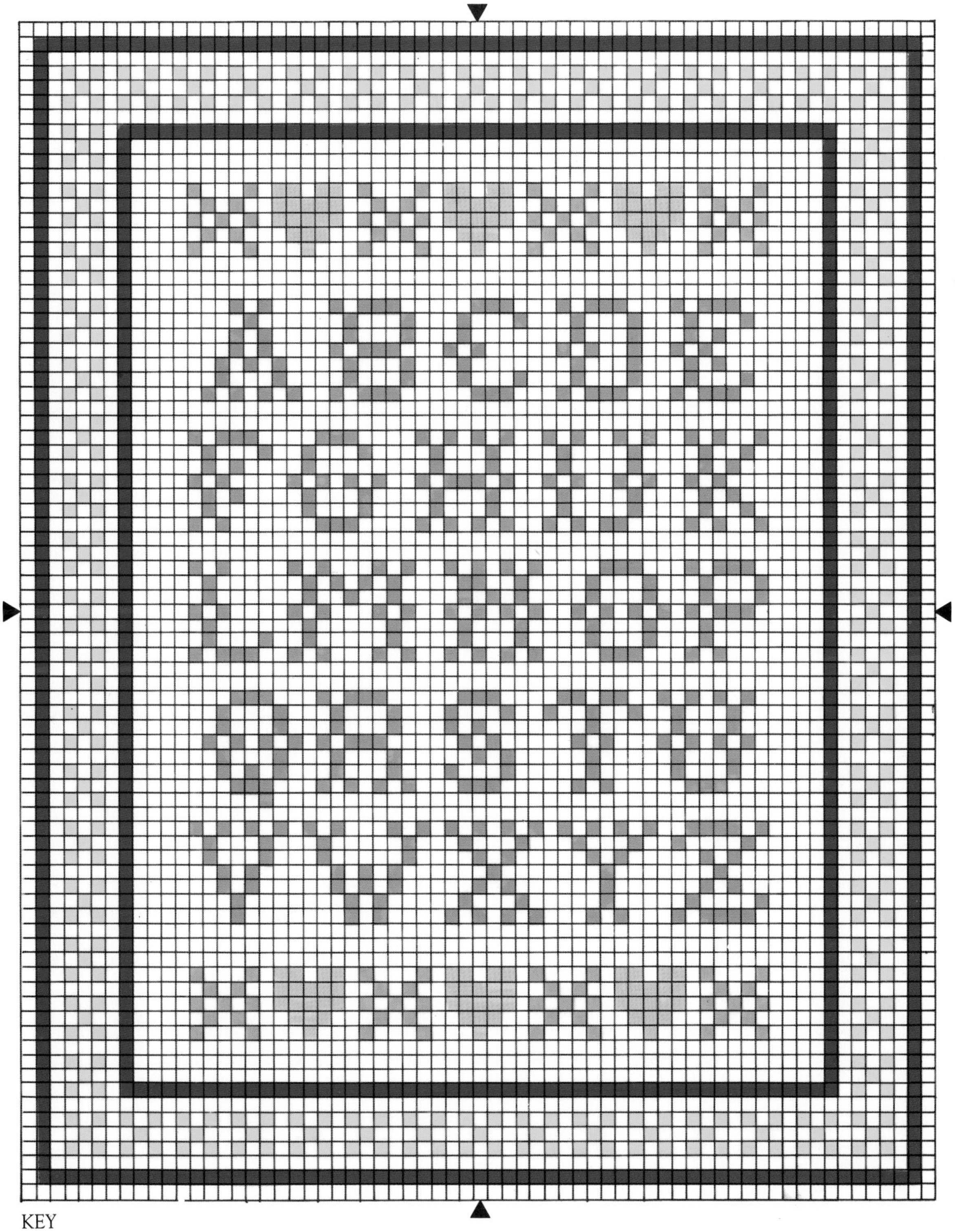

KEY

- 699
- 910
- 993
- 726
- 104

Over to you

Samplers aren't just for new babies; they can be for new homes, new marriages, or for birthdays, anniversaries or any special occasion. Why not design your own? Choose from these borders and motifs, and work out your own design on squared paper.

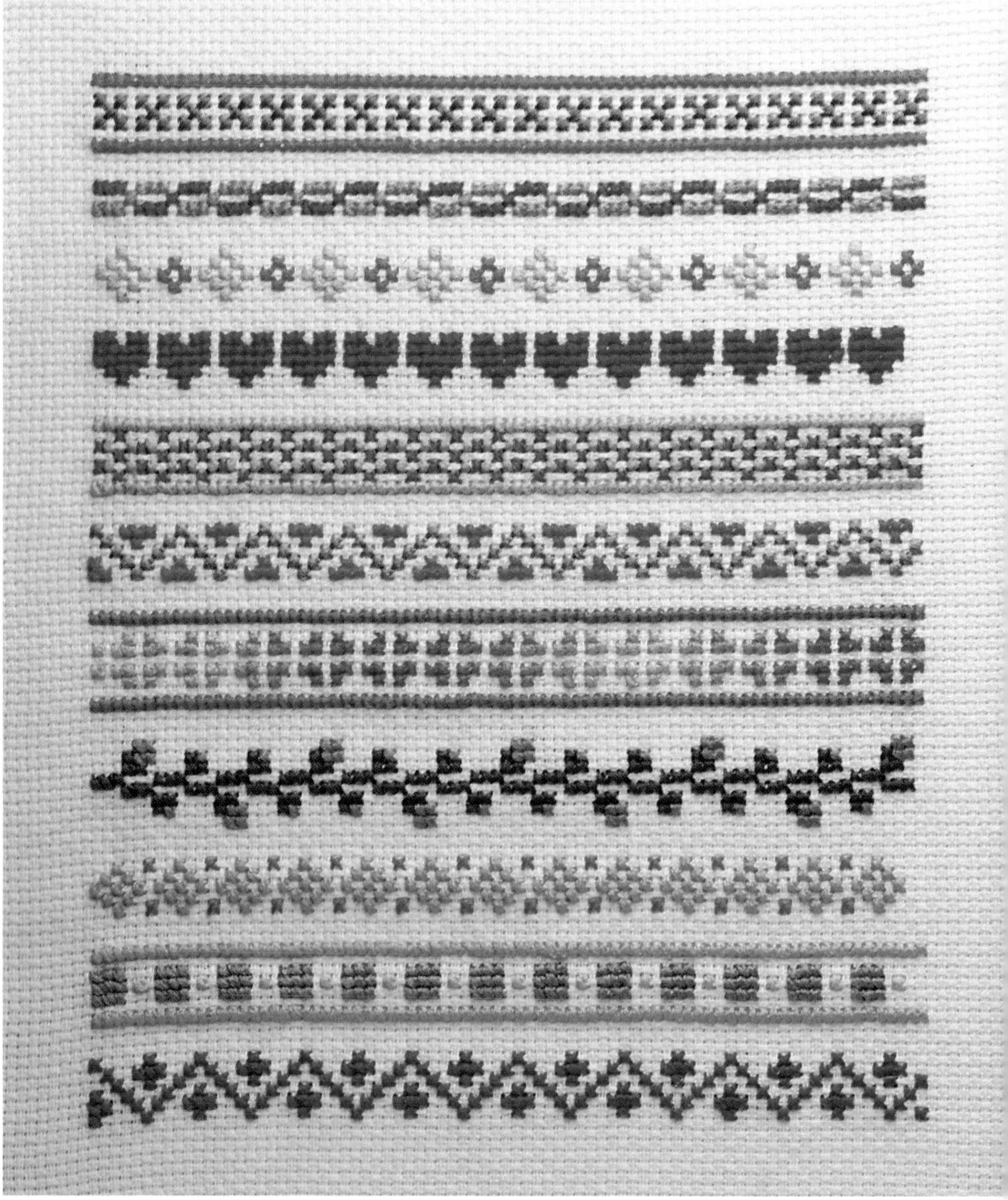

Designing a sampler
Sampler designs are first worked out on squared paper. Decide the finished size then choose your fabric. (The motifs and borders can be worked to any size you like.) Squares on the squared paper represent cross stitches, worked over a pair of threads, or over three or four threads. It is up to you. It is a good idea to experiment with a few stitches on your chosen fabric first. Once decided, mark the middle of the graph paper with vertical and horizontal lines. Supposing your fabric has a count of 14 threads to 1in (2.5cm) and the sampler is to be 12in (30cm) wide. If you have decided to work cross stitches over two threads, then every square on the paper is two threads. You therefore count off 168 squares across the graph paper for the width of your sampler. Work out the depth in the same way.

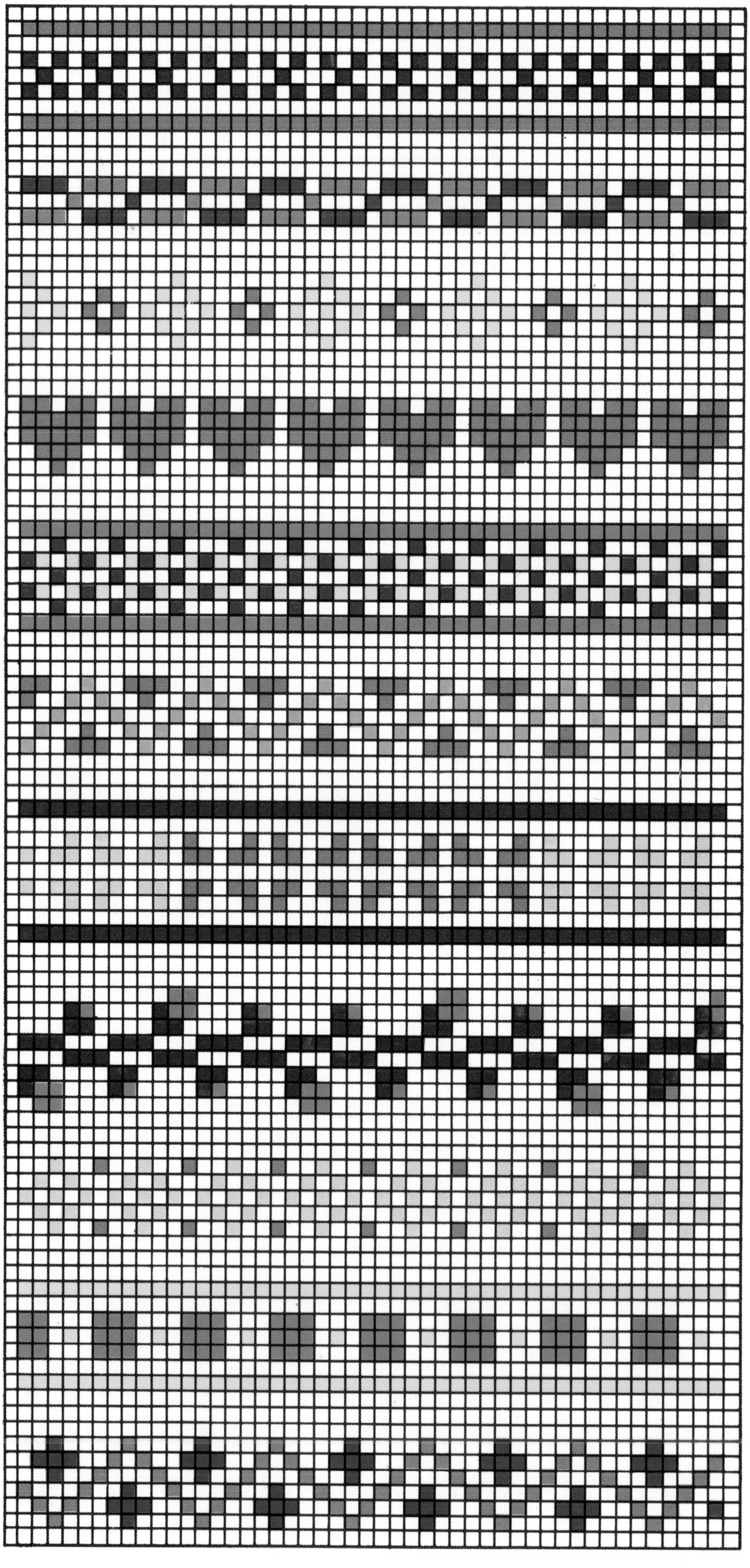

For quiet times

Curling up with a favourite book is always a pleasure – and even more of a pleasure when you can find your page marked with an Egyptian-design bookmark. Embroider yourself a special case for your spectacles too – this design was inspired by Eskimo leatherwork.

Bookmark
Materials

White metal bookmark blank
DMC stranded cottons as follows: one skein each of 797 blue, 3607 pink, 552 purple, 699 green, 606 red, white
Gold metallic thread.

Working the embroidery

Using three strands of thread or three strands of gold thread together, work the bookmark following the chart and the key.

Spectacles case
Materials

Two pieces of cream Binca fabric, 4×9in (10×23cm), six threads to 1in (2.5cm)
DMC soft cottons as follows: one skein each of 726 yellow, 321 red, 825 blue, 943 green
Two pieces each of medium-weight iron-on interfacing and lining, same size.

Preparation

1 Measure and mark the middle of both pieces of fabric with lines of basting stitches, vertically and horizontally.

Working the embroidery

2 The middle of the chart is indicated by arrows on the edges. This corresponds with the middle of your fabric, marked with basting.

3 Using the soft cotton, work the design from the chart and key on both pieces of Binca fabric. Finish thread off neatly at the back so that it cannot be seen from the front of the work.

Finishing

4 Iron the interfacing onto the back of the finished embroidery to prevent fraying.

5 Trim the fabric back to within four holes of the embroidery at the top, and to within two holes on the other three edges.

6 Fold the top edges under and sew down by hand or machine-stitch.

7 Place the two pieces of embroidery together right sides facing, sew or machine-stitch round three sides, leaving the top open. Clip the corners diagonally, turn right side out.

8 Stitch the lining pieces together on three sides, right sides facing. Trim seam allowances back to ɑin (6mm), slip into the case, slipstitch to case on the open end.

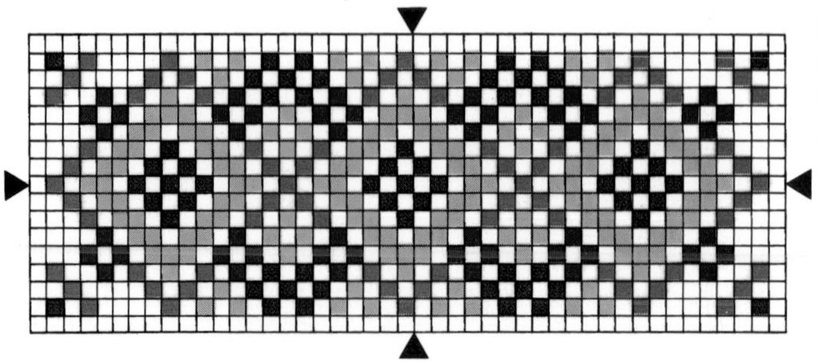

KEY to spectacles case
- 726
- 321
- 825
- 943

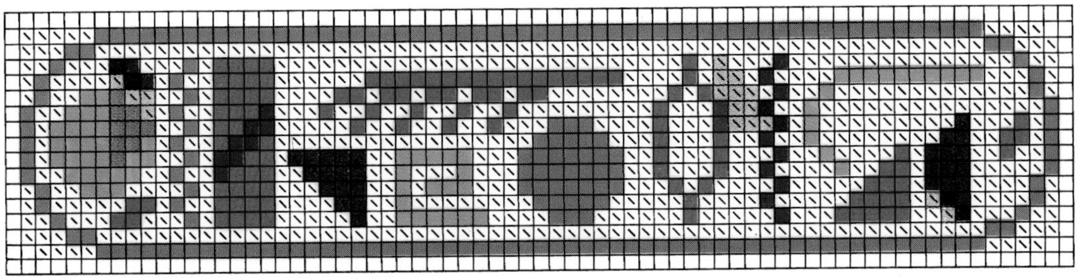

KEY to bookmark

- ■ 797
- ■ 3607
- ■ 552
- ■ 699
- ■ 606
- ■ gold
- ⧅ white

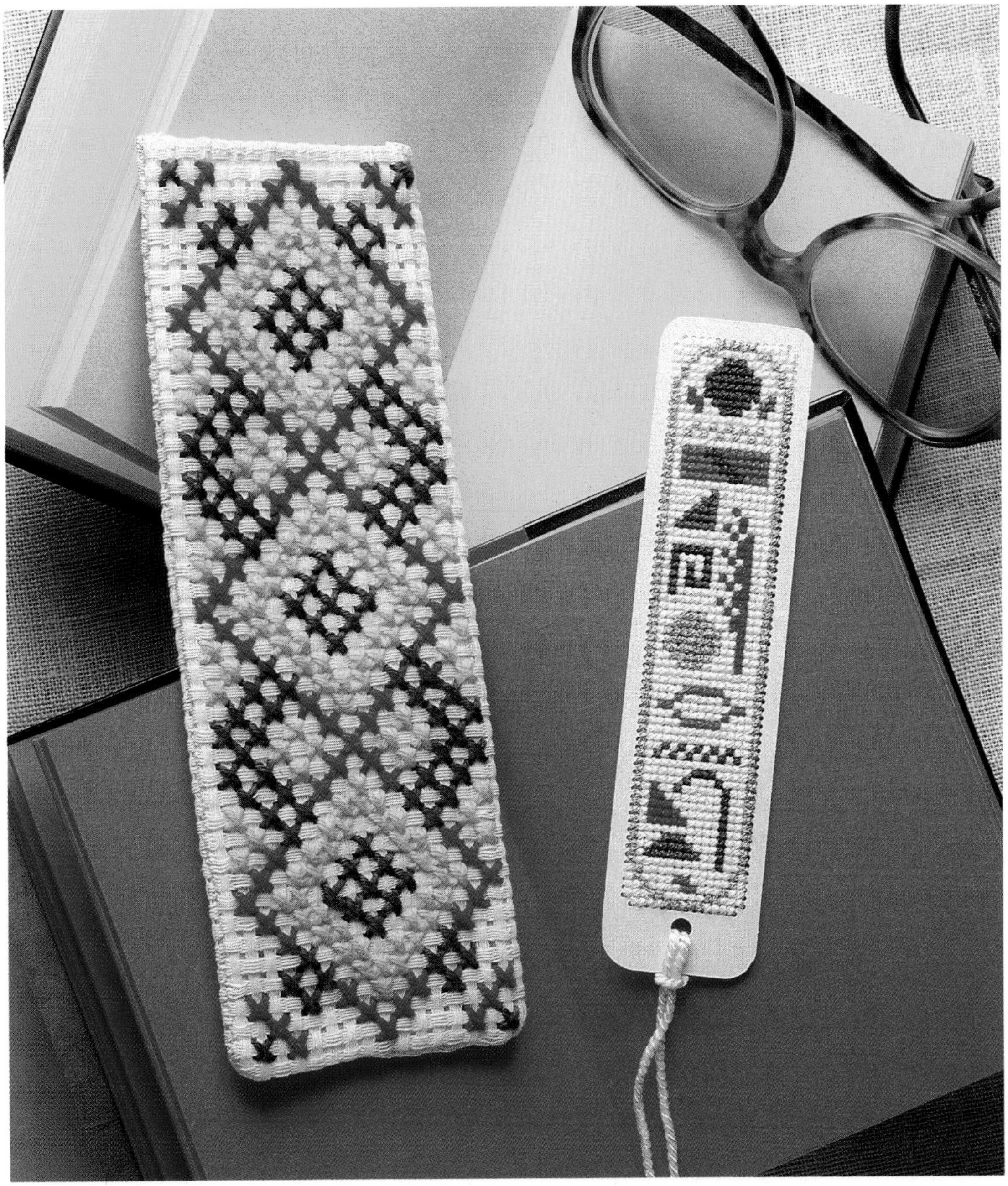

Easy as ABC

This alphabet can be worked up as a sampler just as it is, or individual letters can be used to personalise all kinds of clothes and accessories from dressing gowns and babies' dresses to bags and belts. On page 52, there's a different way of working them in two colours. Choose shades that complement the item you are personalising.

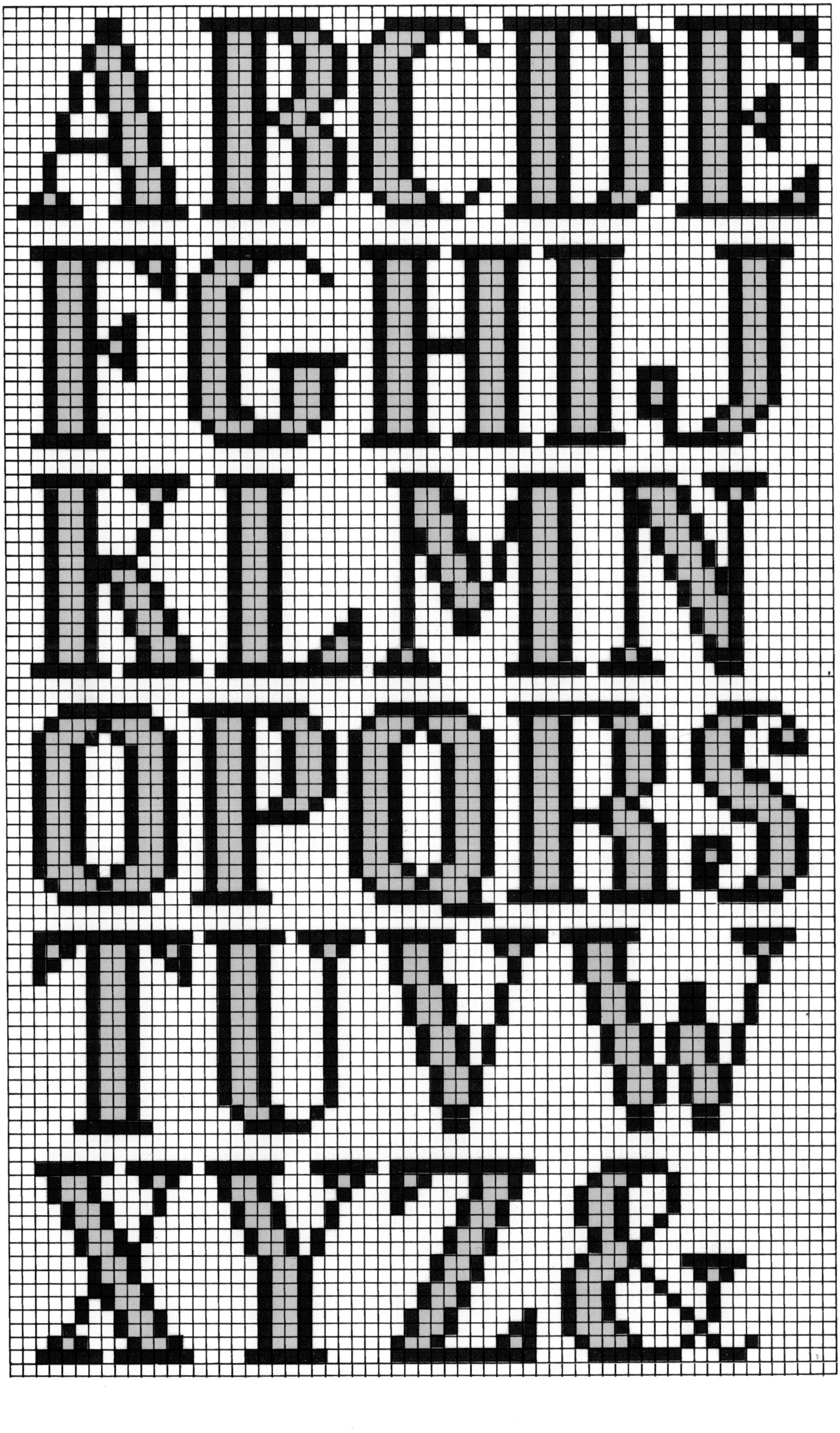
ABCDE
FGHIJ
KLMN
OPQRS
TUVW
XYZ&

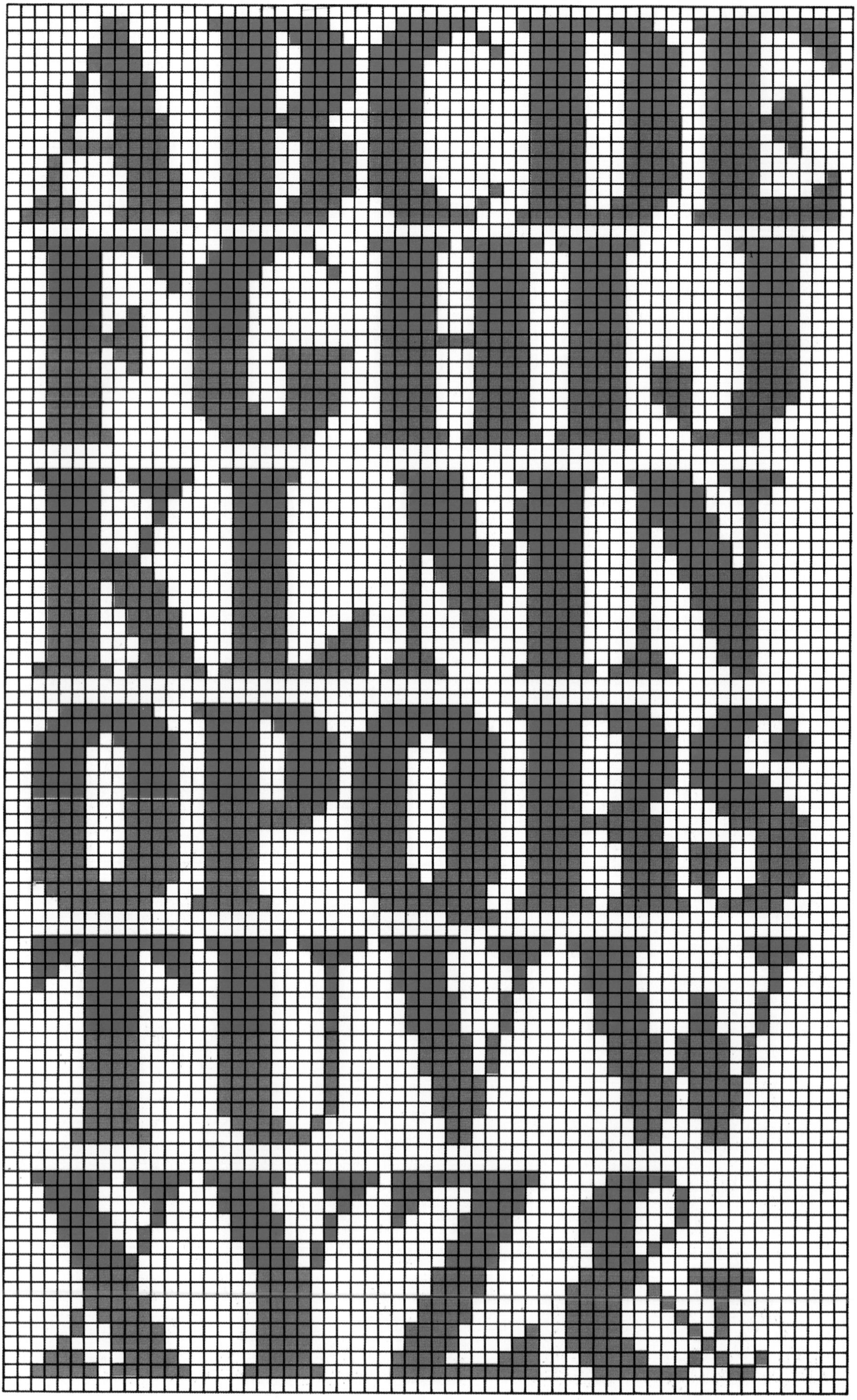

Alphabet letters

In Victorian households, house linens – bedsheets, pillowcases, towels, tablecloths, traycloths and napkins – were often marked with cross-stitched initials, rather than spoiling the linens with marking ink. Initials were also worked on many personal items such as handkerchiefs, purses, scarves and shawls, underclothes and nightgowns, as well as on children's and babies' garments. Sometimes tiny flowers and leaves were incorporated to make the initials even prettier.

The alphabet charts on pages 51 and 52 can be worked to any scale you like. On fabric with 14 threads to 1in (2.5cm), the letters would be just over 1in (2.5cm) high. Worked on a finer weave fabric, the resulting letters will be smaller.

Alphabet letters are an ideal way of decorating and personalizing embroidered items. You can use just one letter, perhaps surrounding it with a garland of flowers, or use two or three letters for the initials of a name. Worked in two colours and with some parts outlined in back stitch, letters from either of the charts can be overlapped. Try working a man's initials on the pocket of a dressing gown – remove the pocket first and use the waste canvas method described on page 36. You can work your own initials on lingerie cases, or handkerchief sachets, or make a prettily embroidered pillow, complete with initials for a bridal gift.

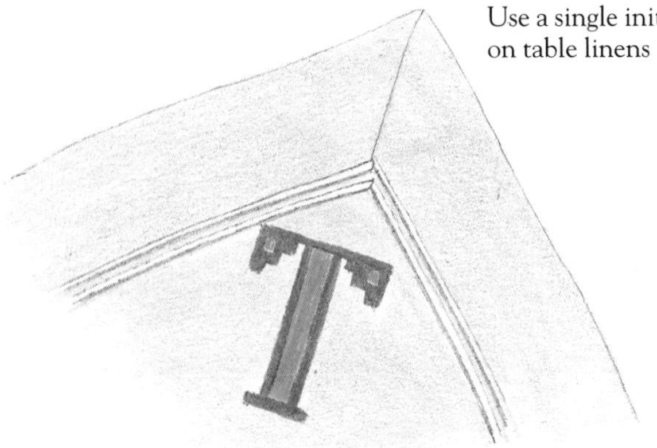

Use a single initial on table linens

Ready-made items require the waste canvas method

Large initials will personalize a diary

Work an initial on a scarf for a gift

Under glass

Chinese brocades were the inspiration for this beautiful pattern, made even more exotic by the use of bright shiny threads. A backing of imitation gold kid adds to the richness.

Materials
$3\frac{1}{2}$in (9cm) diameter glass paperweight blank
White Hardanger fabric, 4in (10cm) square, 11 threads to 1in (2.5cm)
DMC stranded cottons as follows: one skein each of 3607 pink, 792 blue, 552 purple
Light-weight iron-on interfacing, 4in (10cm) square
Gold metallic thread
Circle of imitation gold leather, $3\frac{1}{2}$in (9cm) diameter; clear glue.

Preparation
1 Measure and mark the middle of the fabric with lines of basting stitches, vertically and horizontally.

Working the embroidery
2 The middle of the chart is indicated by arrows on the edges. This corresponds with the middle of your fabric, marked with basting.

3 Using all four strands of the viscose thread, then four strands of gold thread together, work the design following the chart and key.

Finishing
4 Iron the interfacing on to the back of the embroidery to prevent fraying. Make sure the iron is not too hot or the metallic threads could melt.

5 Trim carefully round the circle of embroidery, close to the stitching, but taking care not to cut the stitches.

6 Slip the embroidery into the indentation at the bottom of the paperweight, right side up, so that it shows through the glass top. Spread clear glue across the top of the gold circle and press into position on the bottom of the paperweight, so that the gold shows through the glass. Leave to dry.

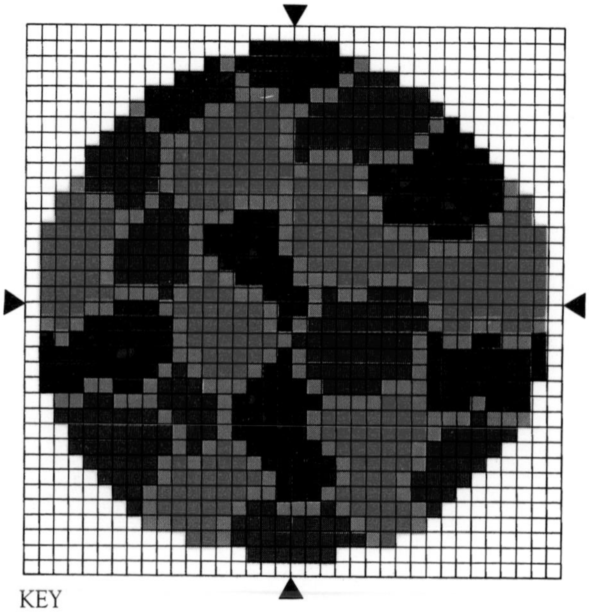

KEY
■ 3607
■ 792
■ 552
■ gold

Shy violets

Here's a pretty flower motif that can be worked on a pocket of a skirt or blouse. It is a motif you'll use again and again, for clothes, accessories or even for home furnishings.

Materials

DMC stranded cottons as follows: one skein each of 327 dark purple, 552 mid-purple, 209 mauve, 211 pale mauve, 986 dark green, 562 pale green, 743 yellow

Note: If you are making your own garment, embroider the pocket before you attach it. On a ready-made garment, remove the pocket, and then stitch it back into place once it is embroidered. If you are using an evenweave fabric, such as linen or a linen-look weave, you will be able to embroider the motif directly onto the fabric working the cross stitches over an even number of threads – three or four, depending on the thickness of the weave. If the fabric is satin, cotton twill or a similar type, use the waste canvas method (see page 157).

Preparation

1 Measure and mark the middle of the pocket with lines of basting stitches, vertically and horizontally.

Working the embroidery

2 The arrows on the chart edges indicate the middle of the design. This corresponds with the marked middle of your fabric. Embroider the design, starting in the middle, following the chart and key.

Finishing

3 When the embroidery is completed, press lightly on the wrong side to 'emboss' the design. Sew the pocket to the garment.

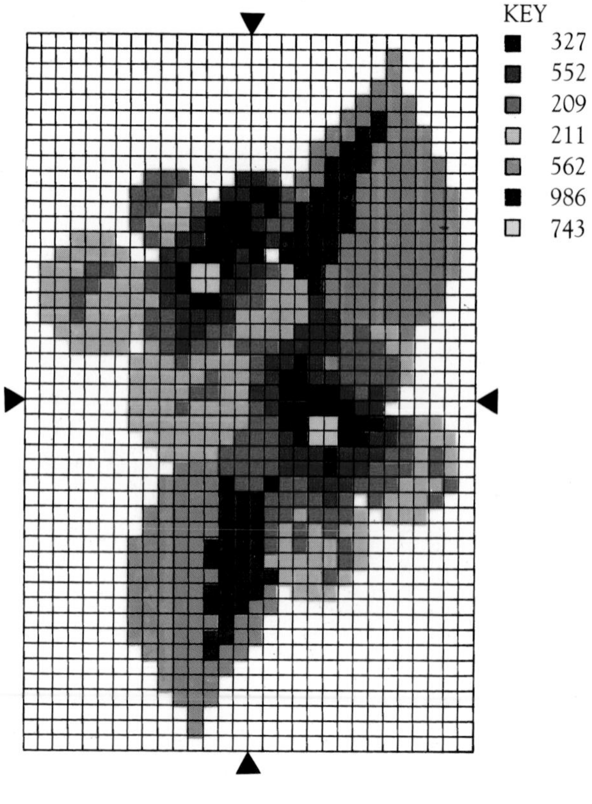

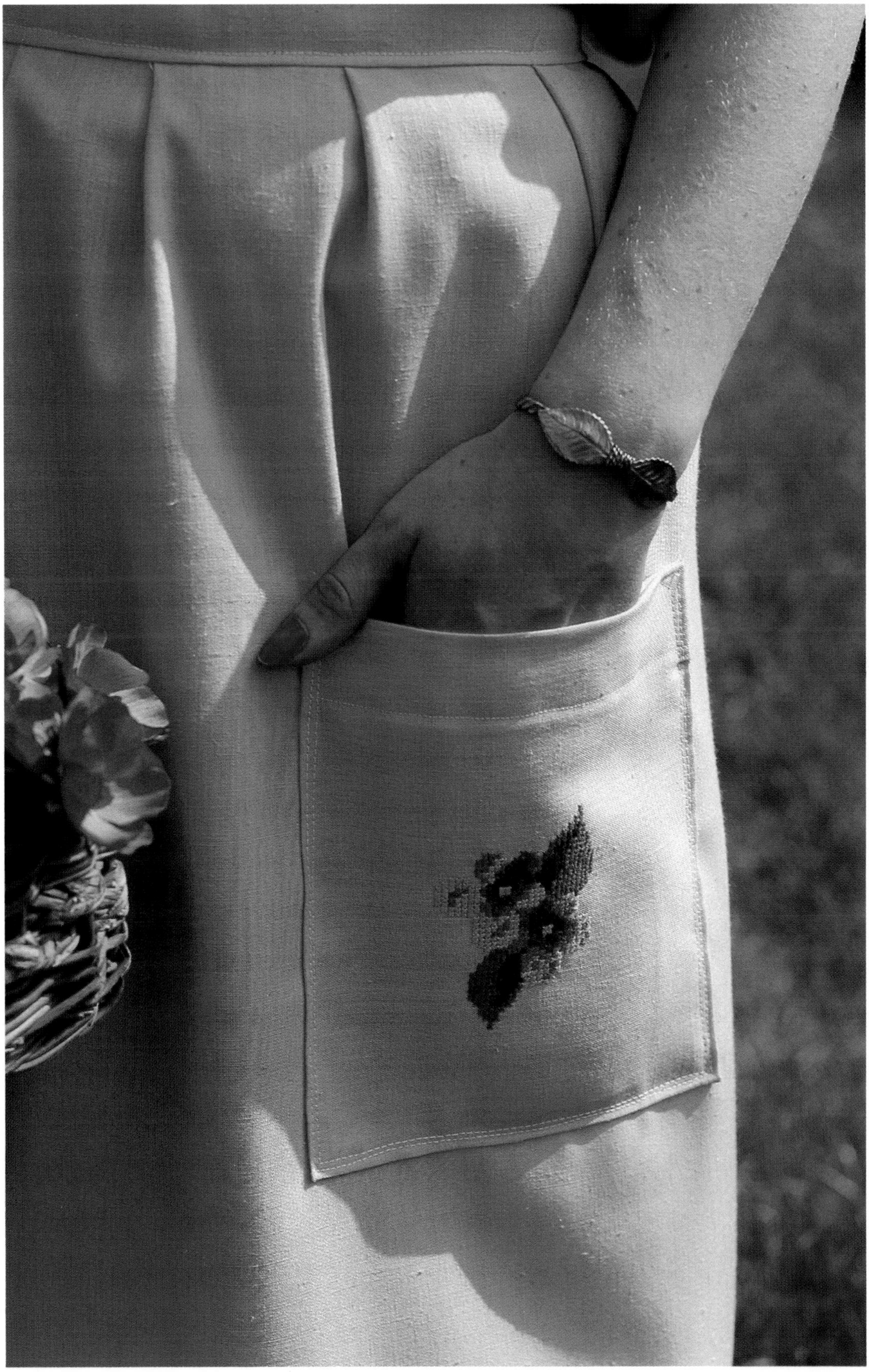

Luxurious lingerie

Add a touch of luxury to lingerie, with a columbine embroidered onto a satin negligée. The traditional English wayside flower has been turned into a delicate motif, and using the waste canvas method means that you can work the embroidery onto the most delicate fabrics.

Materials

Piece of waste canvas, 4in (10cm) square, 12 threads to 1in (2.5cm)

Embroidery silks as follows: one skein each of 605 pale pink, 604 mid-pink, 603 dark pink, 772 pale green, 3364 mid-green, 3363 dark green.

Preparation

1 Baste the waste canvas onto the shoulder of the negligée over the place where the motif is to be. Measure and mark the middle of the canvas with basting stitches both vertically and horizontally.

Working the embroidery

2 Using 2 strands of the silk together, stitch the design following the chart and key, and starting in the middle indicated by arrows on the edges of the chart.

Finishing

3 Remove the waste canvas by dampening it to dissolve the glue holding the threads together. Pull each strand of canvas from under the embroidery, leaving the cross-stitch design on the surface of the fabric. This technique is described and illustrated on page 157.

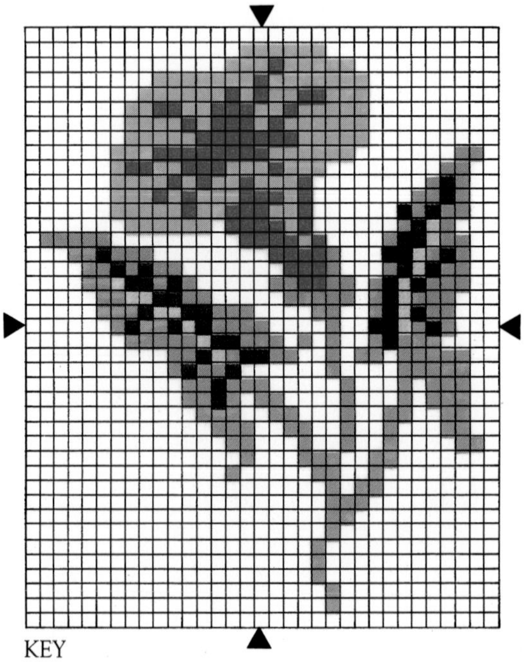

KEY
- 605
- 604
- 603
- 3364
- 3363
- 772

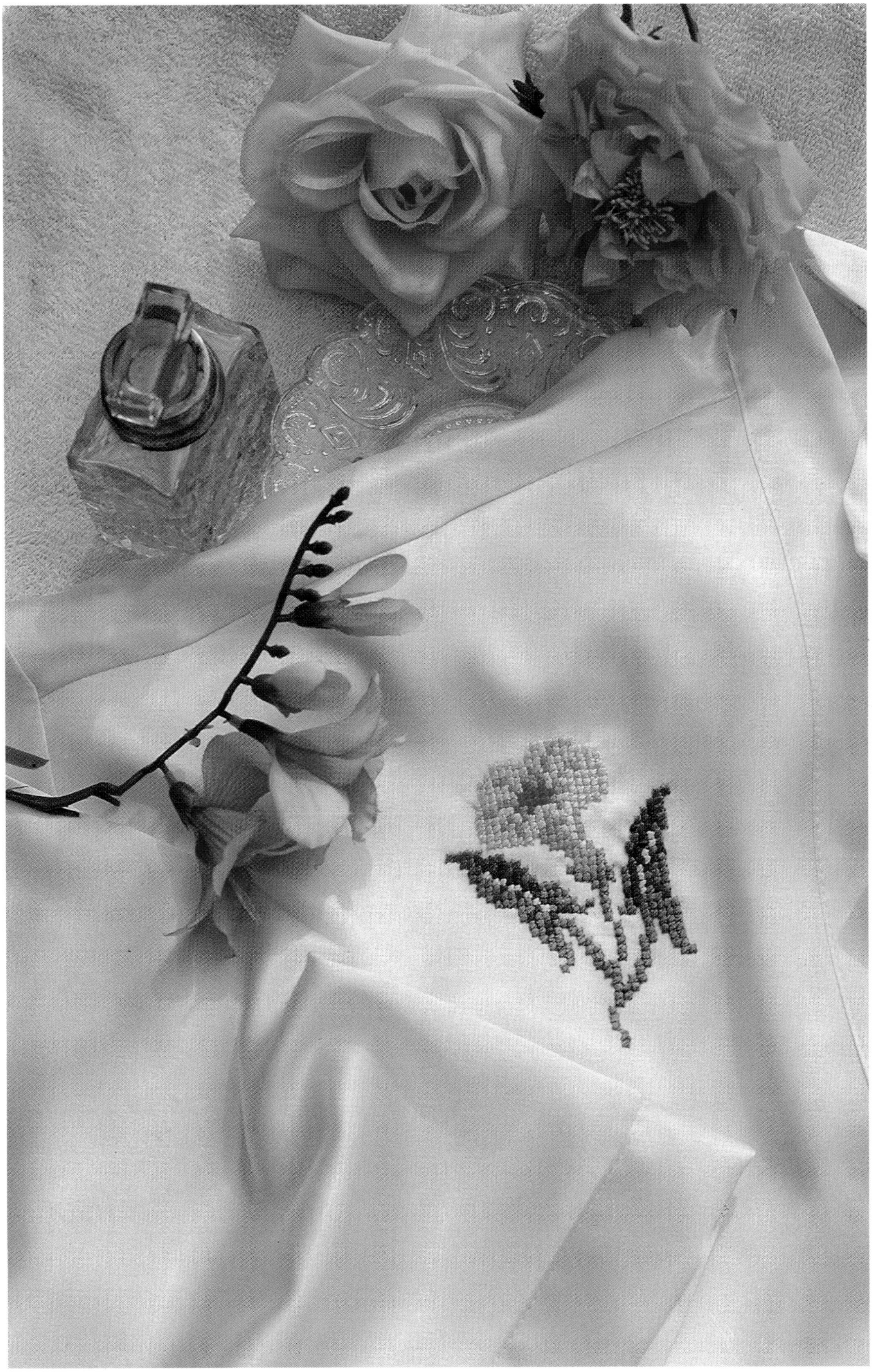

Oriental splendour

The shape of an oriental fan is used for this pretty clutch purse. It is worked in wool embroidery on hessian for everyday use, but the design would look magnificent stitched in metallic threads on a glittery fabric for a luxurious evening bag.

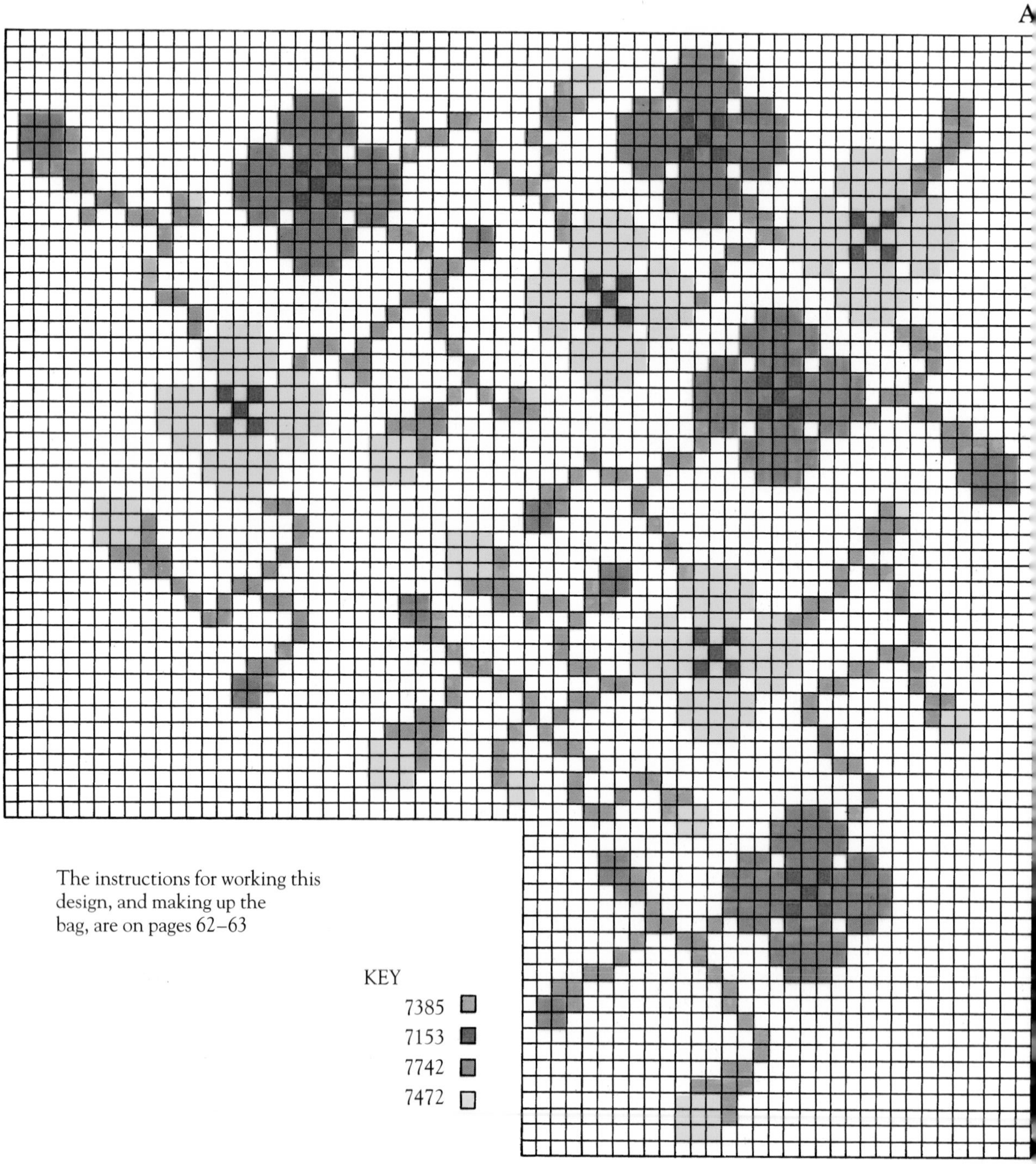

The instructions for working this design, and making up the bag, are on pages 62–63

KEY

7385
7153
7742
7472

Materials

Circle of blue hessian, 19in (48cm) diameter, approximately 16 threads to 1in (2.5cm)

Circle of pelmet-weight iron-on interfacing the same size

Circle of blue lining fabric the same size

DMC tapisserie wools as follows: one skein each of 7472 pale yellow, 7742 dark yellow, 7153 pink, 7385 green.

Preparation

1 Divide the fabric circle into quarters with basting stitches.

Working the embroidery

2 Work the design in one quarter, following the chart and key, making sure that point A on the design is towards the centre of the circle. Work each cross stitch across two threads of the hessian.

Finishing

3 Press the finished embroidery on the wrong side with a warm iron. Check that the fabric is square. Press again and pull into shape if it has distorted. Iron the interfacing circle to the wrong side of the embroidery.

4 Cut out one quarter of the embroidered fabric (see illustration) leaving a ½in (12mm) seam allowance.

5 Cut out one quarter of the lining fabric. With right sides together, pin and baste the embroidered fabric to the lining, leaving the edge marked B open.

6 Machine-stitch ½in (12mm) from the edge along all the edges except edge B (see illustration). Clip the corner and into the seam allowance, then turn right side out. Press seams flat with a warm iron.

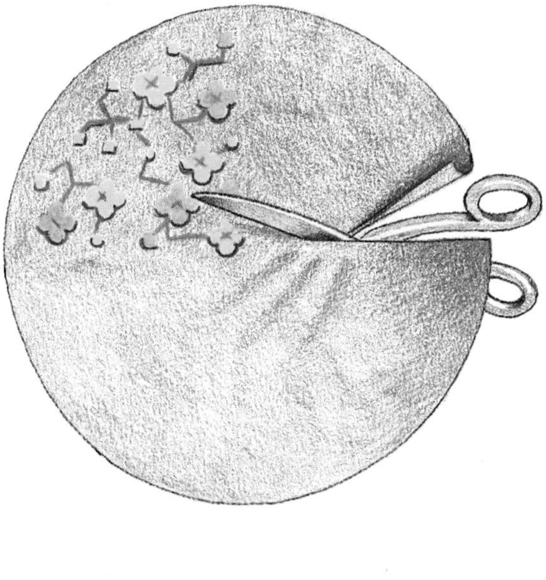

1 Cut out one quarter of hessian, leaving a seam allowance.

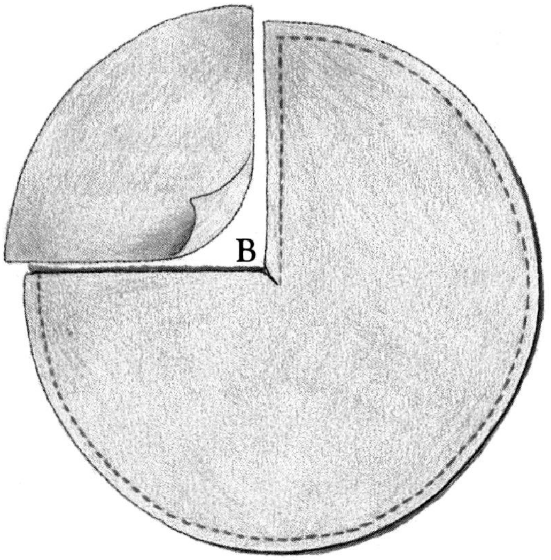

2 Cut out one quarter of the lining, and stitch lining to hessian.

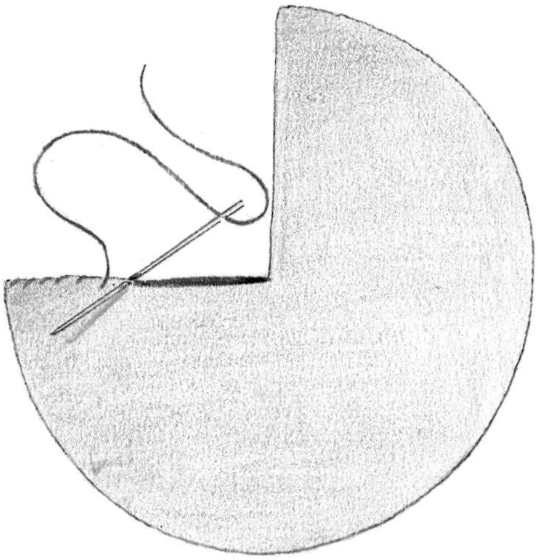

3 Turn right side out, and stitch edge B.

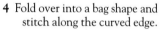

4 Fold over into a bag shape and stitch along the curved edge.

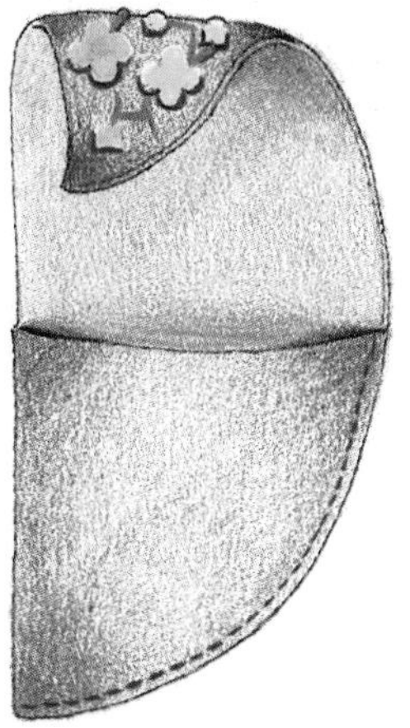

7 Fold in the seam allowances of edge B, and sew together by hand or machine-stitch.

8 Fold the bag (see illustration) and stitch together around the curved edge. Topstitch around the other edges of the bag.

9 Fasten the purse with a press fastener, or work a loop on the flap with matching stranded threads and sew a pretty button on the purse to correspond.

This design is such an unusual shape that it would work well in different sizes. Scale the design down and embroider it on Hardanger or other evenweave fabric for a pincushion, or scale it up and embroider a quarter-circle cushion.

Midnight blues

This amusing cat design shows just how versatile cross-stitch designs can be. Here it is used for a card and on page 67 it becomes a picture.

Materials (for card)

Piece of cream Hardanger fabric, $4 \times 5\frac{1}{2}$in (100×14cm), 11 threads to 1in (2.5cm)

Piece of blue card, $13\frac{1}{2} \times 7$in (34×17.5cm)

Clear glue (or rubber solution)

DMC stranded cottons as follows: one skein each of 310 black, 606 red, 726 yellow, 798 dark blue, 800 mid-blue, 3753 light blue, 702 green, 677 light brown, 832 mid-brown, 838 dark brown, white

Blue rectangular-window card blank.

Preparation

1 Measure and mark the middle of the fabric with lines of basting stitches, vertically and horizontally.

Working the embroidery

2 The middle of the chart is indicated by arrows on the edges. This corresponds with the middle of your fabric, marked with basting.

3 Using three strands of thread together, work the design following the chart and key.

KEY

310	606	726	798
800	3753	702	677
832	838	White	

The cat-in-the-window picture here is worked from the same chart as the Midnight blues card on page 65.

4 Fold the blue card into three, and cut a window in the central panel big enough for the embroidery to show through.

Finishing

5 Press the design lightly on the wrong side with a warm iron. Spread glue thinly around the margins of the embroidery.

6 Glue the embroidery behind the window in the central panel.

7 Glue the back of the left-hand panel and fold it over behind the embroidery.

CAT-IN-THE-WINDOW

Materials

Piece of cream Binca fabric, 12×14 (30×35cm), 6 threads to 1in (2.5cm)
DMC soft cottons as follows: one skein each of 606 red, 726 yellow, 3753 light blue, 702 green, 677 light brown, 832 mid-brown, 838 dark brown, white; two skeins of 310 black; three skeins of 798 dark blue; four skeins of 800 mid blue
Piece of press-on adhesive board
Masking tape.

Preparation

1 Prepare the fabric as for the card.

Working the embroidery

2 Stitch the design, following the chart and key for Midnight blues on page 64.

3 Press the embroidery on the wrong side with a warm iron.

4 Peel the protective covering from the press-on board, and position the embroidery carefully on the top. Smooth the embroidery in place, outwards from the centre.

5 Fold the fabric over the edges of the board and secure at the back with masking tape. The embroidery is now ready for framing.

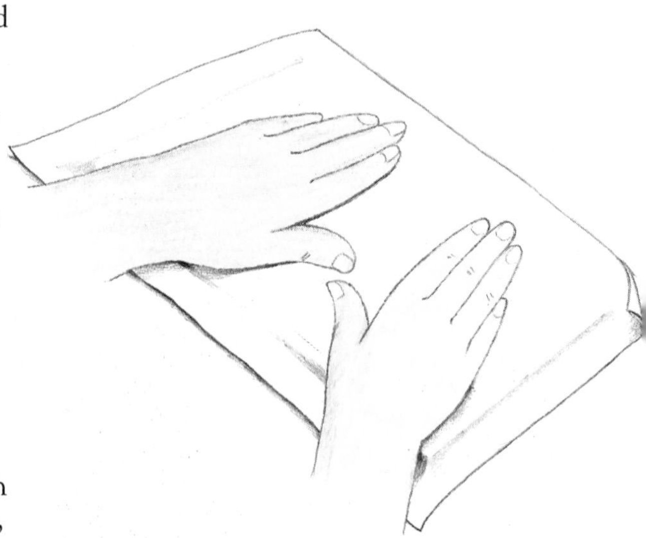

Smooth the fabric on the adhesive surface.

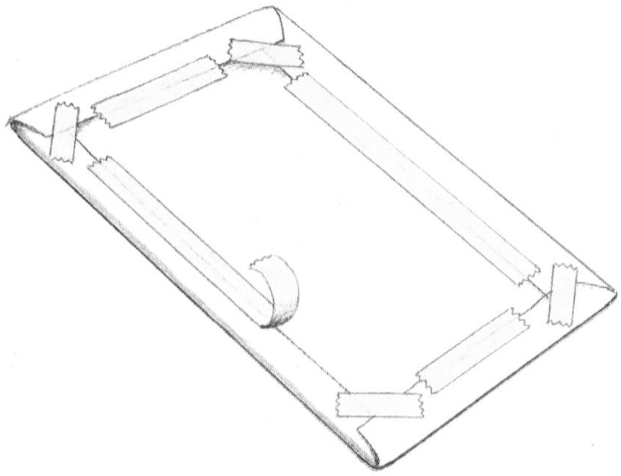

Secure the fabric on the back of the board with masking tape.

Happy ever after

An embroidered frame for a favourite wedding photograph makes an ideal wedding present and it's a lovely idea for a special anniversary gift too. Work it in the pastel colour scheme given or match the colours to the bride's bouquet. The chart is on pages 70–71.

Materials
Piece of white Hardanger, 16×20in (40×51cm), 22 threads to 1in (2.5cm)
DMC stranded cottons as follows: one skein each of 341 pale blue, 809 mid-blue, 605 pale pink, 894 mid-pink
Silver metallic thread
Piece of press-on adhesive board, 11×12½in (28×32cm)
Masking tape.

Preparation
1 Measure and mark the middle of the fabric with lines of basting stitches, vertically and horizontally.

Working the embroidery
2 The middle of the chart is indicated by arrows on the edges. (See pages 70–71.) This corresponds with the middle of your fabric marked with basting.

3 Using three strands of thread together, or three strands of metallic thread together, work the design following the chart and key. Work stitches over two threads of fabric.

4 Press the completed embroidery on the wrong side with a cool iron. (A too-hot iron may melt the metallic threads.)

5 Choose a suitable photograph to fit the frame and mark the position on the back of the fabric. Cut a hole from the middle, allowing 1½in (37mm) of fabric for turning.

6 Lay the fabric over the adhesive board, and carefully mark the position where the photograph will go, using a pin. Cut out the centre of the board with a crafts knife.

7 Peel off the protective backing and press the embroidery firmly onto the adhesive surface. Turn the fabric edges over to the back and secure with masking tape. Clip the corners of the inner edges so that they fold over neatly.

8 Mount the photograph in the centre of the frame, and secure at the back with masking tape.

The hearts and ribbons would look pretty worked on a cushion

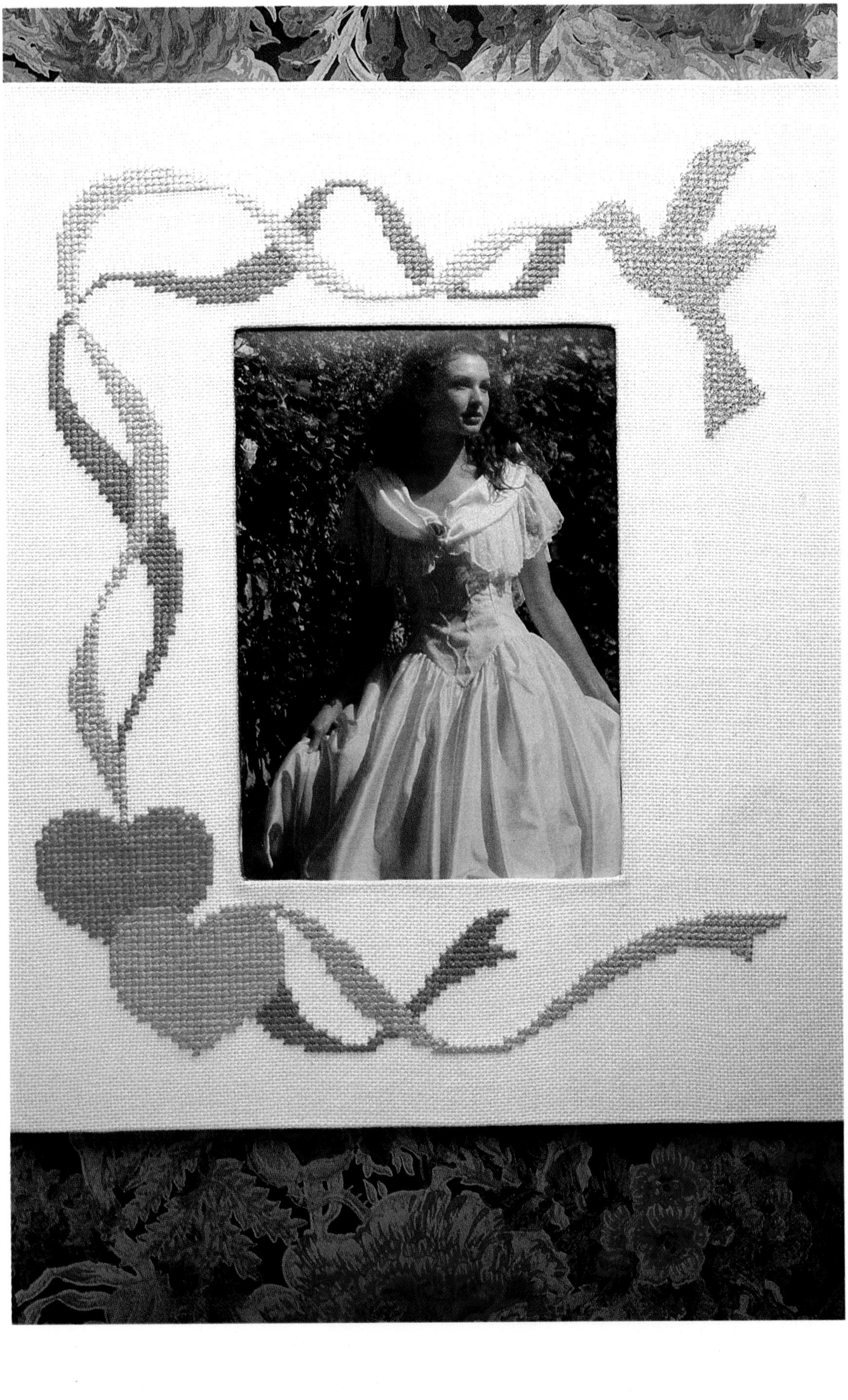

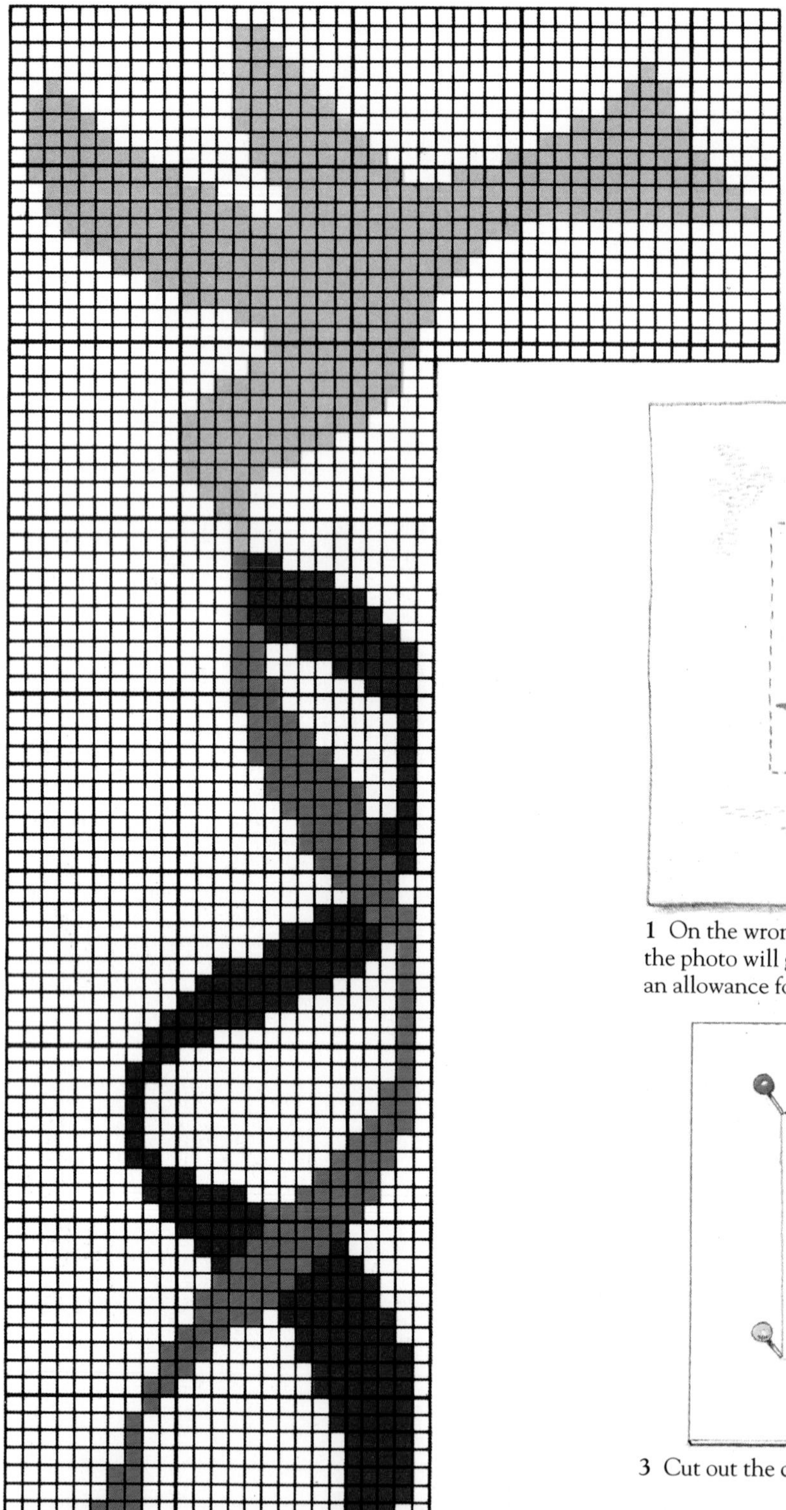
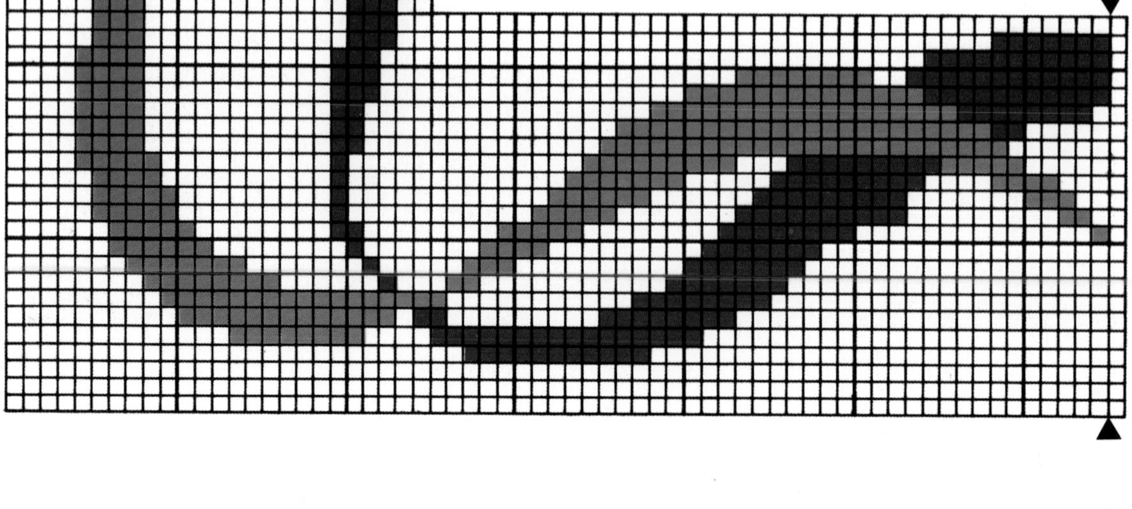

KEY
- Silver
- 809
- 341
- 605
- 894

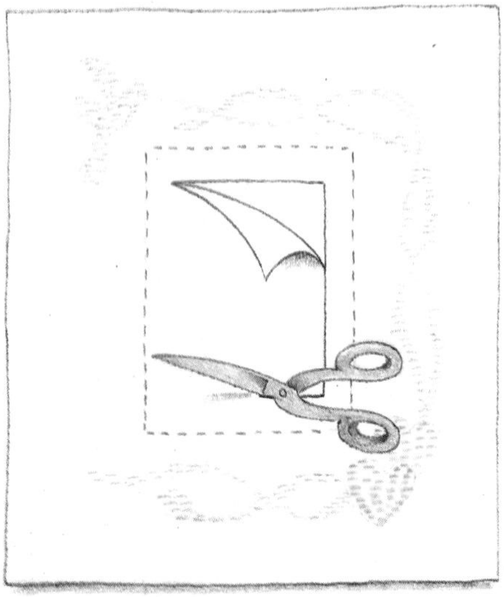

1 On the wrong side of the fabric, mark where the photo will go. Cut inside this line, leaving an allowance for turning.

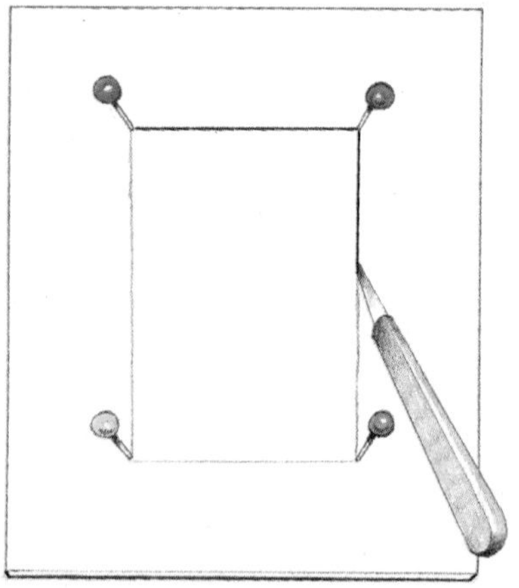

3 Cut out the central piece of the adhesive board.

Chart for the Happy ever after frame

The two sections of the chart join where indicated with arrows

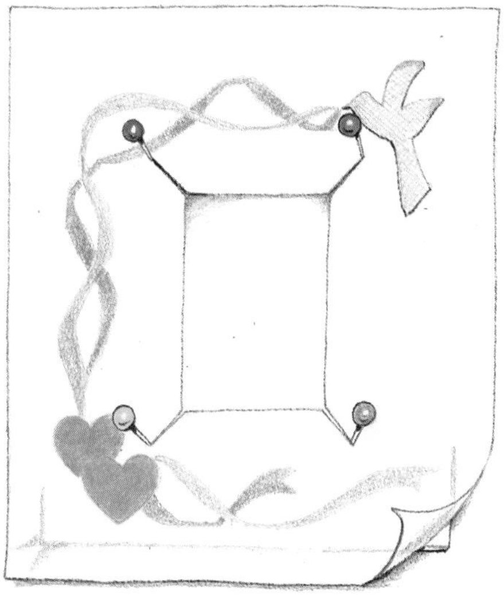

2 Position the fabric over the press-on board, use pins to mark the photo position.

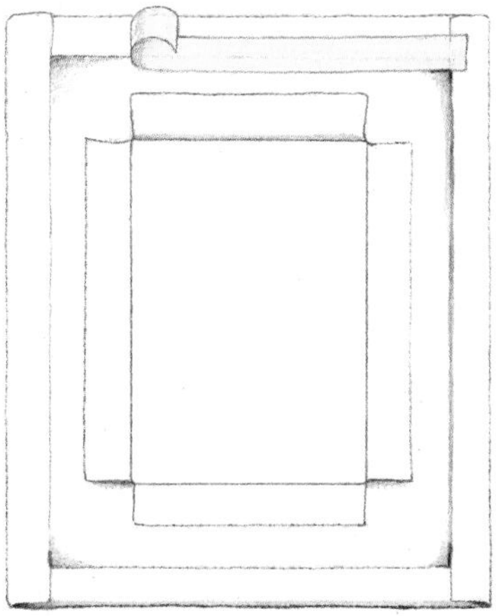

4 Secure the fabric edges on the back with masking tape.

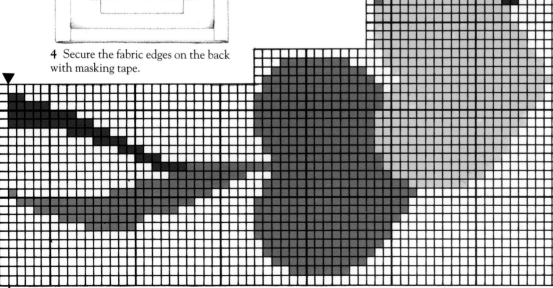

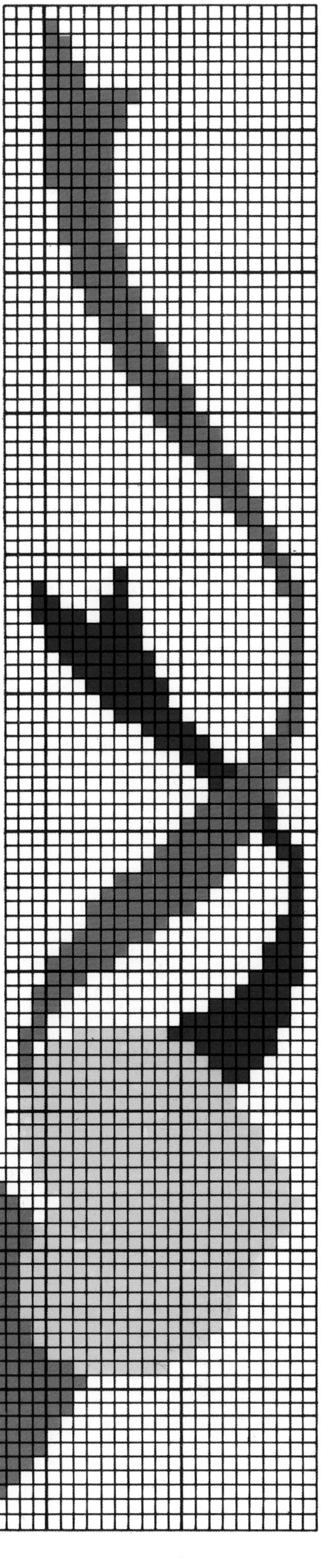

Glittering beauty

Pretty trinkets deserve a special place to keep them; what could be nicer than a glittery dragonfly jewellery box? Plastic canvas is used to construct the box.

Materials
Plastic canvas as follows:
Four pieces 11 × 31 holes (box sides)
Four pieces 5 × 33 holes (lid sides)
Piece 33 × 33 holes (lid top)
Piece 31 × 31 holes (box bottom)
DMC soft cottons as follows: two skeins of white, 1 skein of 209 mauve
Metallic embroidery threads: one spool each of light blue, dark blue.

Working the embroidery
1 The middle of the chart is indicated by arrows on the edges. This corresponds with the middle of your canvas for the lid top.

2 Following the chart and key, embroider the dragonfly design and background on the lid top. Use two strands of metallic thread together for the dragonfly.

3 Embroider the lid sides and box sides following the colours shown on the charts.

4 Work the box bottom entirely in white or choose one of the other colours if you prefer.

Constructing the box
5 Make the lid by stitching the pieces of plastic canvas together with cross stitch, using two strands of the light blue metallic thread.

6 Make the box bottom the same way, using the dark blue metallic thread.

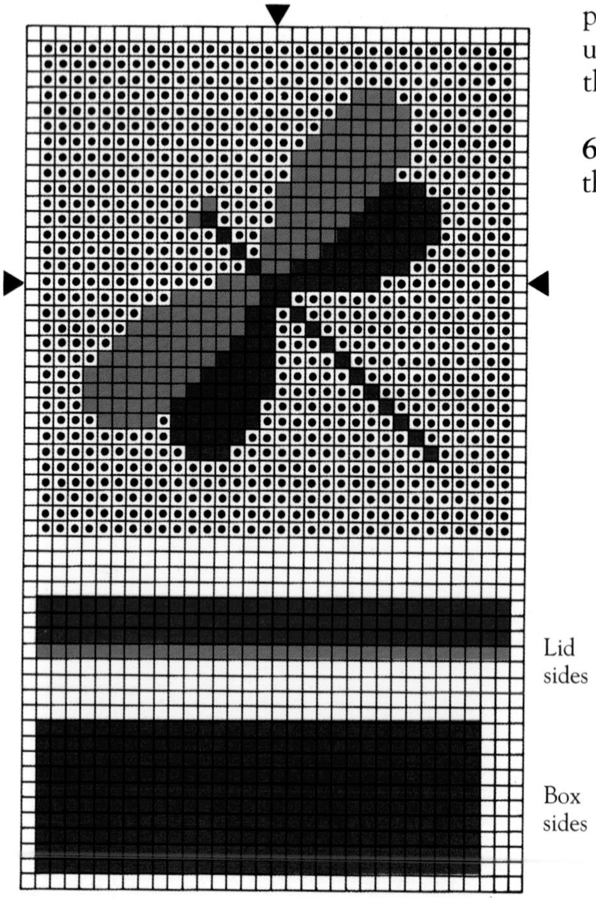

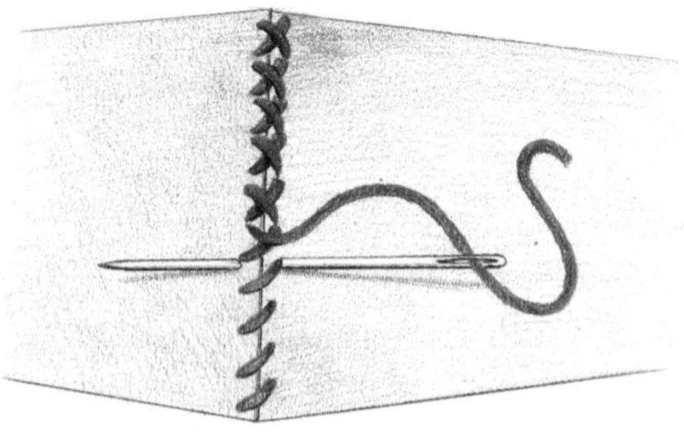

Join pieces of canvas with cross stitches

KEY
- Light blue metallic thread
- 209
- Dark blue metallic thread
- White

Baubles, bangles and beads

Cross stitch can also be used to make jewellery using metal embroidery blanks. Stitch yourself a rainbow bracelet and add some gold beads to the embroidery to make a pair of evening earrings.

Bracelet
Materials

Cross stitch bracelet blank in silver finish
DMC stranded cottons as follows: one skein each of 798 blue, 209 mauve, 603 pink, 3341 orange, 743 yellow, 563 green.

Working the embroidery

Using three strands of thread together, work the design following the chart and key.

Earrings
Materials

Pair of metal cross stitch earring blanks in gold finish
DMC stranded cotton as follows: one skein of 208 purple
84 tiny gold beads.

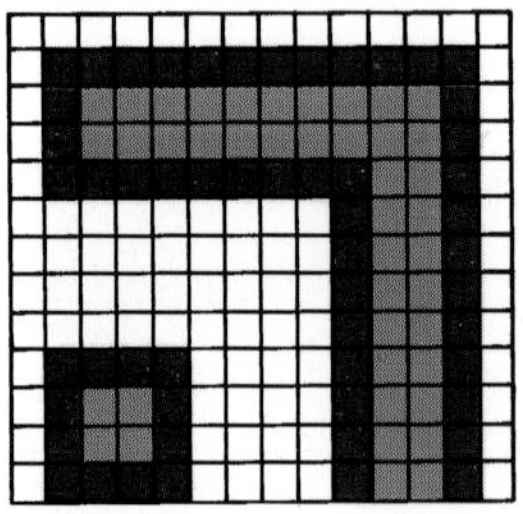

KEY
Gold beads
208

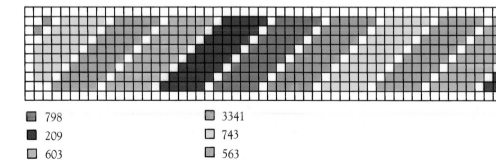

Working the embroidery

1 Stitch the plain outside squares of the design first on each earring.

2 For the inner squares, work the first half of the cross stitch, then thread a gold bead onto the needle before completing the top half of the stitch. You may find that you have to change to a finer needle so that it will go through the centre hole of the beads.

Make a pair of earrings to match your most exotic evening gown; choose either gold or silver backgrounds, and beads in the same colour, then pick a shade of stranded cotton which complements the dress. Or, omit the beads and work the central stitches in a glittery metallic thread to catch the light. For a different mood, work a bracelet to match your favourite summer dress. Instead of the rainbow colours shown here, pick the colours from a floral print or striped dress, and use stranded cottons in those shades to produce a unique piece of jewellery.

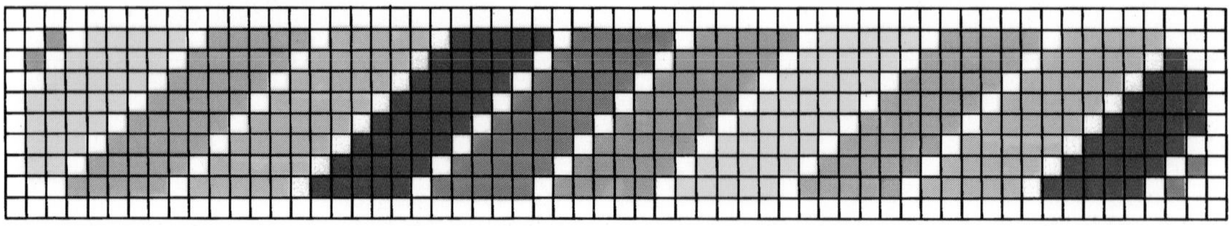

798
209
603
3341
743
563

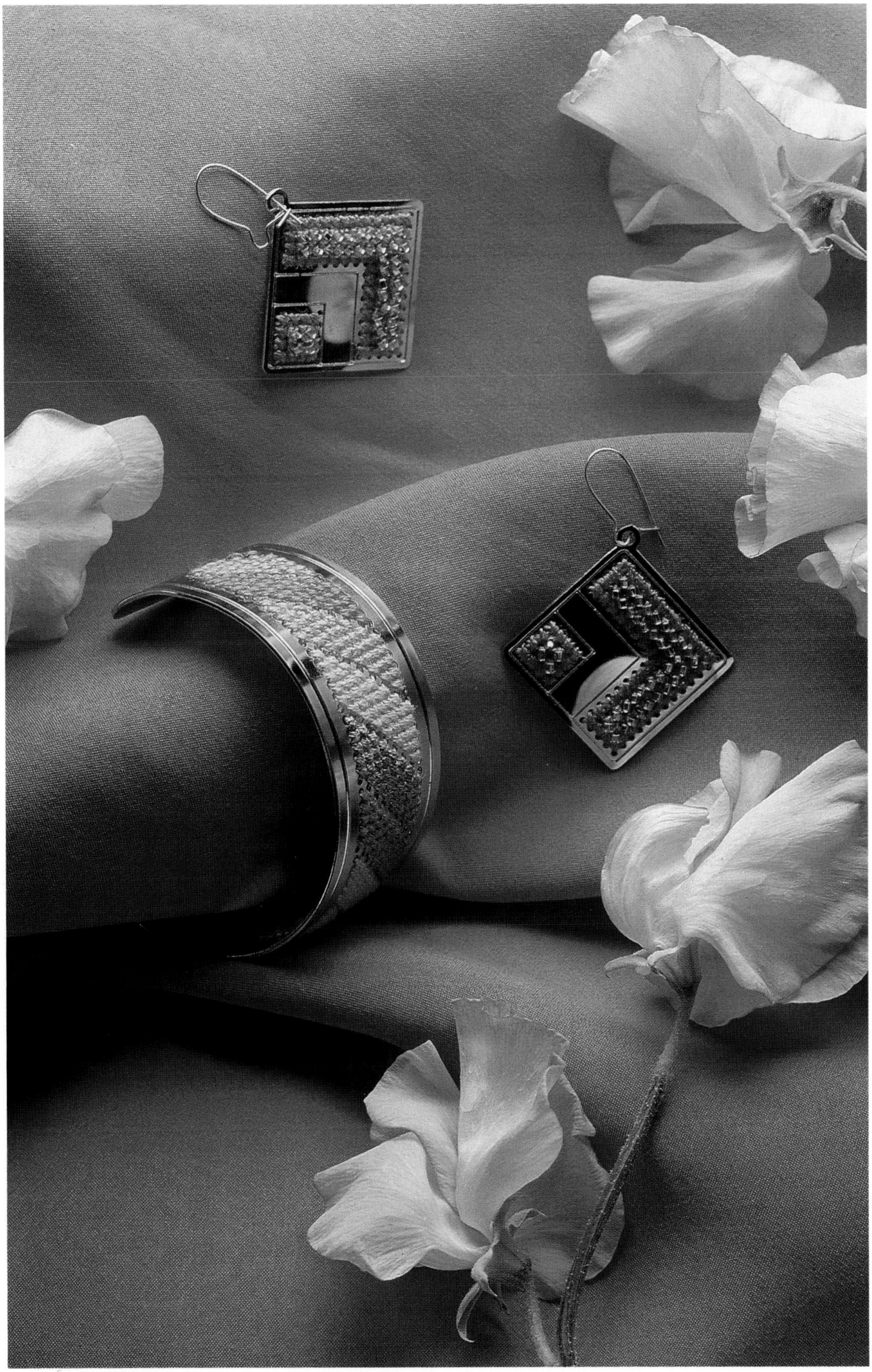

Plains Indian belt

Indian beadwork designs are echoed in this bold zigzag belt; team it with co-ordinating colours, or wear it with white for fashion impact.

Materials

Strip of single-thread canvas 12 threads to 1in (2.5cm), 2in (5cm) wide, and to the waist measurement plus 3in (8cm)
DMC soft cottons as follows: two skeins each of 996 turquoise, 701 green, 956 pink; three skeins of 797 blue
Strip of medium-weight iron-on interfacing 1in (2.5cm) wide by the belt length
Metal buckle to fit a 1in (2.5cm) belt

Working the embroidery

1 Begin at the diagonal end of the chart, 12mm (½in) from the canvas bottom edge, and the same distance from the right-hand end. Work repeats of the design to the other end of the canvas.

2 Press the unworked canvas edges to the wrong side with a warm iron. Trim one end of the iron-on interfacing to the shape of the diagonal end. Iron the interfacing strip onto the back of the belt.

3 Turn the square end of the belt over the bar of the buckle and sew into place.

4 Try the belt on, and make a hole for the buckle tongue at the appropriate place. (The tongue will slip in between the stitches.)

Using this method, it's easy to make a belt to match any of your favourite outfits. Simply pick out the colours you want to use to match or complement a skirt, dress, summer blouse or pair of trousers, and work the belt in those shades. You could use a coloured buckle, too. Or, if you want something extra-special, work a belt in metallic threads to add the finishing touch to a glamorous evening outfit.

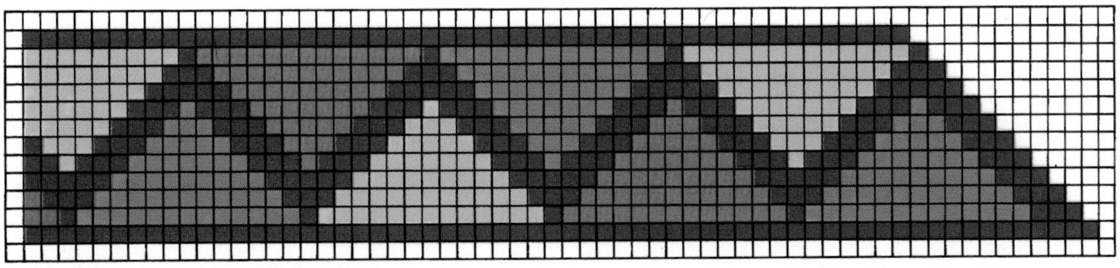

KEY
- 996
- 797
- 701
- 956

Special Occasions

Deck the tree

These pretty glittering Christmas tree ornaments are so easy to make that you could work several in an evening, but they'll last for many Christmases to come.

Materials

Pack of three metal cross stitch mini-ornaments in gold finish.

DMC stranded cottons as follows: one skein each of 606 red, 774 orange, 973 yellow, 445 pale yellow, 797 dark blue, 827 pale blue, 910 green, white.

Working the embroidery

Using three strands of cotton, work the designs following the charts and keys.

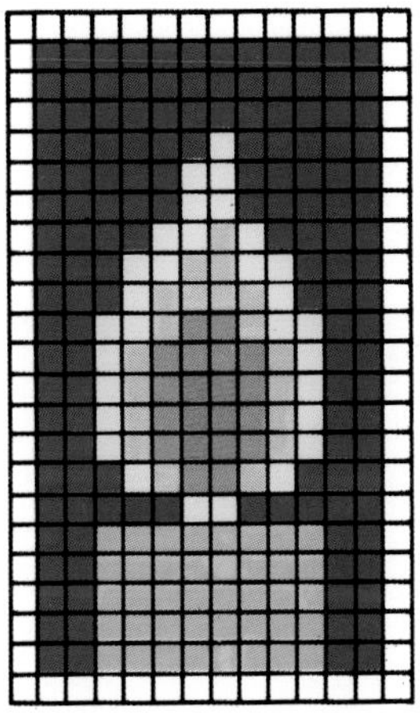

KEY
- 827
- 797
- 606
- 774
- 973
- 445

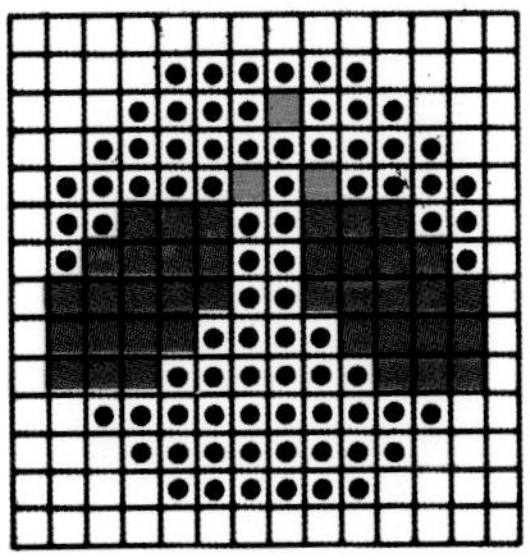

KEY
- 606
- 910
- White

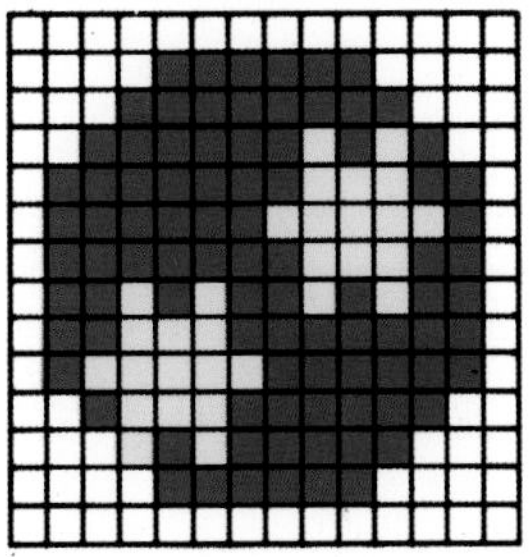

KEY
- 973
- 797

For extra glitter, work the stitches in metallic threads or add a few tiny metallic beads, sewing them to the stitches afterwards.

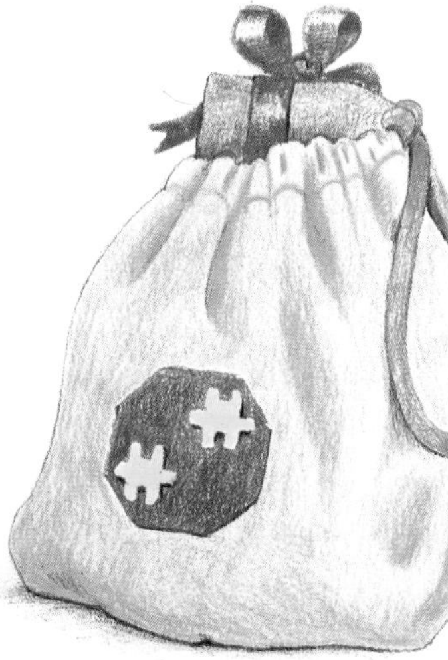

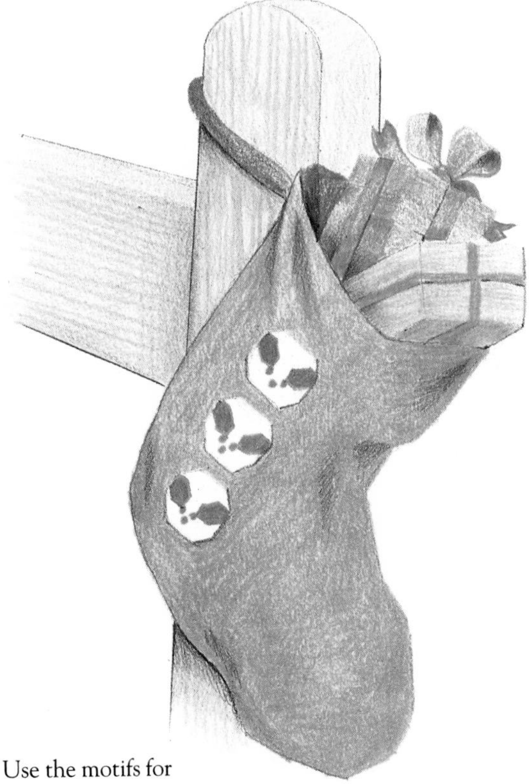

Use the motifs for other Christmas embroidery

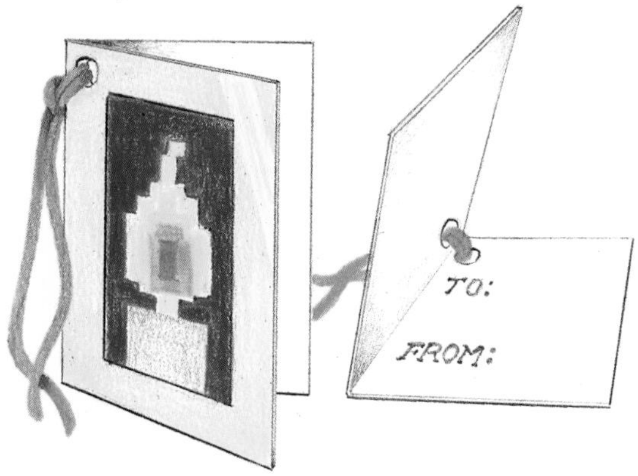

Presents galore

Tree cloths are both pretty and practical and this one with its border of brightly-wrapped presents is sure to get everyone in a festive mood. This is a pattern you'll find other uses for on Christmas embroideries – such as a party tablecloth with matching napkins.

Materials

Piece of green Binca fabric, 44in (112cm) square, 11 threads to 1in (2.5cm)

DMC stranded cottons in assorted bright colours, 15 skeins.

Preparation

1 Measure and mark a line 3in (7.5cm) from the fabric edge all round. Use basting stitches which can be unpicked afterwards, or chalk pencil.

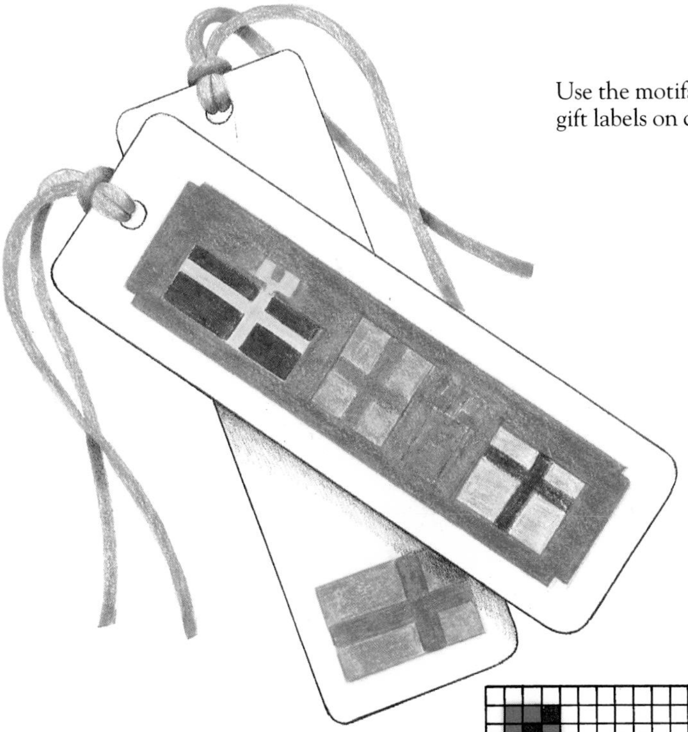

Use the motifs to work gift labels on cross-stitch paper

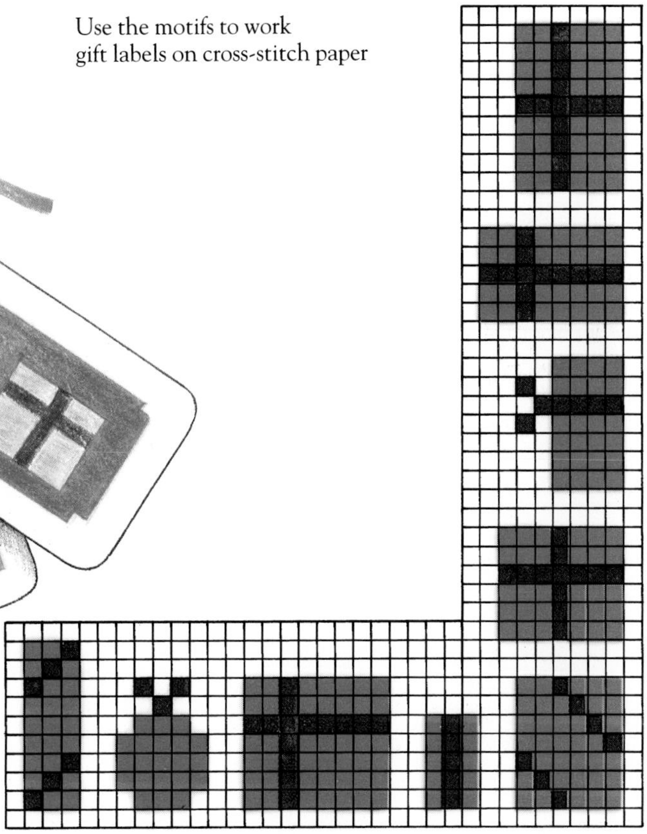

> If you don't want to use Binca as a base for the cloth, use a large-thread, evenweave fabric such as hessian, in green or red.

Working the embroidery

2 Beginning at one corner and referring to the chart, embroider a border of presents along one edge on the marked line. Use six strands of thread together and vary the colours at random as you work; make the colour of each present different from the ones next to it, with the ribbons on the presents in contrasting colours.

3 At the next corner, work the next present at right angles to the one just stitched, still working on the marked line.

4 Continue working repeats of the pattern until a border has been worked round the cloth.

Finishing

5 Fold under ½in (12mm) all round the cloth, press and baste in place. Set the sewing machine to narrow zigzag stitch, and stitch the hem. If you prefer, apply a border of red bias binding to neaten the edges. Alternatively, sew 1in (2.5cm)-wide gold polyester/Lurex ribbon to the hem.

> Use the gift motifs on cross-stitch paper to make special Christmas decorations or unusual gift labels. Work a row of three or four for a hand-made Christmas card. You could also use them as a border for a Christmas buffet cloth instead of the holly leaves (see page 85). If you're feeling adventurous, work the motif on four pieces of plastic canvas (see page 72) to be built up into a three-dimensional Christmas decoration. Decorate with beads.

Seasonal design

Invite friends for an informal buffet supper over the Christmas season and present the food on a bright buffet cloth embroidered with holly leaves and berries.

Materials

Two pieces of white evenweave cotton fabric, $32 \times 2\frac{1}{2}$in (81×6cm), 28–30 threads to 1in (2.5cm)

Piece of Christmas-print cotton fabric, 44×32in (112×81cm)

DMC stranded cottons as follows: four skeins of 910 green, one skein of 321 red.

Working the embroidery

1 Using all six strands of embroidery cotton together, work the holly design along the centre of each length of white fabric. Work cross stitches across four threads.

2 Cut a strip off each end of the Christmas print fabric, $4\frac{1}{2}$in (11.5cm) from the selvedge.

3 Insert the embroidered strips between the two pieces of Christmas fabric. Work a double line of top stitching on both edges. Trim off the excess white fabric on the wrong side.

4 Turn under and stitch a hem on the long edges. Use a contrasting thread if you like.

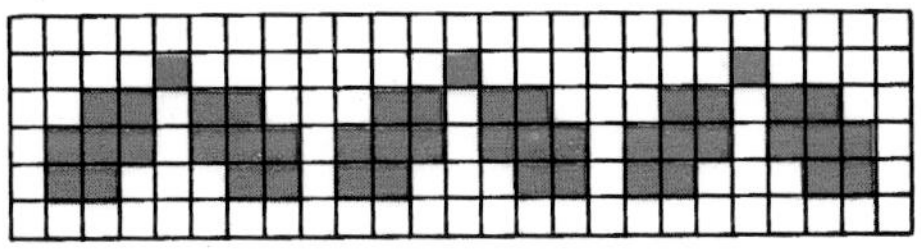

KEY

■ 321

■ 910

Work the holly and berry motif on a strip of hessian and stitch to the edges of a felt Christmas tree cloth for a seasonal decoration

Season's greetings

Make an extra-special Christmas card by embroidering your own; these three designs are very simple. For variety, work the designs on different-coloured backgrounds; the snowflake, for instance, would look effective on rich green or midnight blue.

Materials

Candy stick card

Piece of pale green Aida fabric, 5×4in (13×10cm), 11 threads to 1in (2.5cm)

DMC stranded cottons as follows: one skein each of 606 red, 910 green, white

White oval-window card blank.

Christmas tree card

Piece of white Aida fabric, 5×4in (13×10cm), 11 threads to 1in (2.5cm)

DMC stranded cottons as follows: one skein each of 702 green, 973 yellow, 606 red, 718 pink

Red rectangular-window card blank.

Season's greetings

Snowflake card
Piece of red Aida fabric, 4in (10cm) square, 14 threads to 1in (2.5cm)
DMC stranded cotton as follows: one skein of white
White round-window card blank.

Preparation
1 Measure and mark the middle of the fabric with lines of basting stitches, vertically and horizontally.

Working the embroidery
2 On all three charts, the middle of the design is indicated with arrows on the edges. This corresponds with the marked middle of the fabric. Using all six strands of thread for the candy stick and Christmas tree, and three strands for the snowflake, work the designs following the charts and keys.

Finishing
3 Press the finished embroidery on the wrong side with a warm iron.

4 Spread glue around the edges of the window on the inside of the card blank, and position the embroidery behind the window.

5 On the inside of the card, cover the left-hand flap with a layer of glue and fold it over to enclose the embroidery. Leave to dry.

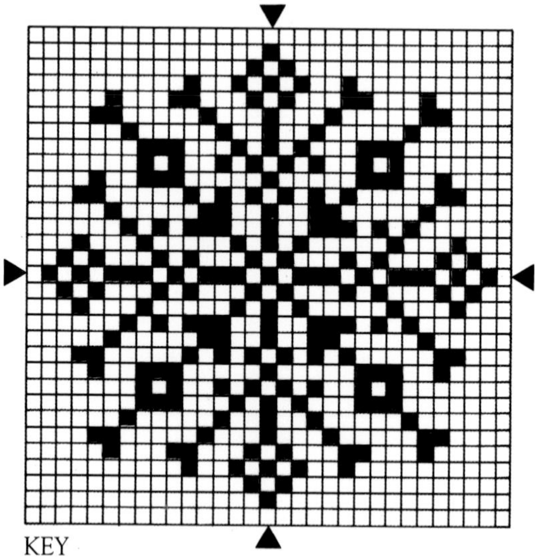

KEY
■ White

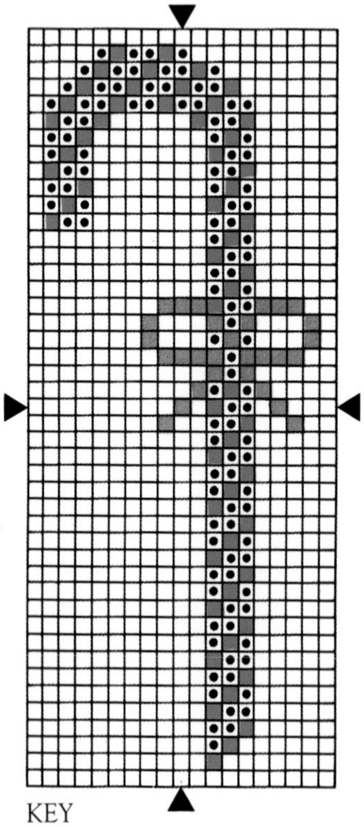

KEY
■ 910
■ 606
▣ White

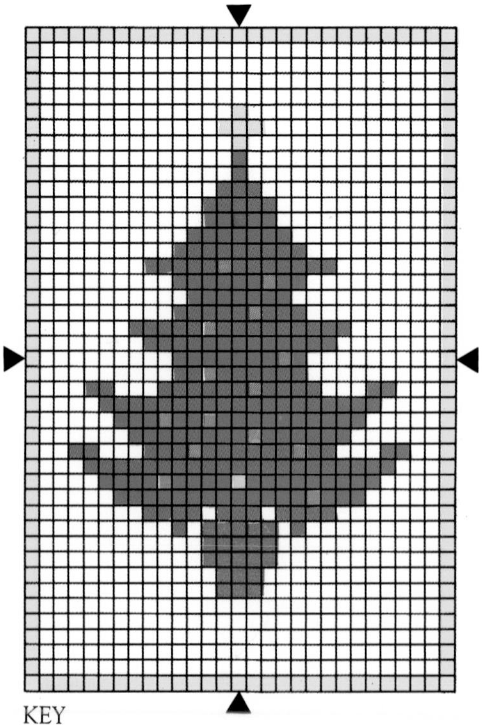

KEY
■ 702
■ 606
■ 718
□ 973

Motifs for cross stitch, like those on the opposite page, and others in this book, can be used to decorate not only gift items but are also ideal for embroidery on clothing, using the waste canvas method described on page 157. Cross stitch can also be worked on knitted items. Simply position your cross stitches, using the knitted stitch as a guide. Ready-made or hand-made garments and accessories can be personalised in this way and made to look very special. Use 4-ply or DK knitting wool, or tapisserie wool.

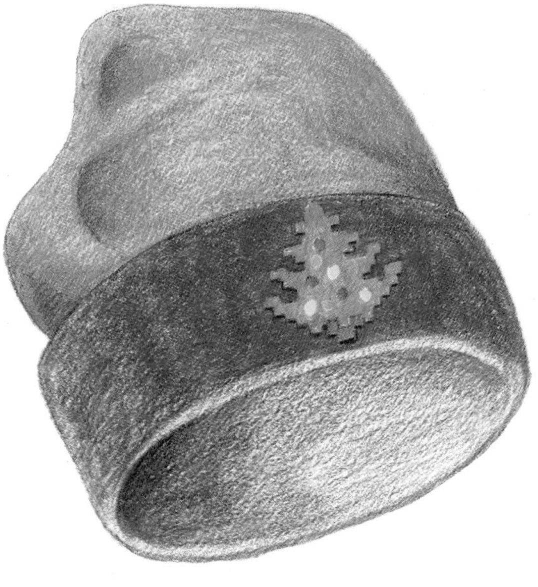

Embroider a motif on a hand-knitted winter cap

Cross stitch a motif on woolly gloves so that you can recognise your own

Amusing motifs, like the candy stick, are fun to embroider on casual clothes

ABCDEFGHIJ
KLMNOPQRS
TUVWXYZ
abcdefghijklmnopq

PART IV

Cross Stitch Pictures

Country fruits

This bright sprig of richly-coloured country fruits makes a delightful picture, but it could also be used singly or as a repeating motif on co-ordinated table linen.

Materials
11in (28cm) square of ecru evenweave linen with a thread count of 16 to 1in (2.5cm)
DMC stranded cottons as follows: 1 skein each of 975 light beige, 782 oak, 563 Windsor green, 3051 viridian green, 606 crimson, 892 bright pink, 209 mid-mauve, 552 dark purple, 920 copper.
Note: Define the straight lines on the chart in back stitch using the shades shown.

Preparation
1 Measure and mark the middle of the fabric with basting threads (refer to Better Embroidery).

(refer to Better Embroidery)

- 975
- 782
- 563
- 3051
- 606
- 892
- 209
- 552
- 920

Size of finished embroidery: 4½ × 3in (11.5 × 7.5cm)

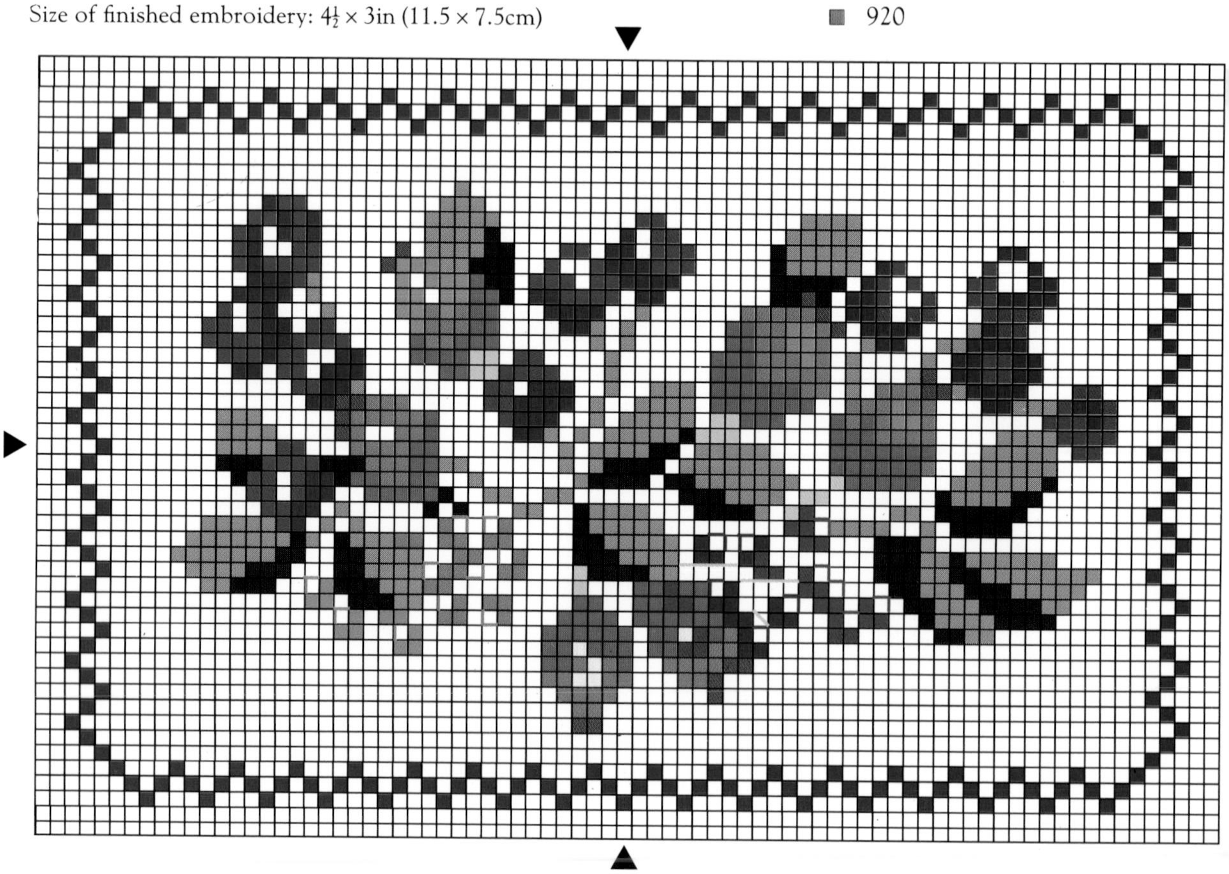

Working the embroidery
2 The centre of the chart is indicated by arrows on the edges. This coincides with the basted stitches. Following the chart and the colour key, begin by embroidering the middle block of colour, using 2 strands of thread together. Complete the design as shown on the chart.

Finishing
3 Remove the basting stitches. Press the finished embroidery lightly on the wrong side.

Mounting
4 Mount on cardboard for framing (refer to Better Embroidery).

Before beginning to embroider, it is often useful to tape a short length of each of the thread shades required to a small piece of card, noting its number. This can be invaluable if the thread band becomes detached and lost as the work progresses.

Tiger lilies

These elegant blooms would look superb in any formal setting, perhaps framed and hung in the dining room, or in a gracious bedroom. Adapt the colours to match your decor.

Materials

12in (30cm) square of white evenweave linen with a thread count of 14 threads to 1in (2.5cm)

DMC stranded cottons as follows: 1 skein each of 725 pine, 743 orange, 744 mid-yellow, 471 mid-olive green, 3346 dark olive green, 310 black

Size of finished embroidery: 5½ × 6in (14 × 15cm)

▨	725	▨	471
▨	743	■	3346
▢	744	■	310

Preparation

1 Measure and mark the middle of the fabric (see Better Embroidery).

Working the embroidery

2 The centre of the chart is indicated by arrows on the edges. This coincides with the basted stitches. Following the chart and the colour key, begin by embroidering the middle block of colour, using 2 strands of thread together. Complete the design as shown on the chart.

Finishing

3 Remove the basting stitches. Press the finished embroidery lightly on the wrong side and mount for framing.

Sweet violets

These delicate blossoms have been captured forever in a spring picture, which would look particularly pretty in a young girl's bedroom. You could also work a set of scatter cushions.

Size of finished embroidery: $5\frac{1}{4} \times 5\frac{3}{4}$in (13 × 15cm)

783	905	963	208	890
906	561	210	3347	

Materials

10 × 12in (25 × 30cm) piece of ecru evenweave linen with a thread count of 16 to 1in (2.5cm)

DMC stranded cottons as follows: 1 skein each of 783 sienna brown, 906 leaf green, 905 mid-leaf green, 561 dark leaf green, 963 soft pink, 210 dark lavender, 208 mid-purple, 890 bottle green, 3347 lime green

Preparation

1 Measure and mark the middle of the fabric (see Better Embroidery).

Working the embroidery

2 The centre of the chart is indicated by arrows on the edges. This coincides with the basted stitches. Following the chart and the colour key, begin by embroidering the middle block of colour, using 2 strands of thread together. Complete the design as shown on the chart.

Finishing

3 Remove the basting stitches. Press the finished embroidery lightly on the wrong side and mount for framing.

A sprig of roses

Besides making a charming picture, this romantic motif could be used, omitting the border, on the corner of a pillow case or repeated along the edge of a crisp white sheet.

Materials
8in (20cm) square of ecru evenweave linen with a thread count of 14 to 1in (2.5cm)

DMC stranded cottons as follows: 1 skein each of 501 dark green, 954 dark lime green, 3793 dark dusky pink, 948 pale pink, 957 light pink, 604 pink

Size of finished embroidery: 4 × 5in (10 × 12.5cm)

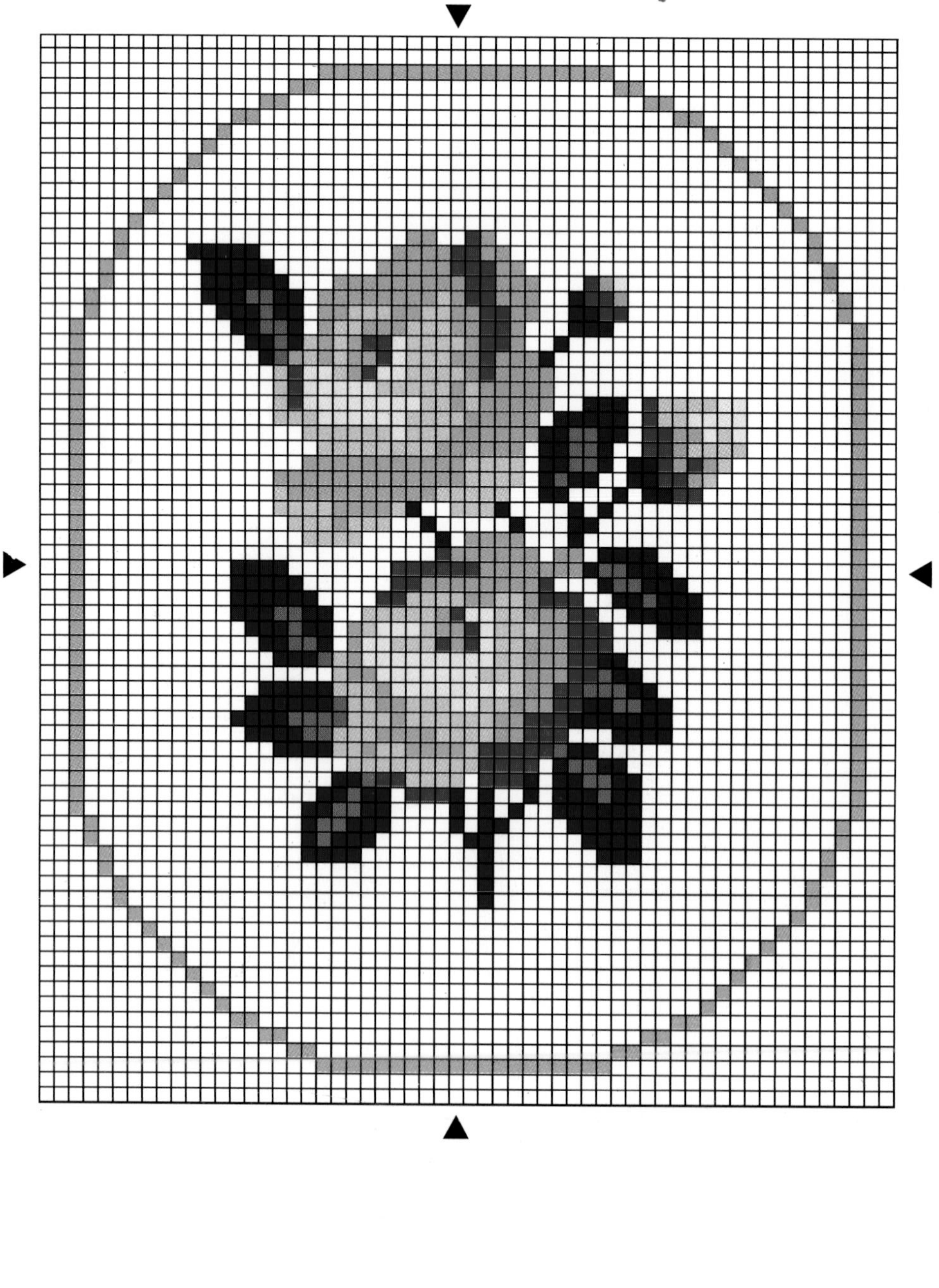

- 501
- 954
- 3793
- 948
- 957
- 604

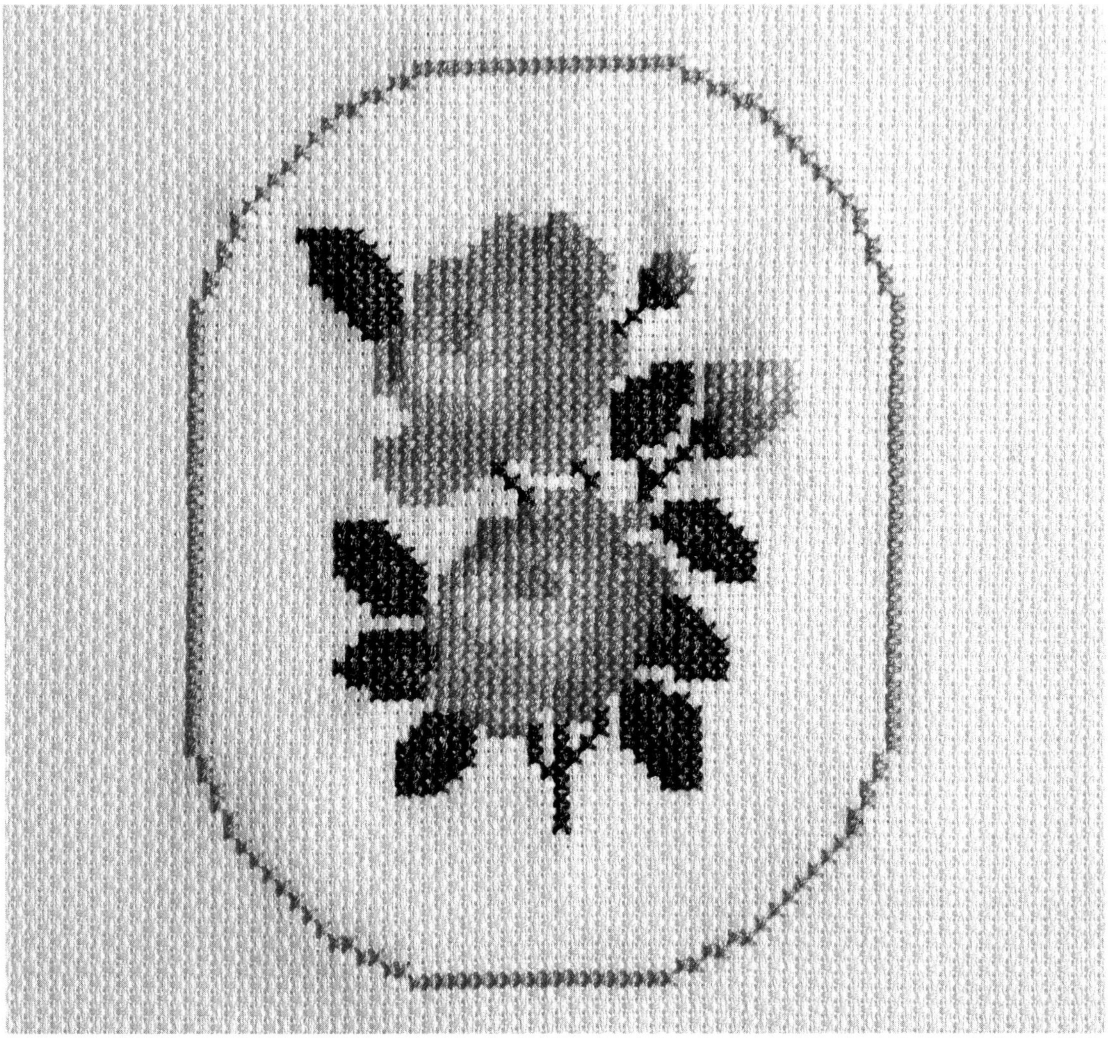

Preparation
1 Measure and mark the middle of the fabric with basting threads (see Better Embroidery).

Working the embroidery
2 The centre of the chart is indicated by arrows on the edges. This coincides with the basted stitches. Following the chart and the colour key, begin by embroidering the middle block of colour, using 2 strands of thread together. Complete the design as shown on the chart.

Finishing
3 Remove the basting stitches. Press the finished embroidery lightly on the wrong side.

Mounting
4 Mount on cardboard for framing (see Better Embroidery).

Try working the design in other colourways, such as yellow and cream for example, to make a pair of stunning pictures for the sitting room or bedroom. On a very fine evenweave fabric this motif would make a delicate design for a diary cover or a box top. You might also try abstracting the lower rose with its leaves for a smaller motif.

A pot of geraniums

Reminiscent of sunny summer days this flower picture will be a cheerful and welcome addition to your kitchen. The colour of the flowers could be changed to peach or pink.

Materials
12 × 10in (30 × 25cm) piece of ecru evenweave linen with a thread count of 14 to 1in (2.5cm)
DMC stranded cottons as follows: 1 skein each of 3772 stone, 680 chestnut, 778 light chestnut, 801 mid-brown, 471 mid-olive green, 3346 dark olive green, 740 pillar box red, 666 mid-red, 310 black

Preparation
1 Measure and mark the middle of the fabric with basting threads (see Better Embroidery).

Working the embroidery
2 The centre of the chart is indicated by arrows on the edges. This coincides with the basted stitches. Following the chart and the colour key, begin by embroidering the middle block of colour, using 2 strands of thread together. Complete the design as shown on the chart.

3 Define the lines on the leaves and the flower pot in back stitch, using 1 strand of shade 310 black. (See Better Embroidery for working back stitch.)

Finishing
4 Remove the basting stitches. Press the finished embroidery lightly on the wrong side.

Mounting
5 Mount the embroidery for framing (see Better Embroidery).

Cross stitch charts can also be used for canvaswork. Why not echo the design of your cross stitch picture in a canvas work cushion which could be worked in either cross or tent stitch.

Size of finished embroidery: 4 × 6in (10 × 15.5cm)

3772	3346
680	740
778	666
801	310
471	

Strawberry circlet

Dainty and delicate, this tiny circlet could be framed to decorate a bedroom, or it could be used in a greetings card to delight a special friend on a birthday.

Materials

9in (23cm) square of ecru evenweave linen with a thread count of 14 to 1in (2.5cm)

DMC stranded cottons as follows: 1 skein each of 725 pine, 774 dark orange, 444 light orange, 369 pale leaf green, 471 mid-olive green, 3348 light olive green, 3346 dark olive green, 740 pillar box red, 310 black

Preparation

1 Measure and mark the middle of the fabric with basting threads (see Better Embroidery).

Working the embroidery

2 The centre of the chart is indicated by arrows on the edges. This coincides with the basted stitches. Following the chart and the colour key, begin by embroidering the middle block of colour, using 2 strands of thread together. Work straight lines in 310 black back stitch. Complete the design as shown on the chart.

Finishing

3 Remove the basting stitches. Press the finished embroidery lightly on the wrong side.

Mounting

4 Mount the embroidery on cardboard for framing (see Better Embroidery).

Size of finished embroidery 2¾in (7cm) square

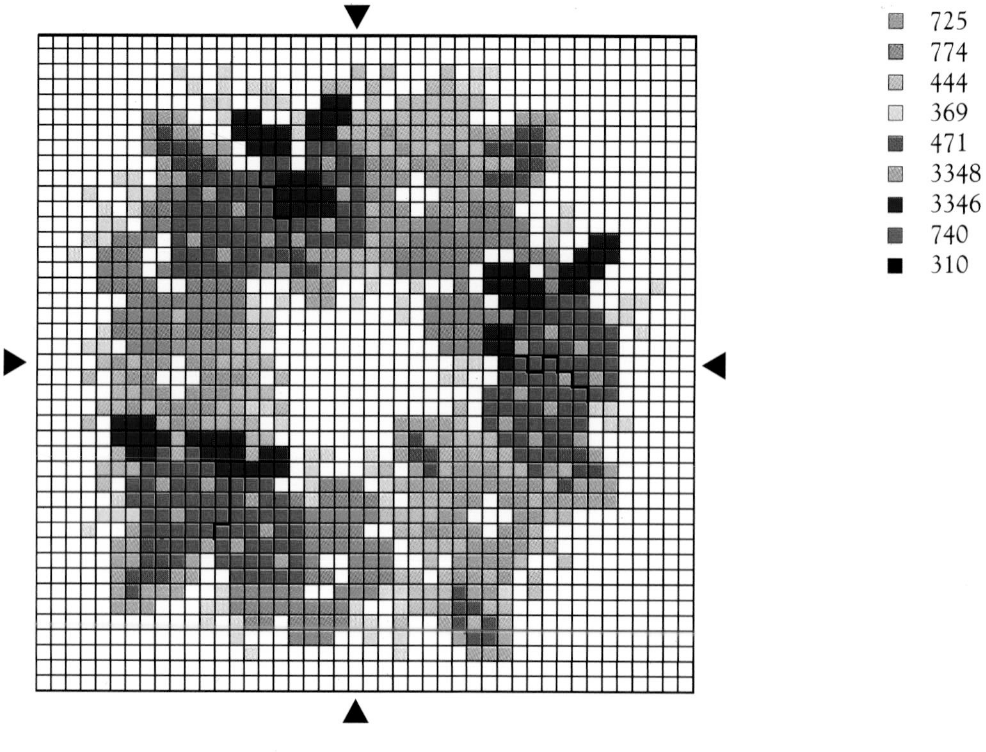

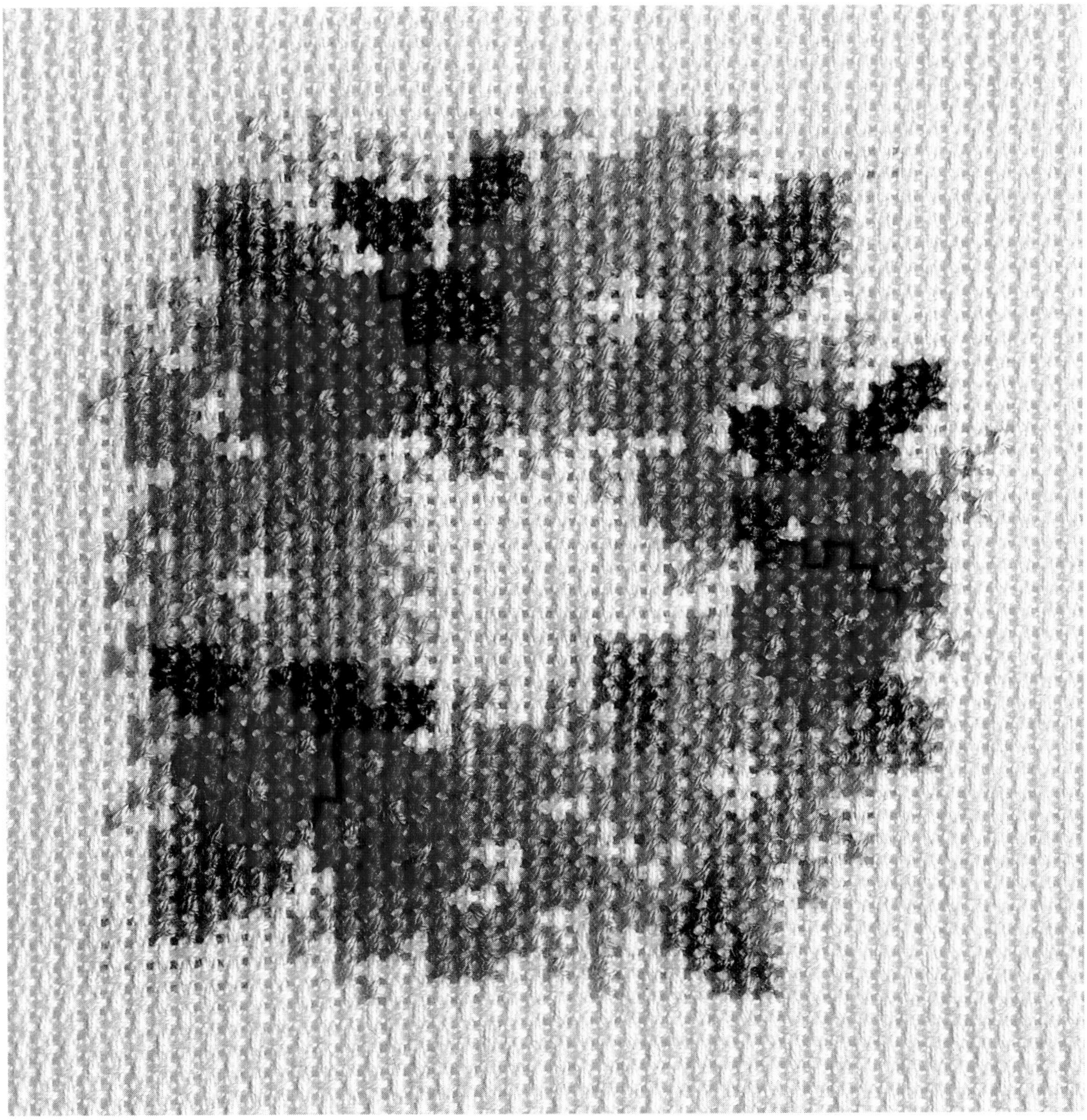

Strawberry pincushion After working the motif, trim the fabric back to a 4in (10cm) square, cut a second piece and sew together. Edge the cushion with a twisted cord.

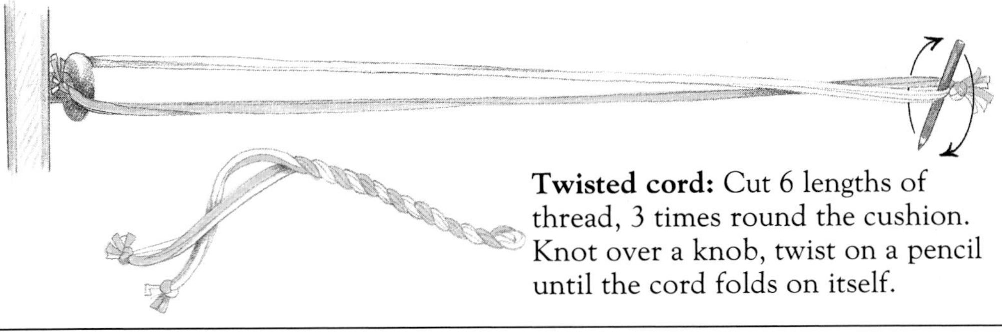

Twisted cord: Cut 6 lengths of thread, 3 times round the cushion. Knot over a knob, twist on a pencil until the cord folds on itself.

Summer nosegay

This bunch of summer flowers is tied with a ribbon and makes a pretty picture for you to frame as a gift. The colours could be changed to blend with any room setting.

Materials

12½in (32cm) square of white evenweave linen with a thread count of 14 to 1in (2.5cm)

DMC stranded cottons as follows: 1 skein each of white, 760 mid-salmon, 744 mid-yellow, 905 mid-leaf green, 471 mid-olive green, 504 light hooker green, 501 dark green, 3793 dark dusky pink, 948 pale pink, 3713 light lavender, 208 mid-purple, 3746 dark mauve, 310 black, 943 violet, 3078 cream

Preparation

1 Measure and mark the middle of the fabric with basting threads.

Working the embroidery

2 The centre of the chart is indicated by arrows on the edges. This coincides with the basted stitches. Following the chart and the colour key, begin to embroider the middle block of colour, using 2 strands of thread together. Complete the design as shown on the chart.

3 Define the lines between the petals with a single strand of shade 310 black in back stitch. Define the lines of the bow with a strand of shade 3793 dark dusky pink in back stitch.

Size of finished embroidery: 6 × 4½in (15 × 11.5cm)

Finishing

4 Remove the basting stitches. Press the finished embroidery lightly on the wrong side and mount on cardboard for framing.

⊡	White	▦	504	■	208
▨	760	■	501	■	3746
▨	744	▨	3793	■	310
■	905	▨	948	▨	943
▨	471	▨	3713	▨	3078

Blue vase

This striking flower display has the appeal of a Dutch painting. Besides making an imposing picture, it could also be used to stunning effect as a fire screen.

Materials

16 × 14in (40 × 35cm) piece of white evenweave linen with a thread count of 14 to 1in (2.5cm)

DMC stranded cottons as follows: 1 skein each of white, 3078 yellow, 561 dark hooker green, 320 olive green, 3346 dark olive green, 954 dark lime green, 321 cerise, 498 dark cerise, 3755 wedgwood blue, 798 dark blue, 813 mid-cobalt blue, 414 charcoal grey, 727 yellow, 815 maroon

Preparation

1 Measure and mark the middle of the fabric with basting threads (see Better Embroidery).

> When adapting a cross stitch chart for needlepoint take care in choosing your background colour. A dark green, blue or chocolate brown will give a heavy Victorian effect, while soft pinks, peaches and sea greens will blend with a more modern setting. Always buy sufficient skeins of background colour to finish your work, as dye lots can vary considerably.

> **Care of embroidered pictures**
> Embroidered pictures should not be displayed in direct sunlight or under strong artificial lights as these will damage the fabric and cause the colours to fade. Embroideries should be kept away from direct sources of heat, such as radiators or open fires. Dry air, fumes and dust will cause damage, even if the work is framed behind glass. Modern, branded embroidery threads are colour-fast and thus washable. If your embroidery becomes soiled it can be gently squeezed through luke warm suds, rinsed, dried and pressed. Antique textiles should never be washed or dry cleaned without expert advice.

Working the embroidery

2 The centre of the chart is indicated by arrows on the edges. This coincides with the basted stitches. Following the chart and the colour key, begin by embroidering the middle block of colour, using 2 strands of thread together. Complete the design as shown on the chart.

3 Work the petal divisions and the veins on the leaves in back stitch using a single strand of shade 414 charcoal grey. Refer to Better Embroidery for back stitch.

Finishing

4 Remove the basting stitches. Press the finished embroidery lightly on the wrong side.

Mounting

5 Mount the embroidery on cardboard for framing (see Better Embroidery).

Size of finished embroidery: 8 × 7in (20 × 18cm)

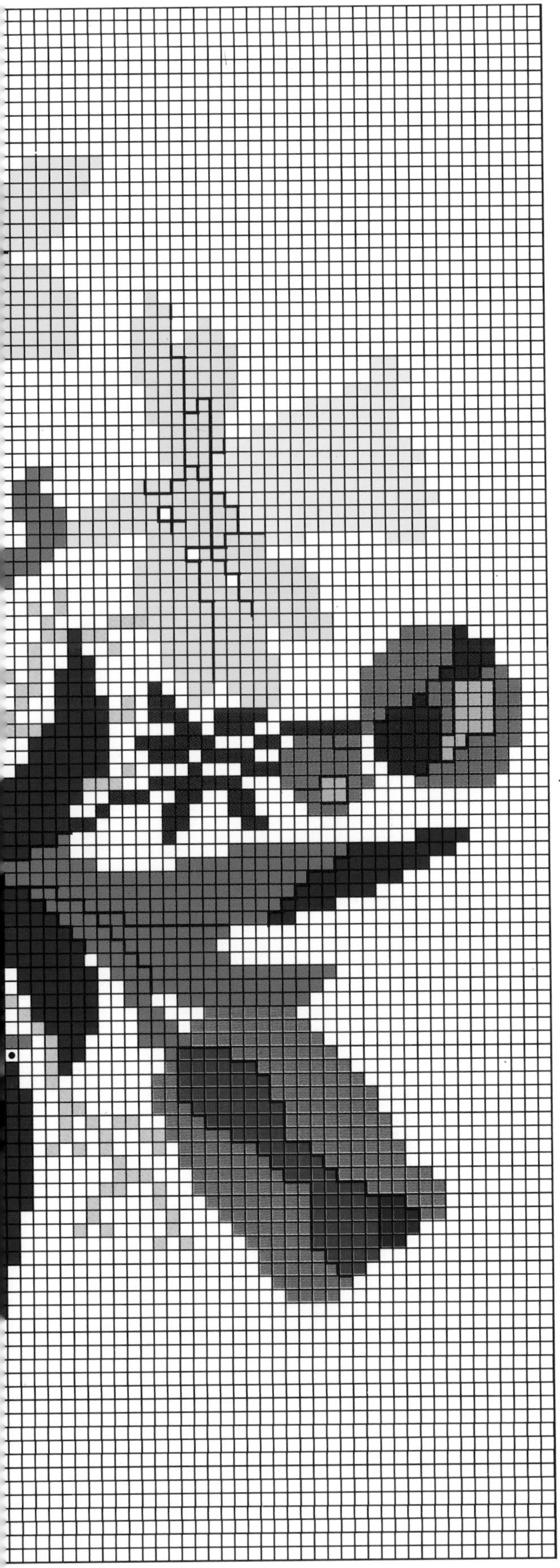

- White
- 727
- 561
- 320
- 3346
- 954
- 321
- 498
- 3755
- 798
- 813
- 414
- 3078
- 815

Butterfly and flowers

Always a popular subject, a small tortoiseshell butterfly settles on a purple periwinkle flower. The colours could be varied to make a group of three matching pictures.

■ 3774
■ 358
■ 774
■ 444
■ 3346
■ 954
■ 606
■ 666
■ 210
■ 208
■ 799
■ 310

Materials

12¾in (32cm) square of white evenweave linen with a thread count of 10 to 1in (2.5cm)

DMC stranded cottons as follows: 1 skein each of 3774 mid-beige, 358 dark oak, 774 dark orange, 444 light orange, 3346 dark olive green, 954 dark lime

Size of finished embroidery: 6¼ (16cm) square

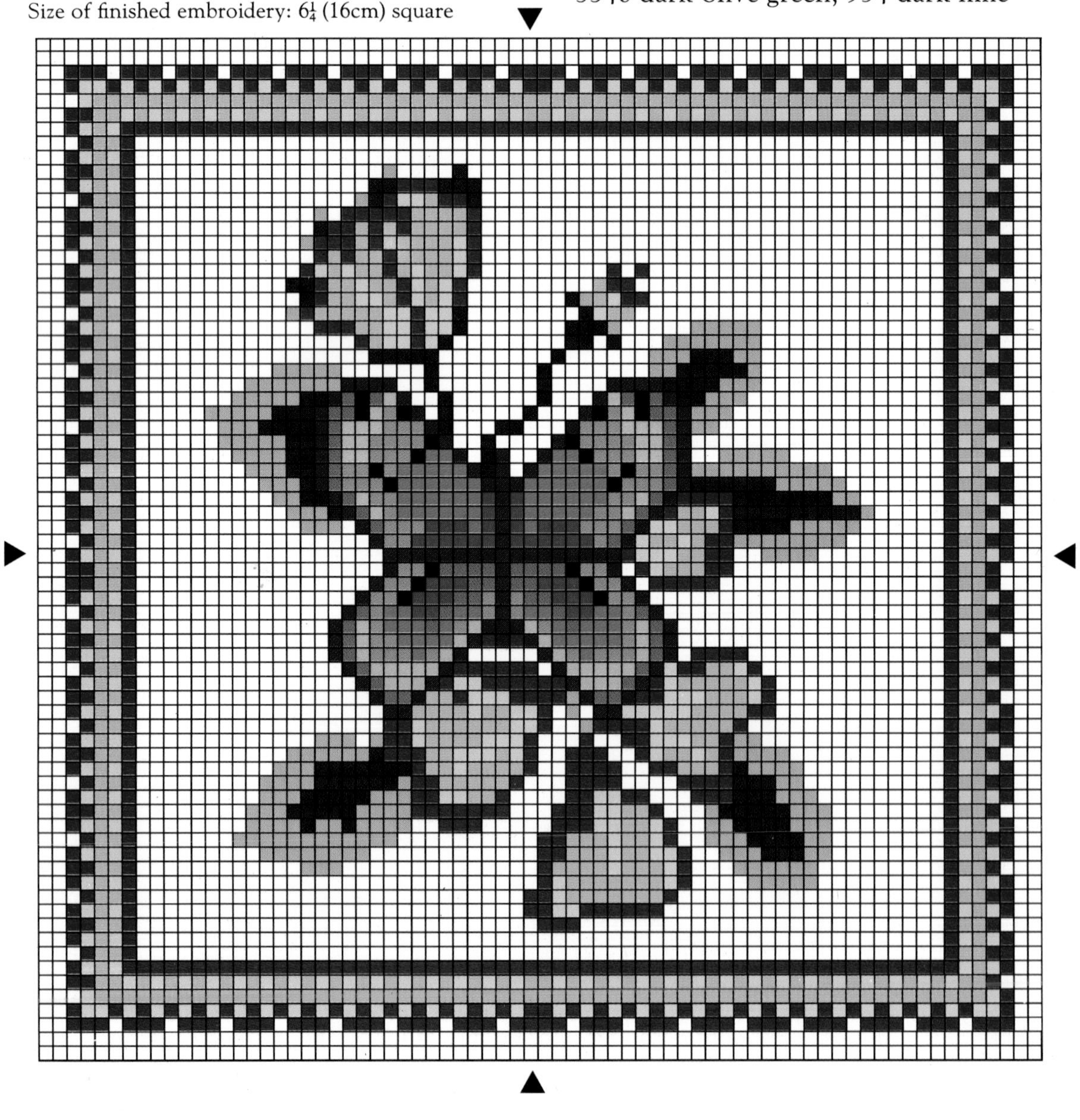

green, 606 crimson, 666 mid-red, 210 dark lavender, 208 mid-purple, 799 blue, 310 black

Preparation
1 Measure and mark the middle of the fabric with basting stitches (see Better Embroidery).

Working the embroidery
2 The centre of the chart is indicated by arrows on the edges. This coincides with the basted stitches. Following the chart and the colour key, begin by embroidering the middle block of colour, using 2 strands of thread together. Complete the design as shown on the chart.

Finishing
3 Remove the basting stitches. Press the finished embroidery lightly on the wrong side and mount on cardboard for framing. (Refer to Better Embroidery.)

March hare

A favourite with adults and children alike, this realistic-looking March hare would look charming framed in a dark, rich wood for a hall or perhaps a boy's bedroom.

Materials
12 × 10in (30 × 25cm) piece of ecru evenweave linen with a thread count of 10 to 1in (2.5cm)

DMC stranded cottons as follows: 1 skein each of white, 3774 mid-beige, 433 dark oak, 310 black, 94 shaded olive green

Size of finished embroidery: 4½in (11cm) square

- White
- 3774
- 433
- 310
- 94

Preparation

1 Measure and mark the middle of the fabric with basting stitches (see Better Embroidery).

Working the embroidery

2 The centre of the chart is indicated by arrows on the edges. This coincides with the basted stitches. Following the chart and the colour key, begin by embroidering the middle block of colour, using 2 strands of thread together. Complete the design as shown on the chart.

3 Define detail on legs, ears and tail in back stitch, using a single strand of shade 310 black.

Finishing

4 Remove the basting stitches. Press the finished embroidery lightly on the wrong side.

Mounting

5 Mount the embroidery on cardboard for framing (see Better Embroidery).

Fabrics and threads

Fine and medium-weight fabrics and embroidery cottons and silks are the most popular materials for cross stitch. However, coarser fabrics and canvas can be worked with soft embroidery cotton and tapestry and crewel wools. Novelty yarns and raffia can also be used for more experimental work. Waste canvas enables you to work cross stitch on plain weave fabrics such as cotton, muslin, cotton lawn and organdie.

Parrot

This bright and cheerful bird design will liven up the kitchen. Besides making a charming picture, the parrot could also be embroidered on accessories such as a coffee pot cover.

Materials

9½ × 10¼in (24 × 26cm) piece of white evenweave linen with a thread count of 14 to 1in (2.5cm)

DMC stranded cottons as follows: 1 skein each of 433 dark oak, 772 pear green, 905 mid-leaf green, 606 crimson, 815 mid-cobalt blue, 310 black, 746 off-white

Size of finished embroidery: 3½ × 4¾in (9 × 12cm)

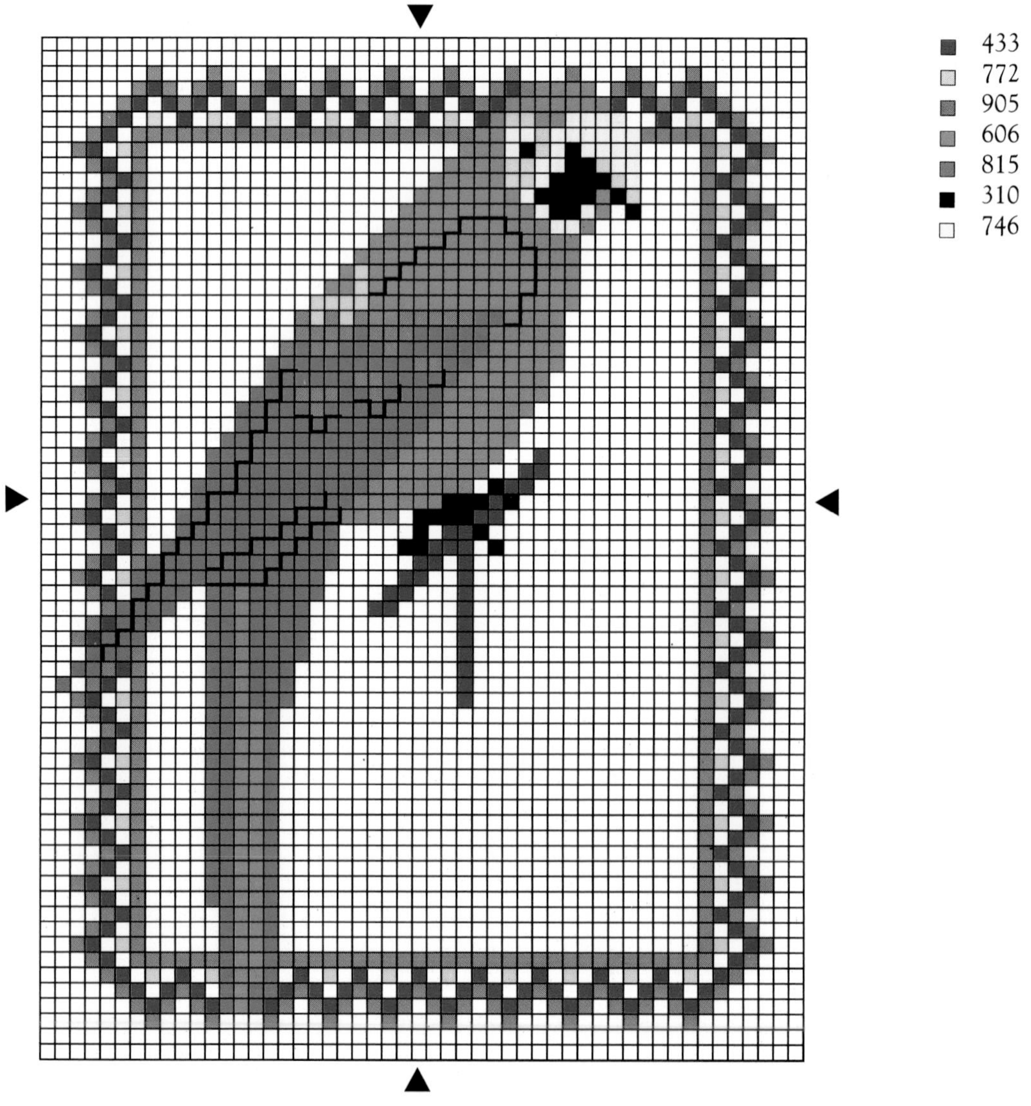

Preparation

1 Measure and mark the middle of the fabric with basting stitches (see Better Embroidery).

Working the embroidery

2 The centre of the chart is indicated by arrows on the edges. This coincides with the basted stitches. Following the chart and the colour key, begin by embroidering the middle block of colour, using 2 strands of thread together. Complete the design as shown on the chart.

Finishing

3 Remove the basting stitches. Press the finished embroidery lightly on the wrong side.

Mounting

4 Mount the finished embroidery on cardboard for framing (see Better Embroidery).

A flock of birds

These familiar garden birds can be framed individually or mounted together to make a long picture. They could also be used to produce very special greetings cards.

BLUE TIT

Materials

8in (20cm) square of ecru evenweave linen with a thread count of 14 to 1in (2.5cm)

Size of finished embroidery: 4 × 2in (10 × 5cm)

DMC stranded cottons as follows: 1 skein each of white, 3774 mid-beige, 680 chestnut, 726 dark lemon, 772 pear green, 799 blue, 3325 light cobalt blue, 310 black

Note: Define the face and beak in back stitch using a single strand of 310 black.

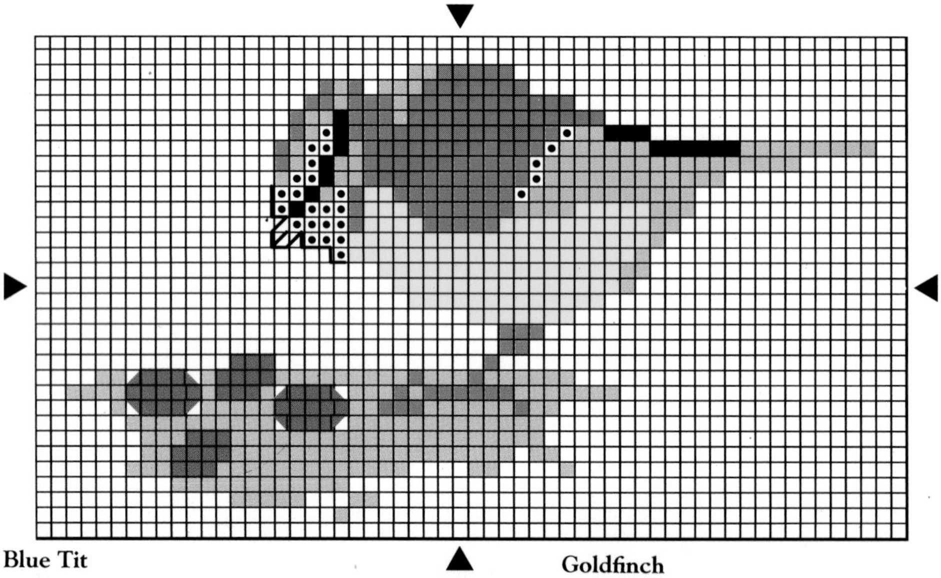

Blue Tit

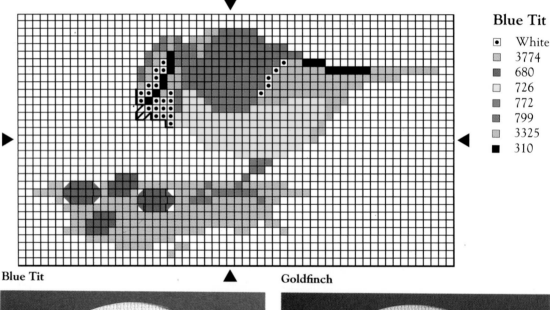

- White
- 3774
- 680
- 726
- 772
- 799
- 3325
- 310

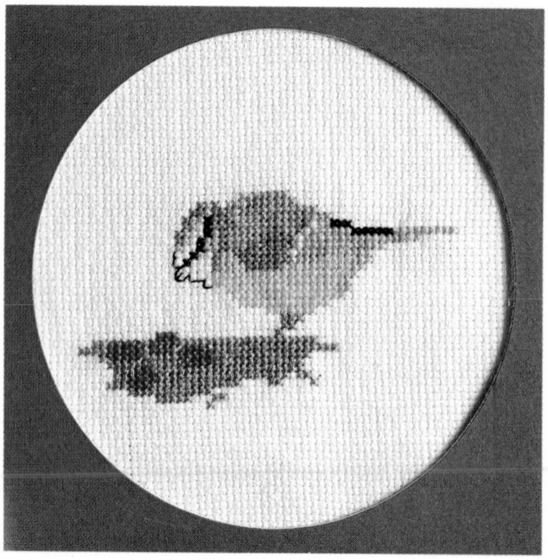

Blue Tit

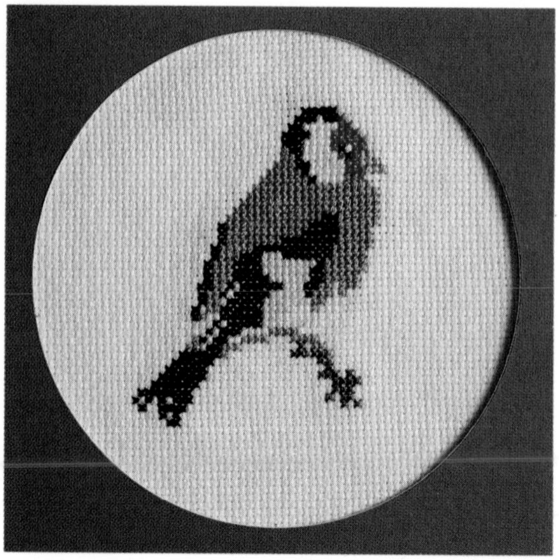

Goldfinch

GOLDFINCH

Materials

8 × 9in (20 × 22cm) piece of ecru evenweave linen with a thread count of 14 to 1in (2.5cm)

DMC stranded cottons as follows: 1 skein each of 3774 mid-beige, 436 sienna brown, 744 mid-yellow, 3346 dark olive green, 740 pillar box red, 310 black, 1746 off-white, 3772 grey

Goldcrest

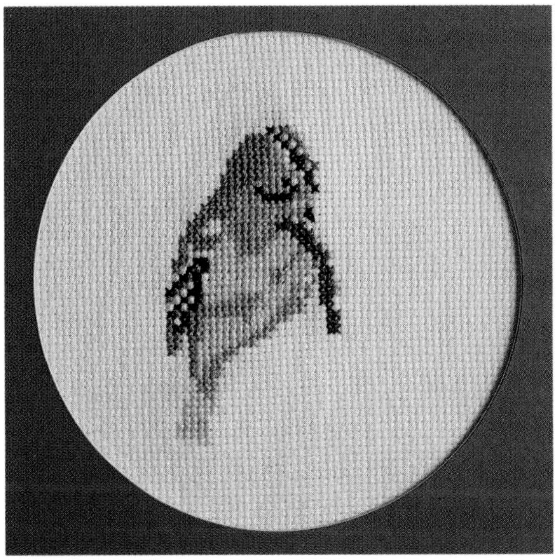

GOLDCREST

Materials

8in (20cm) square of ecru evenweave linen with a thread count of 14 to 1in (2.5cm)

DMC stranded cottons as follows: 1 skein each of 3772 stone, 778 chestnut, 801 mid-brown, 726 dark lemon, 3078 pale yellow, 722 pear green, 471 mid-olive green, 310 black, 746 off-white

Goldfinch

□	3774	□	744	■	310
□	3772	■	3346	□	746
■	436	■	740		

Goldcrest

□	3722	■	471
■	778	■	722
■	801	■	310
□	726	□	746
□	3078		

Size of finished embroidery: $2\frac{1}{2} \times 3\frac{1}{4}$in (6.5 × 8cm)

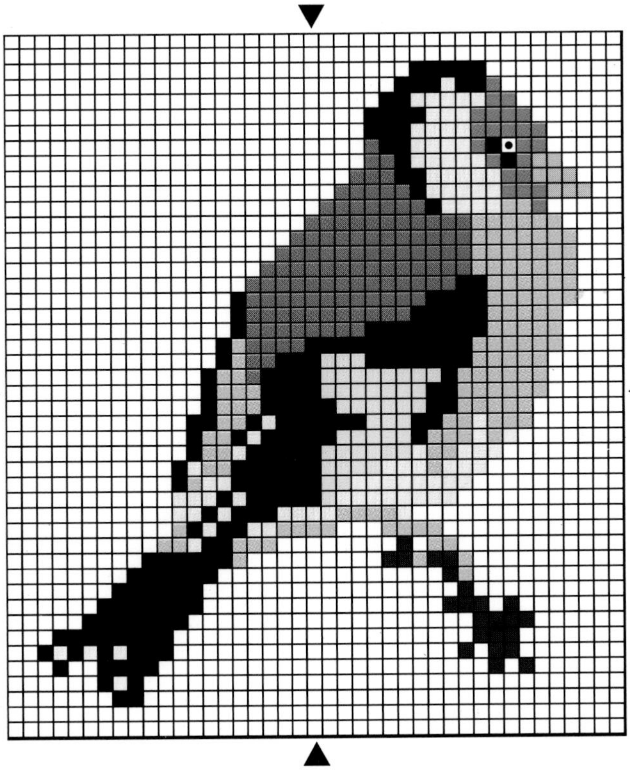

Size of finished embroidery: $1\frac{3}{4} \times 3$in (4.5 × 7.5cm)

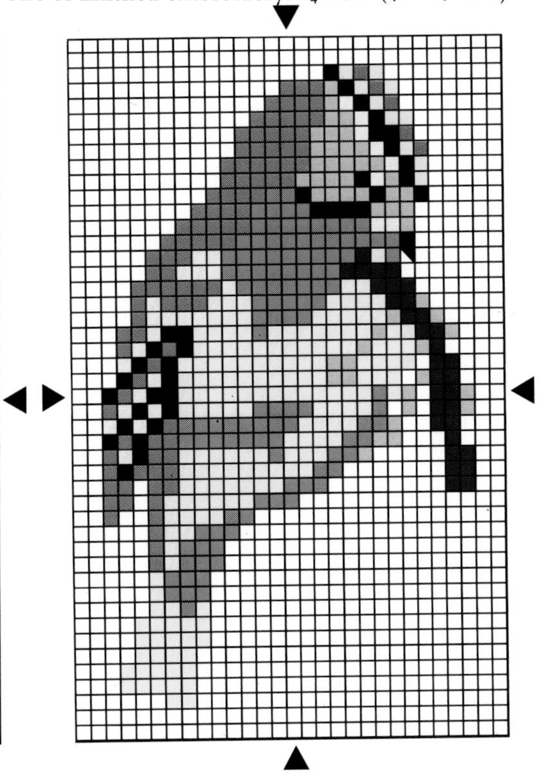

Size of finished embroidery: $3\frac{1}{2} \times 5$in (9×12.5cm)

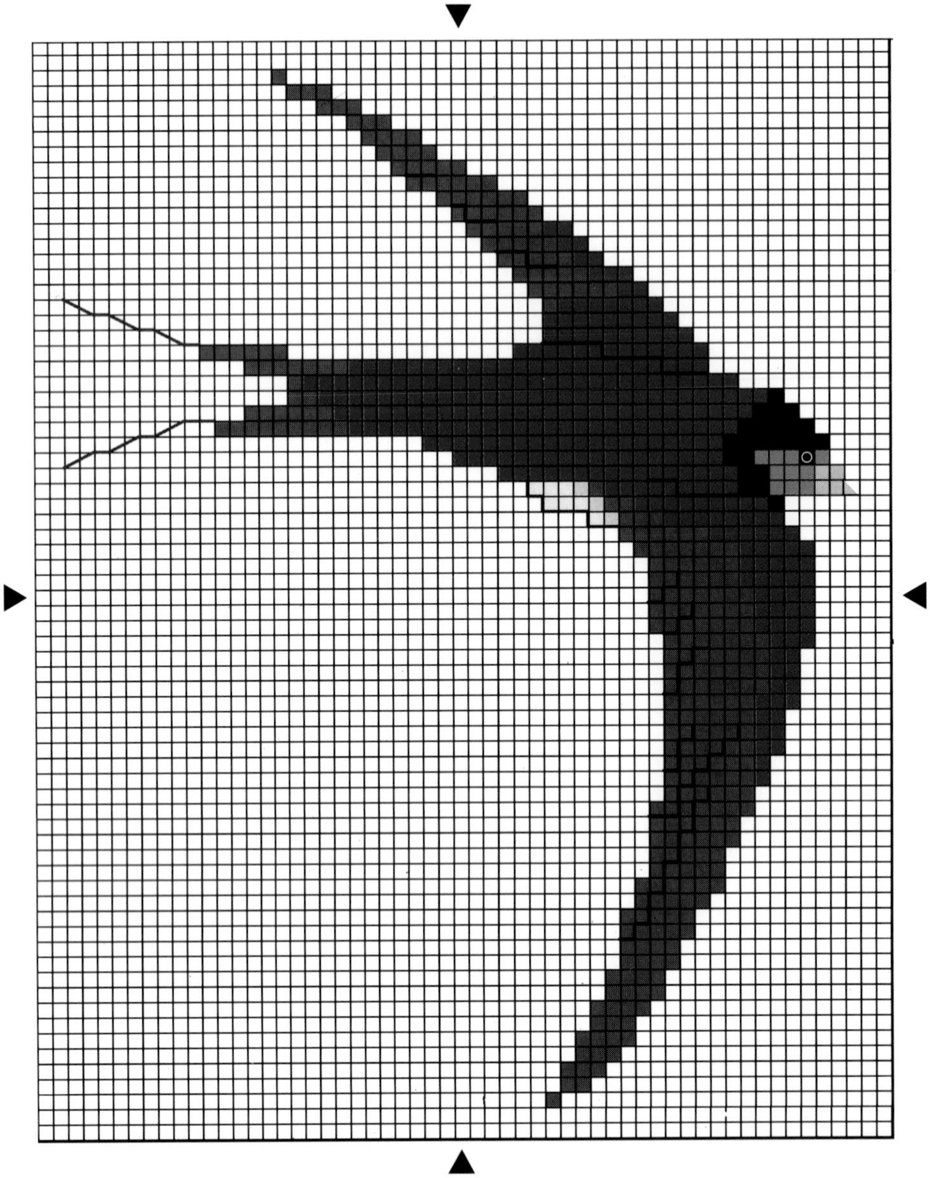

Swallow

- 739
- 729
- 3072
- 414
- 310
- 920
- 746

SWALLOW

Materials

10in (25cm) square of ecru evenweave linen with a thread count of 14 to 1in (2.5cm)

DMC stranded cottons as follows: 1 skein each of 739 beige, 729 dark navy blue, 3072 light grey, 414 charcoal grey, 310 black, 920 copper, 746 off-white

Note: Define the under-body and tail in back stitch, using a single strand of 310 black.

Preparation

1 Measure and mark the middle of the fabric with basting stitches (see Better Embroidery).

Working the embroidery

2 The centre of each of the charts is indicated by arrows on the edges. This coincides with the basted stitches. Following the charts and the colour keys, begin by embroidering the middle block of colour, using 2 strands of thread together. Complete the designs as shown on the charts.

Swallow

Finishing

3 Remove the basting stitches. Press the finished embroideries lightly on the wrong side.

Mounting

4 If you are mounting the embroideries for a picture, refer to Better Embroidery for the technique.

Bead embroidery

Working on canvas, cross stitch motifs can be adapted to bead embroidery for items such as bags, foot stools and pictures and pincushions. Use half cross stitch to attach the beads to the canvas using 2 strands of thread.

Bear with balloons

A firm favourite with children for many years, no nursery is complete without a teddy bear. This picture could also form the basis of a birthday sampler.

Size of finished embroidery: $4\frac{3}{4} \times 6\frac{3}{4}$in (12 × 17cm)

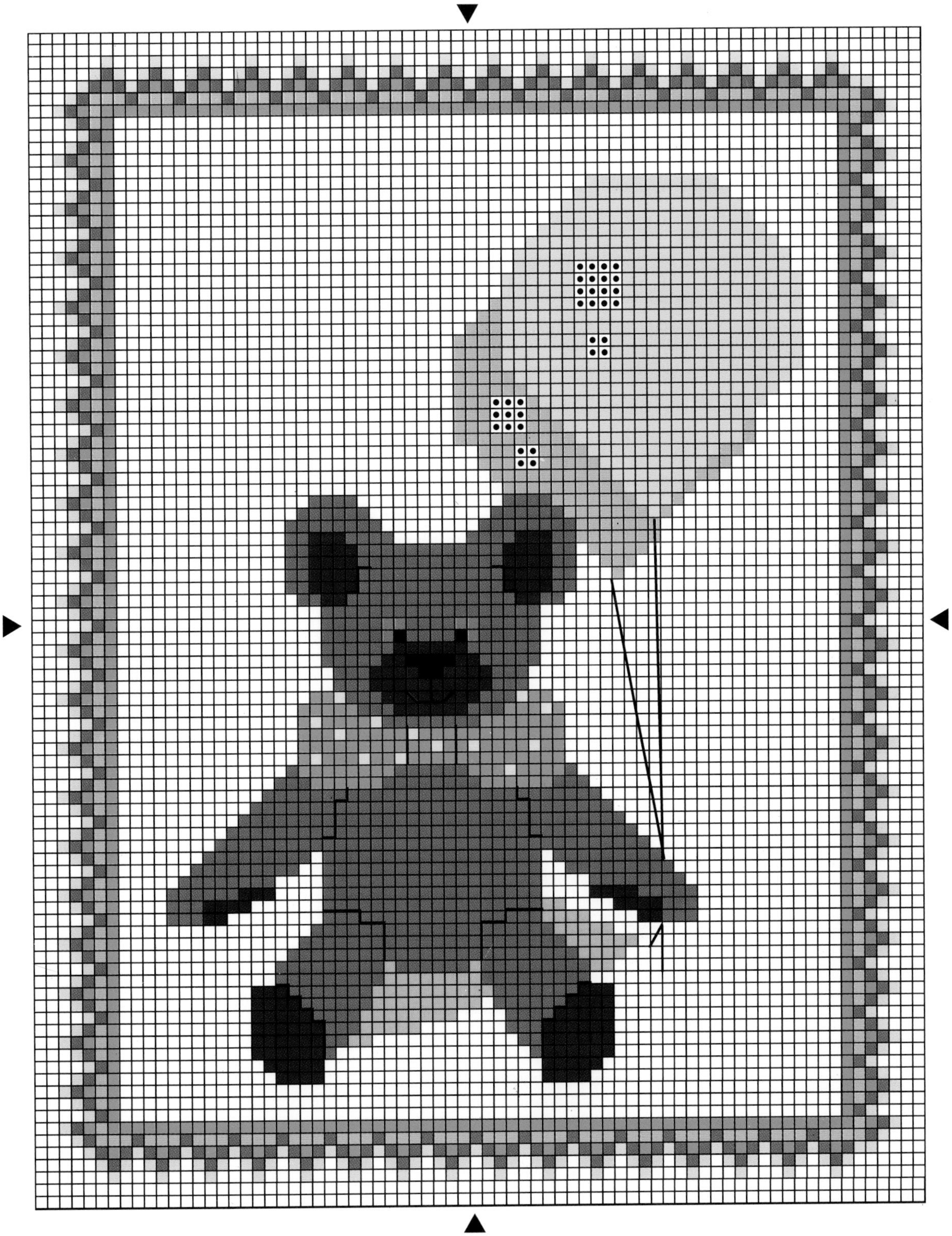

⊡	White	☐	726
▦	3072	▦	906
▦	436	▦	210
■	433	☐	3753
▦	680	■	310

Materials

10 × 12in (25 × 30.5cm) piece of ecru evenweave linen with a thread count of 14 to 1in (2.5cm)

DMC stranded cottons as follows: 1 skein each of 680 chestnut, 433 dark oak, 436 sienna brown, 726 dark lemon, 906 lime green, 210 lavender, 3753 light wedgwood blue, 310 black, white, 3072 grey.

Note: Define the lines shown on the chart using a single strand of 310 black. Fasten 2 strings of 2 strands of 310 black from the balloons to the bear's paw.

Preparation

1 Measure and mark the middle of the fabric with basting stitches.

Working the embroidery

2 The centre of the chart is indicated by arrows on the edges. This coincides with the basted stitches. Following the chart and the colour key, begin to embroider the middle block of colour, using 2 strands of thread together. Complete the design as shown on the chart.

Finishing

3 Remove the basting stitches. Press the finished embroidery lightly on the wrong side.

Mounting

4 Mount the embroidery on cardboard for framing.

Knitted motifs Cross stitch charts can also be used for knitting, to decorate the front of a sweater with a motif, simply by working each square as a stocking stitch. Alternatively, you can embroider the design directly onto the garment.

Tiger bright

Bold and beautiful, this magnificent picture makes a superb gift for a friend who is interested in the conservation of wildlife. You might also use it to make a calendar.

Materials

12in (30cm) square of ecru evenweave linen with a thread count of 14 to 1in (2.5cm)

DMC stranded cottons as follows: 2 skeins of 680 chestnut; 1 skein each of 760 mid-salmon pink, 436 sienna brown, 3348 pale leaf green, 471 mid-olive green, 3346 dark olive green, 3072 light grey, 310 black, 746 off-white, 726 dark lemon

Size of finished embroidery: $6\frac{1}{2} \times 6\frac{3}{4}$in (16 × 17cm)

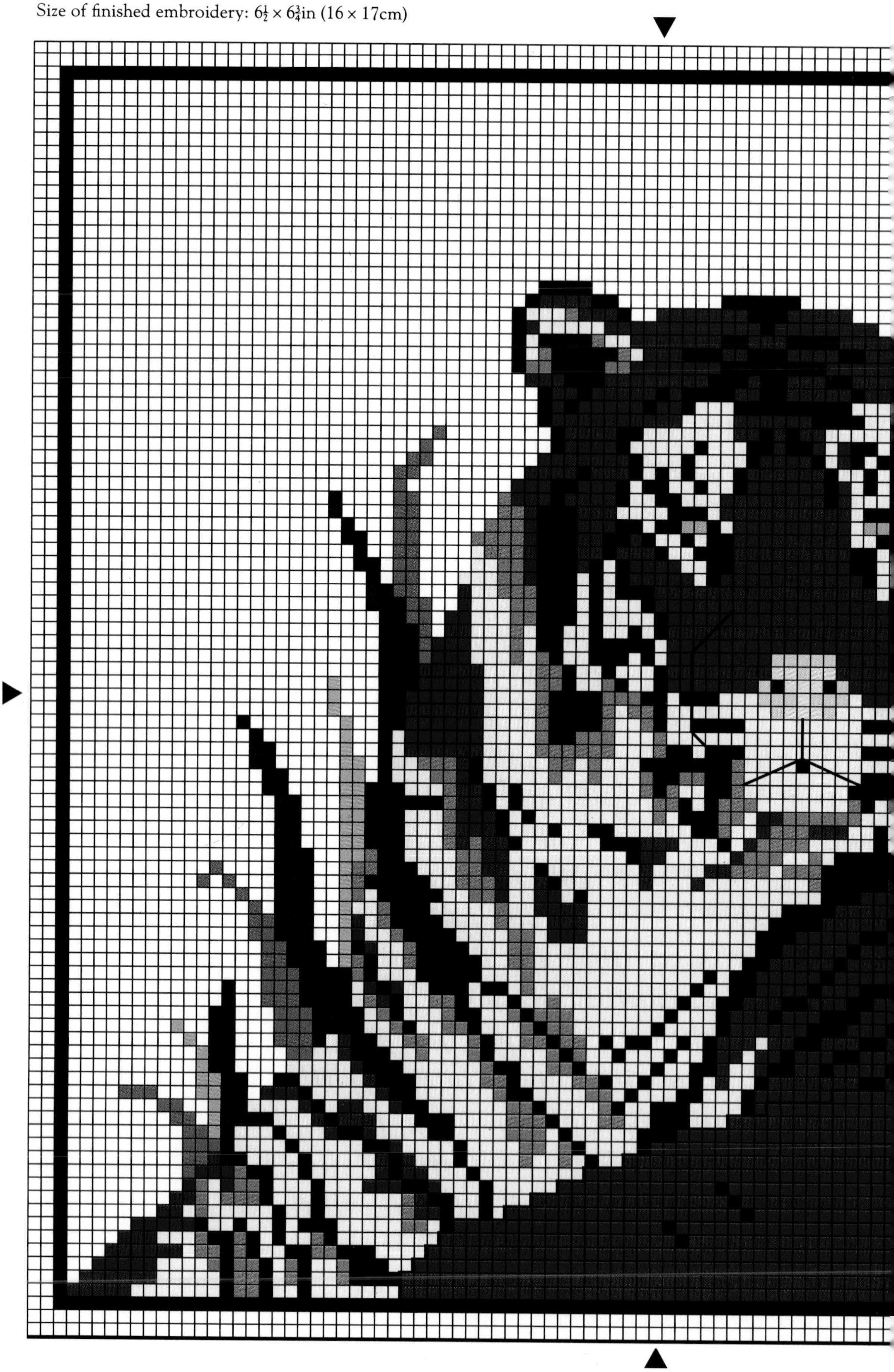

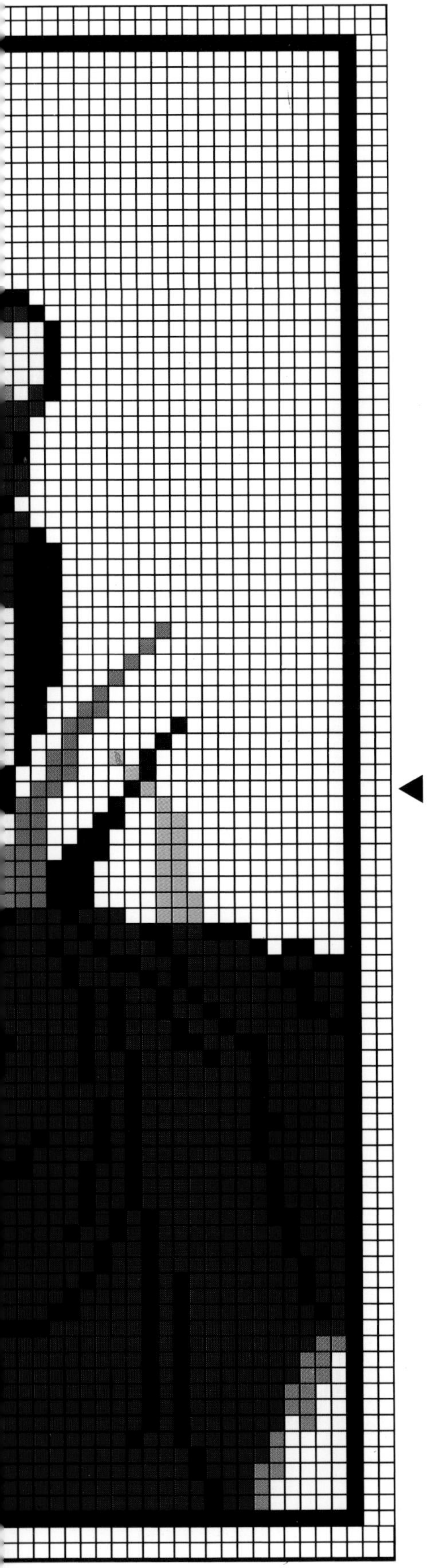

Preparation

1 Measure and mark the middle of the fabric with basting stitches (see Better Embroidery).

Working the embroidery

2 The centre of the chart is indicated by arrows on the edges. This coincides with the basted stitches. Following the chart and the colour key, begin by embroidering the middle block of colour, using 2 strands of thread together. Complete the design. Define the muzzle with black back stitches.

Finishing

3 Remove the basting stitches. Press the finished embroidery lightly on the wrong side.

Mounting

4 Mount the embroidery on cardboard for framing (refer to Better Embroidery).

> This tiger motif would look especially striking worked in cross stitch on a black knitted sweater using tapestry wools, 4-ply or double knitting yarn. Work each cross stitch over a knitted stitch. Alternatively, use Swiss embroidery stitches and duplicate the stocking stitches.

- 760
- 680
- 436
- 726
- 3348
- 471
- 3346
- 3072
- 310
- 746

Tabby cat

Everyone's favourite, this tabby cat proudly sits in a field of summer grass. The colours could be changed to produce a cross stitch portrait of your own special feline friend.

Materials

10in (25cm) square of ecru evenweave linen with a thread count of 14 to 1in (2.5cm)

DMC stranded cottons as follows: 1 skein each of white, 772 pear green, 3348 pale leaf green, 561 dark leaf green, 471 mid-olive green, 776 light dusky pink, 894 dark pink, 3072 light grey, 648 mid-grey, 310 black

Size of finished embroidery: 4¾in (12cm) square

▣	White	□	776
■	772	■	894
■	3348	■	3072
■	561	■	648
■	471	■	310

Preparation

1 Measure and mark the middle of the fabric with basting stitches (see Better Embroidery).

Working with embroidery

2 The centre of the chart is indicated by arrows on the edges. This coincides with the basted stitches. Following the chart and the colour key, begin by embroidering the middle block of colour, using 2 strands of thread together. Complete the design as shown on the chart.

3 Define the mouth and legs with back stitch (see the straight lines shown on the chart) using a single strand of 310 black.

Finishing

4 Remove the basting stitches. Press the finished embroidery lightly on the wrong side. Mount for framing.

Summer's bounty

The three matching pictures in this series could be framed as a single long picture, or individually framed. They would look well framed in a light-coloured wood – pine or maple.

SUMMER SALAD

Materials

12 × 14in (30 × 35cm) piece of white evenweave linen with a thread count of 14 to 1in (2.5cm)

DMC stranded cottons as follows: 1 skein each of white, 729 brick red, 434 brown, 435 dark fawn, 905 mid-leaf green, 471 mid-olive green, 3348 light olive green, 504 light hooker green, 700 hooker green, 954 dark lime green, 321 dark red, 666 mid-red, 3078 cream, 740 pillar box red, 774 dark salmon pink, 310 black

Note: Define the lines on the cucumber in a single strand of 504 light hooker green, using back stitch. Define the lines on the celery stalks and cos lettuce in a single strand of white, using back stitch.

CONTINENTAL VEGETABLES

Materials

12 × 14in (30 × 35cm) piece of white evenweave linen with a thread count of 14 to 1in (2.5cm)

DMC stranded cottons as follows: 1 skein each of 739 beige, 3774 mid-beige, 950 dark beige, 774 dark salmon pink, 712 light fawn, 744 mid-yellow, 3348 pale leaf green, 905 mid-leaf

Continental vegetables

739	3348	342
3774	905	209
774	561	208
712	471	727
950	666	3078
744	321	310
		White

Size of finished embroidery: 5¾ × 3in (14.5 × 7.5cm)

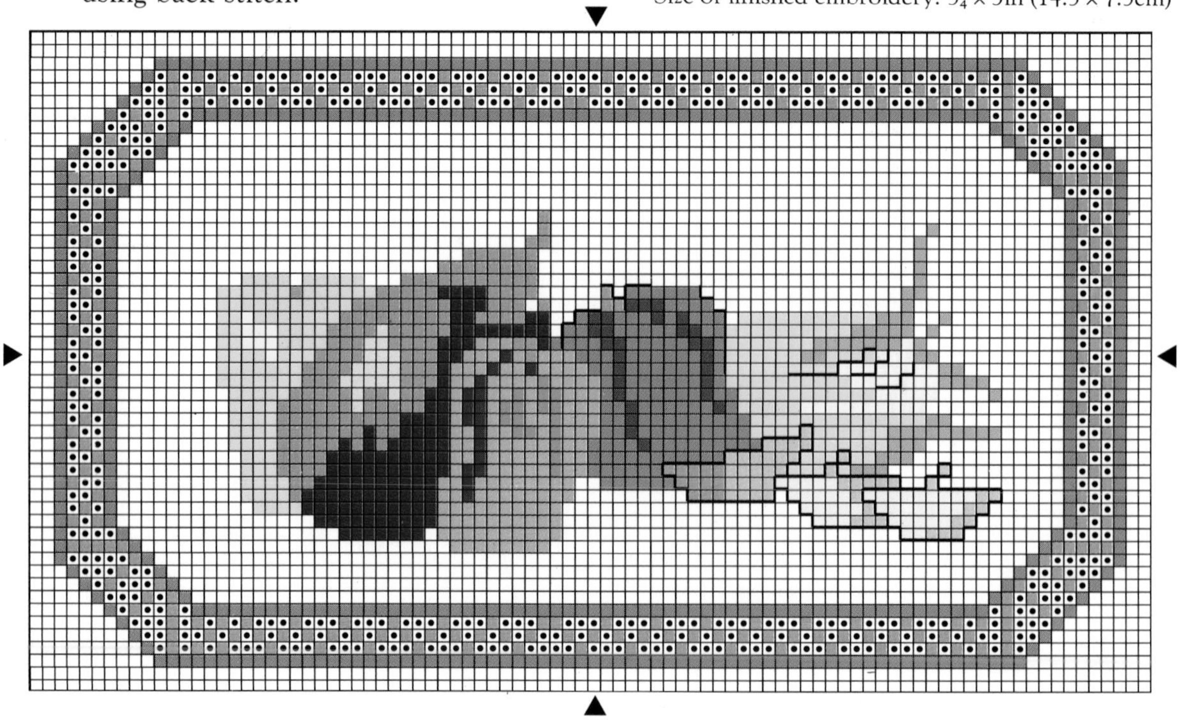

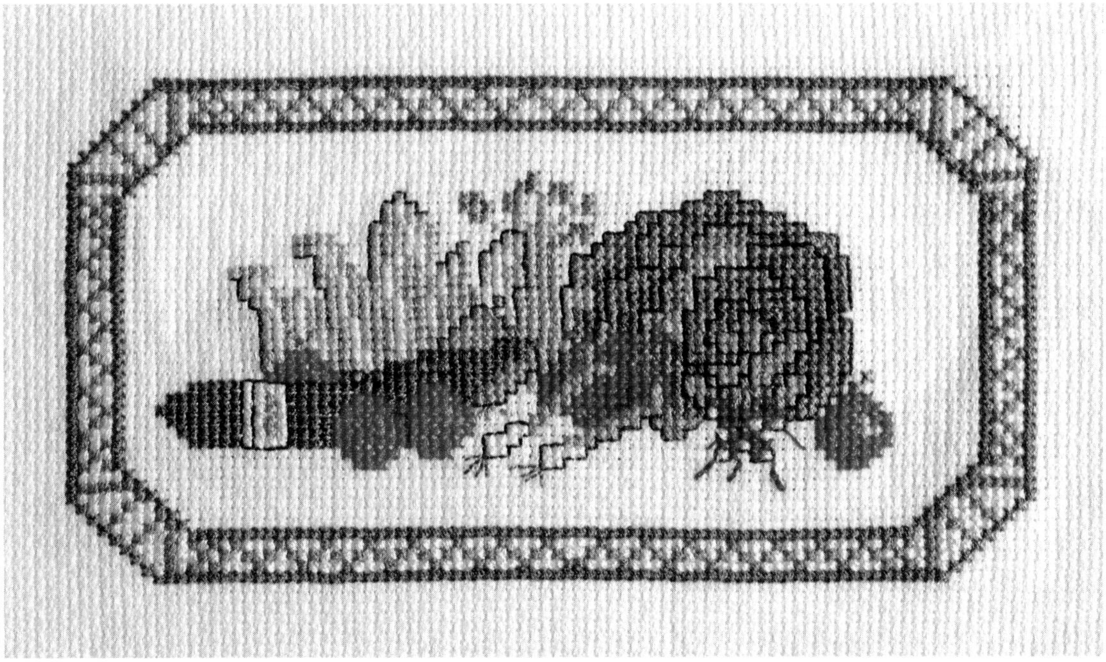

Summer salad

green, 561 dark leaf green, 471 mid-olive green, 666 mid-red, 321 cerise, 342 mid-lavender, 209 mid-mauve, 208 mid-purple, 310 black, 727 yellow, 3078 cream, white

Summer salad

White	700
729	954
434	321
435	666
905	3078
471	740
3348	774
504	310

Size of finished embroidery: 5¾ × 3in (14.5 × 7.5cm)

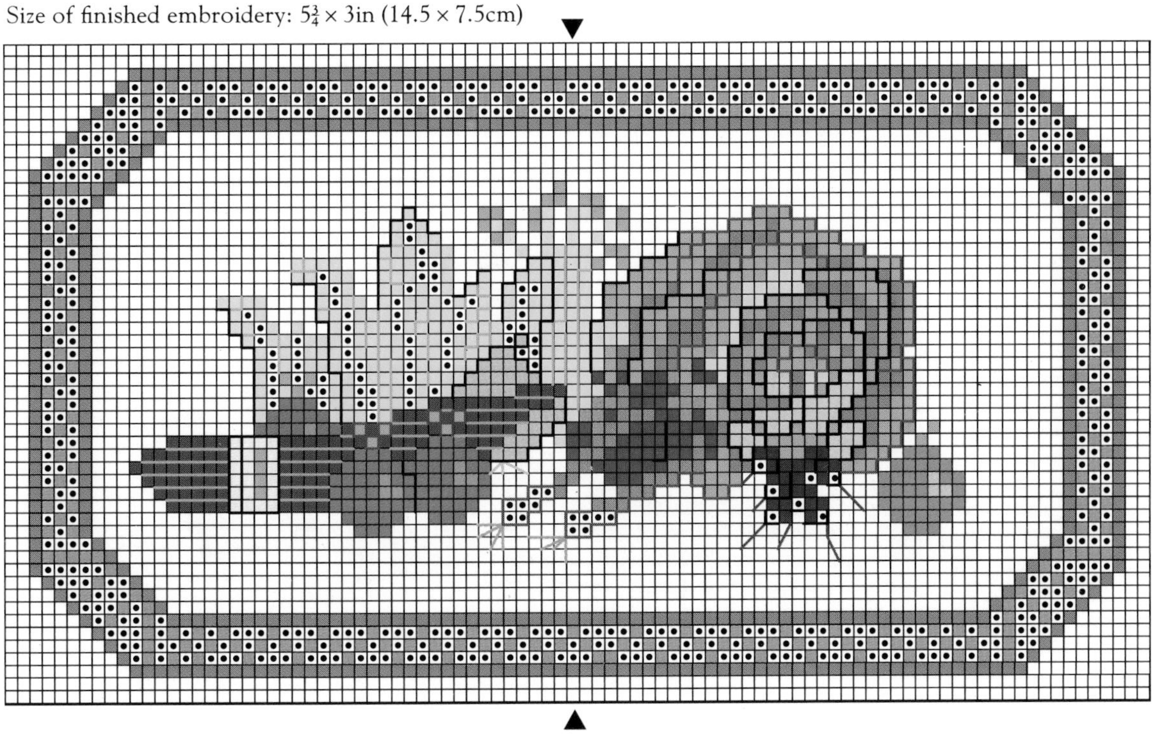

AN ABUNDANCE OF FRUITS

Materials

10 × 12in (25 × 30cm) piece of white evenweave linen with a thread count of 14 to 1in (2.5cm)

DMC stranded cottons as follows: 1 skein each of 975 light beige, 3774 mid-beige, 433 dark oak, 774 dark orange, 743 orange, 772 pear green, 905 mid-leaf green, 471 mid-olive green, 3348 light olive green, 504 light hooker green, 501 dark green, 472 pale olive green, 320 olive green, 666 mid-red, 321 cerise, 3793 dark dusky pink, 3713 light lavender, 3746 dark mauve, 813 mid-cobalt blue, 310 black, 815 maroon, 3078 cream, 48 shaded pink, 57 shaded strawberry, 727 yellow.

Preparation for all designs

1 Measure and mark the middle of the fabric pieces with basting stitches (see Better Embroidery).

Working the embroideries

2 The centre of the charts is indicated by the arrows on the edges. This coincides with the basted stitches. Following the charts and the colour keys, begin by embroidering the middle block of colour, using 2 strands of thread together. Complete the designs as shown on the charts.

3 Using back stitch and a single strand of the relevant colour, embroider definition lines as shown on the charts.

Finishing

4 Remove the basting stitches. Press the finished embroideries lightly on the wrong side.

Mounting

5 Mount the embroideries on cardboard for framing (see Better Embroidery).

Note: The border of An abundance of fruits has been worked in shades of beige. If you are working the three pictures as a set, use white instead of colour 975 beige, with 3774 beige.

An abundance of fruits

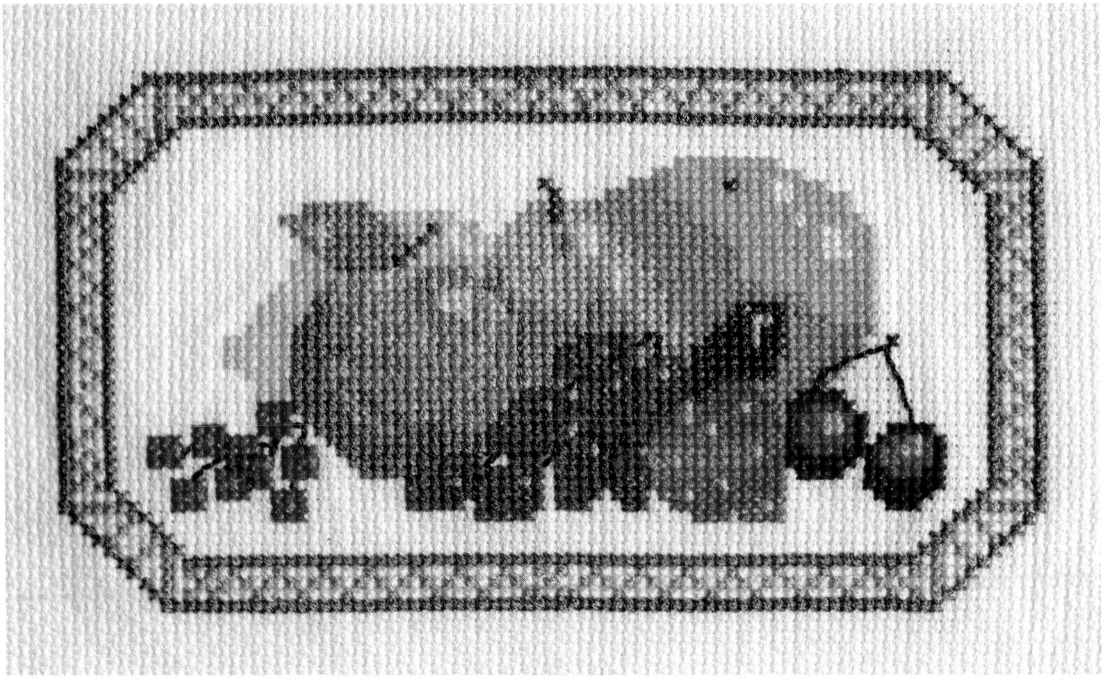

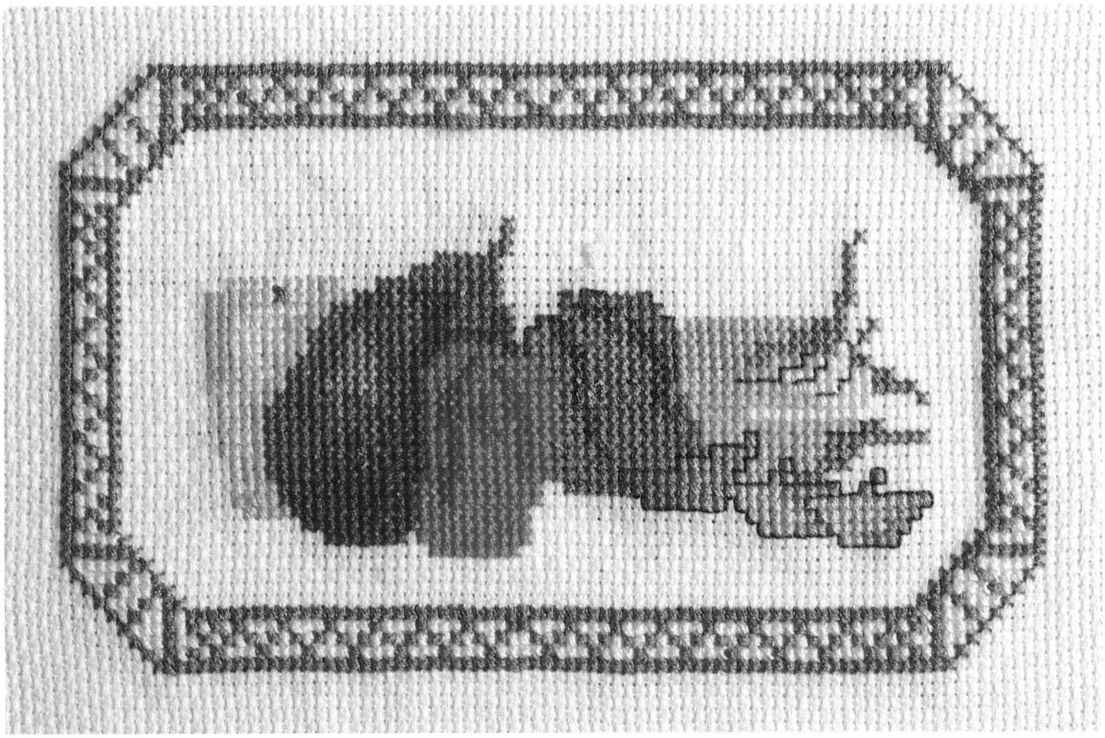

An abundance of fruits

975
3774
433
774
743
772
905
471
3348
504
501
472
320
666
321
3793
3713
3746
813
310
815
3078
48
57
727

Size of finished embroidery: $5\frac{3}{4}$ × 3in (14.5 × 7.5cm)

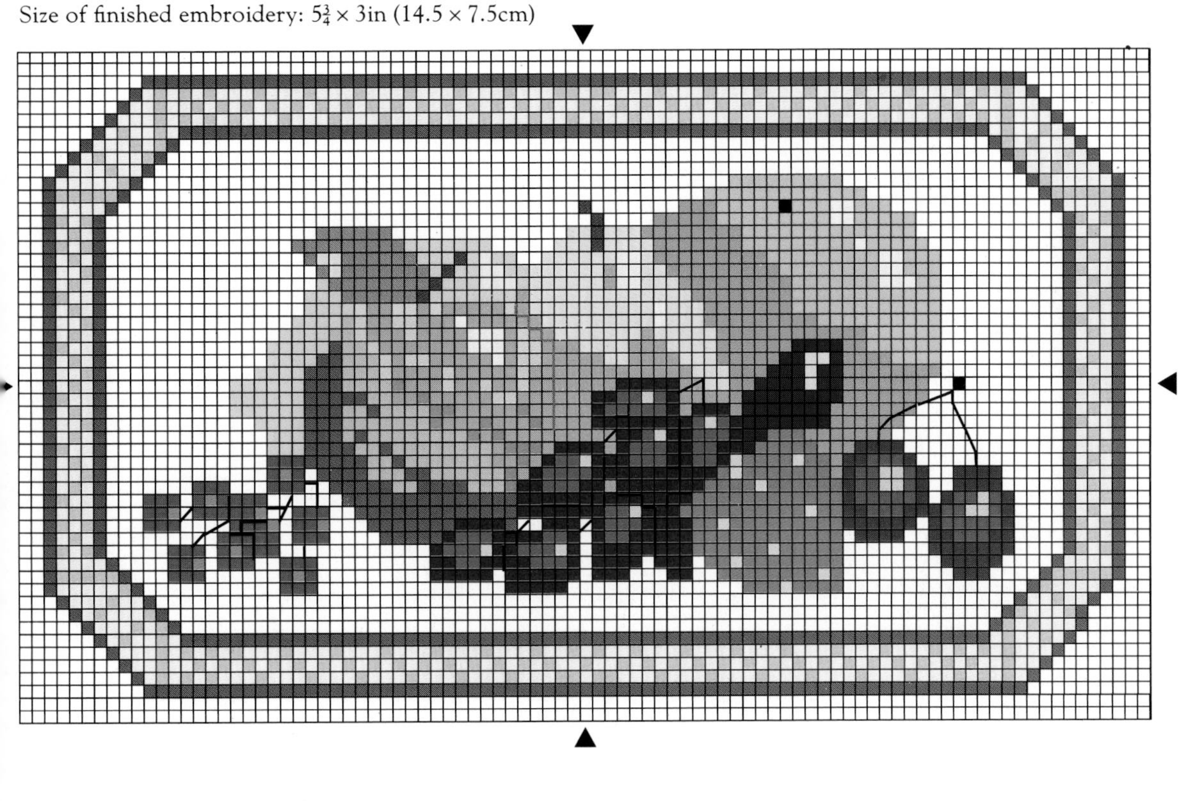

PART V

Romantic Keepsakes

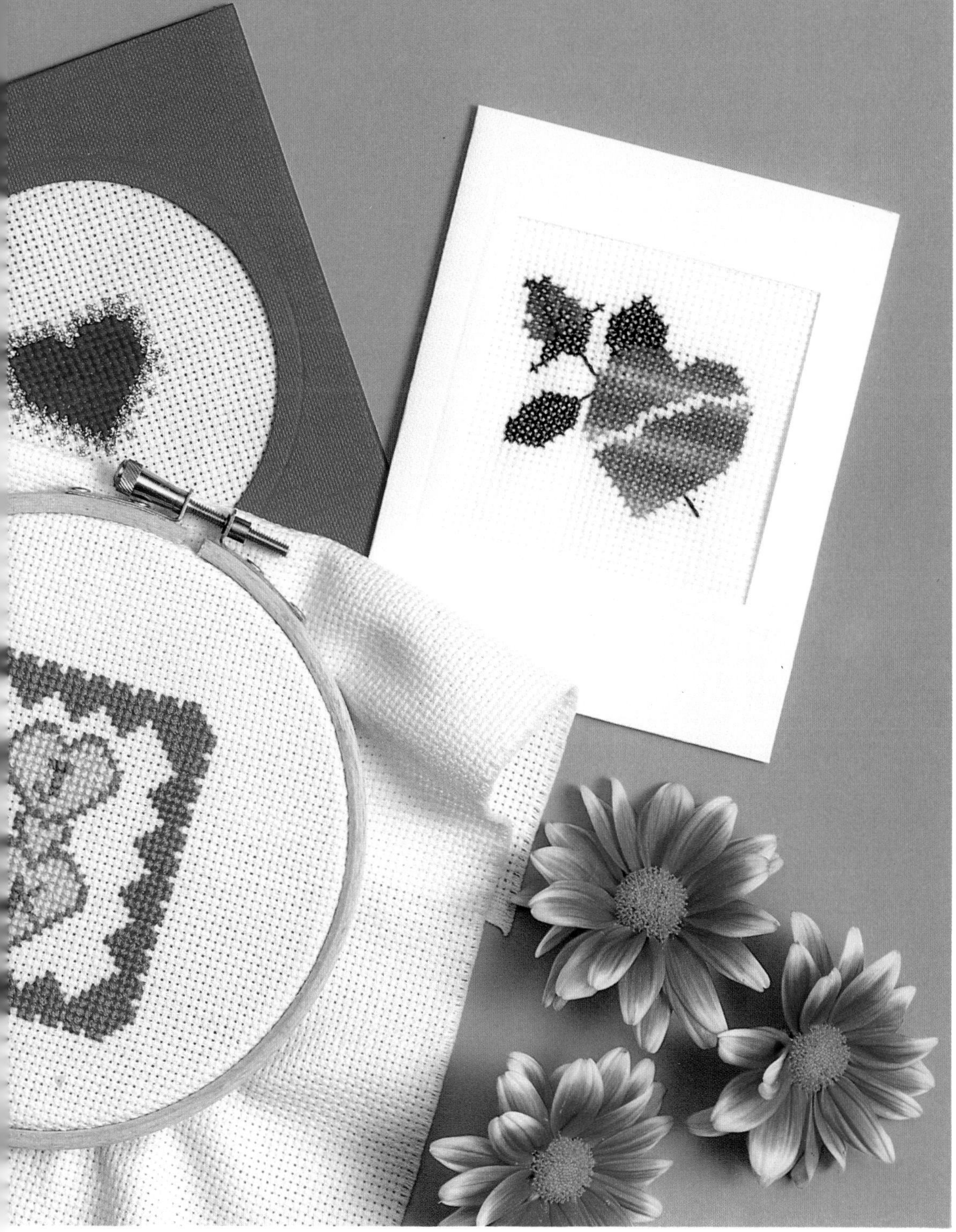

Valentine hearts

Embroider your loved one's initial, surrounded by hearts, for a special token on St Valentine's day. This design can be framed for a small picture or it could be put into a greetings card mount.

Materials

10in (25cm) square of ecru evenweave linen with a thread count of 14 to 1in (2.5cm)

DMC stranded cottons as follows: 1 skein each of 3793 dark dusky pink, 321 red; Silver embroidery thread

Preparation

1 Measure and mark the middle of the fabric with basting stitches (see Better Embroidery).

Working the embroidery

2 The centre of the chart is indicated by the arrows on the edges. This coincides with the basted stitches. Following the chart and the colour key, begin by embroidering the middle block of colour, using 2 strands of thread together. Complete the design as shown on the chart.

Finishing

3 Remove the basting stitches. Press the finished embroidery lightly on the wrong side.

Size of finished embroidery: $3\frac{3}{4}$in (9.5cm) square

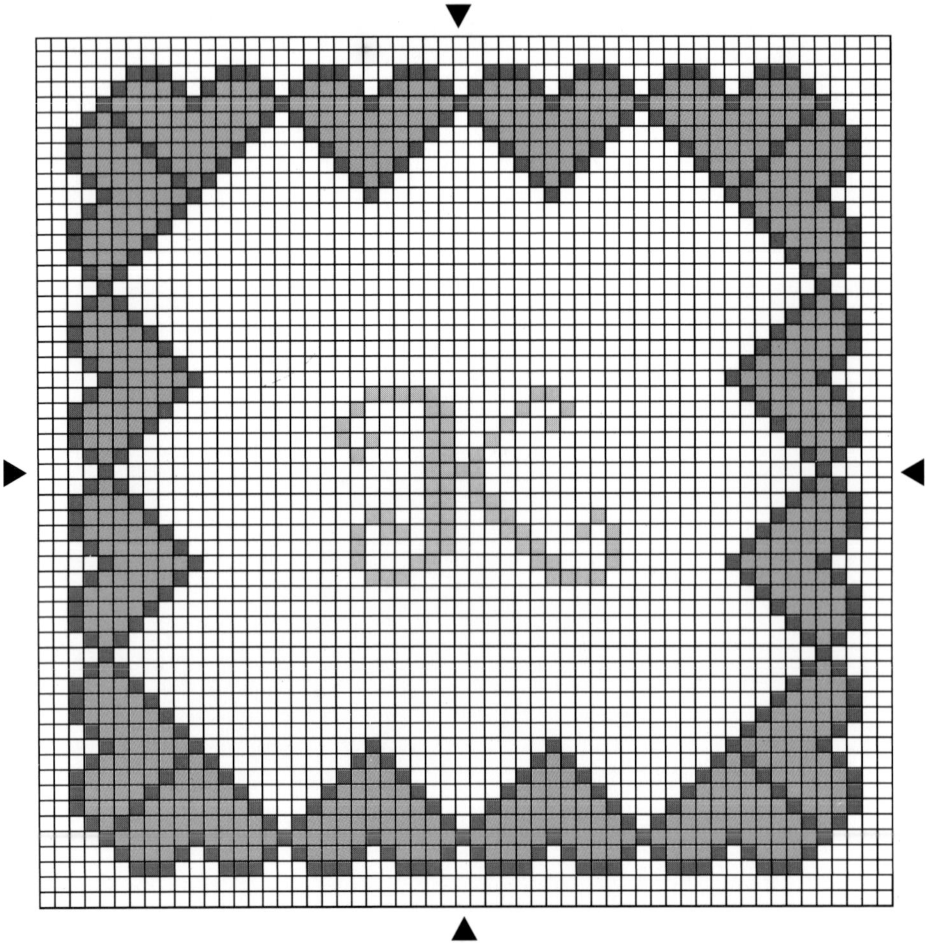

- 3793
- 321
- Silver

Mounting
4 Mount the embroidery on cardboard for framing (see Better Embroidery).

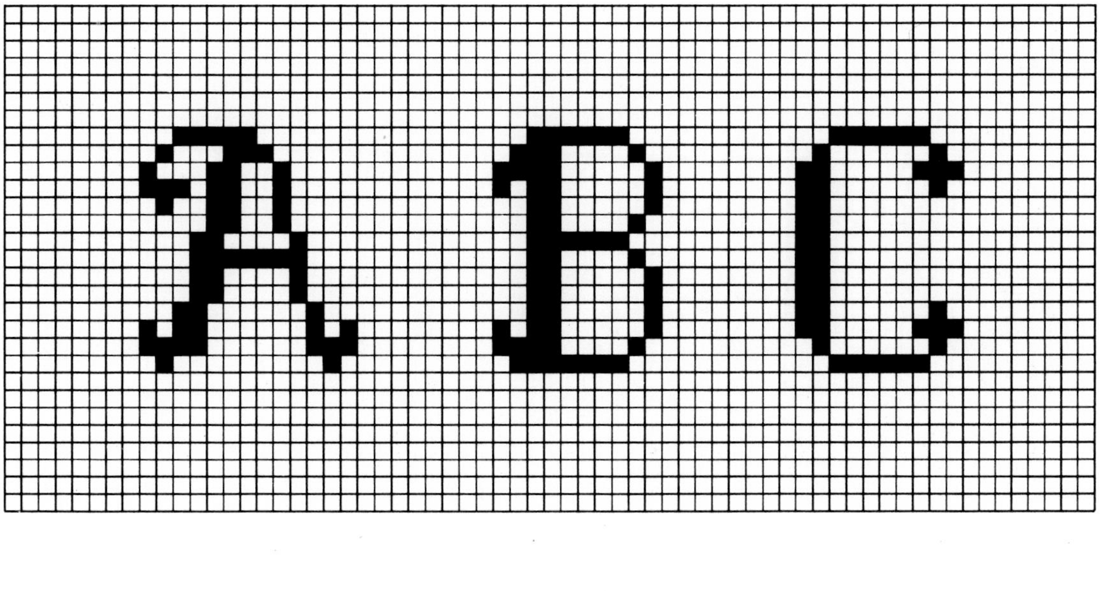

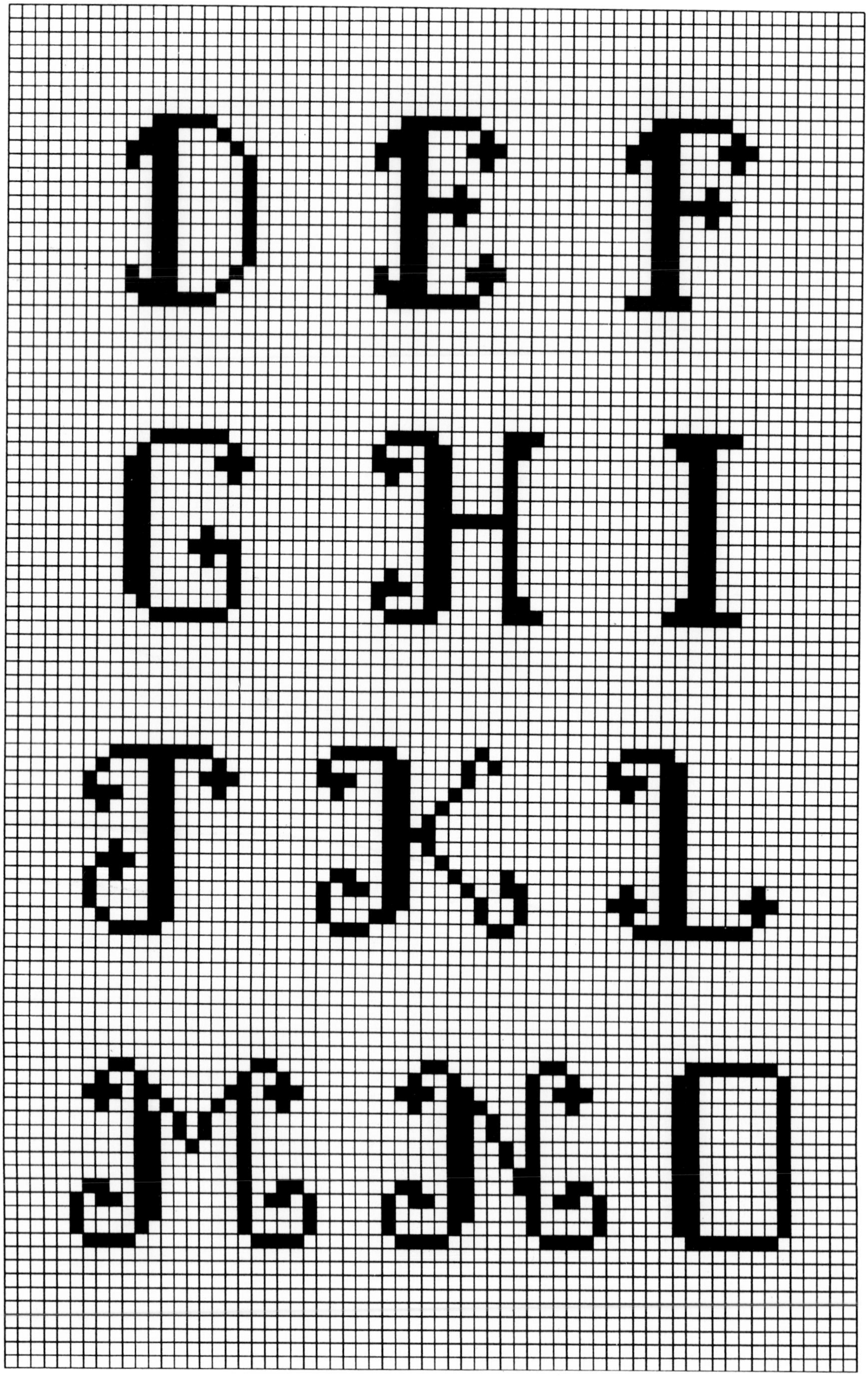

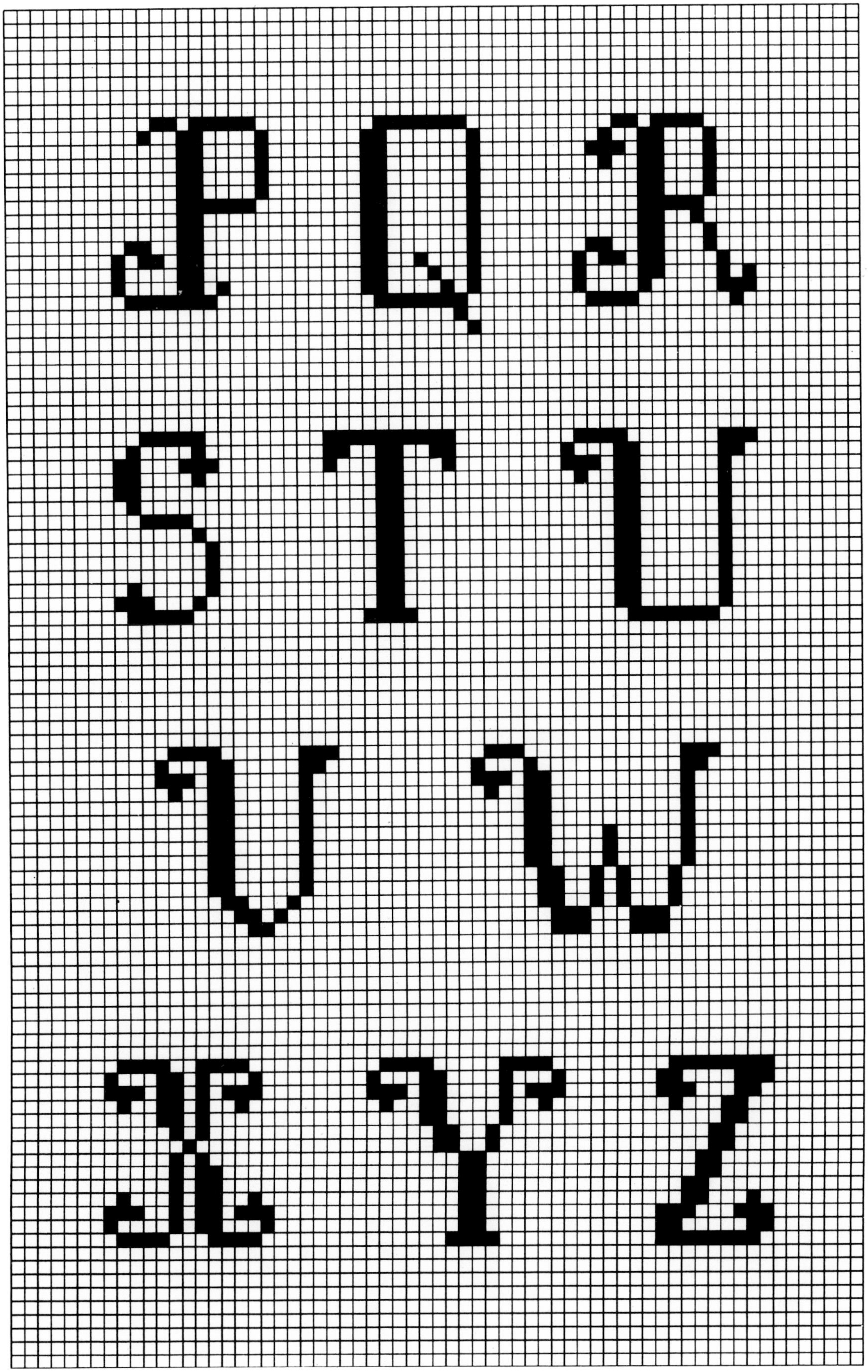

Two hearts as one

Two interlocking hearts embroidered with initials have their own special message. The central motif could also be embroidered on table linens as a wedding gift.

Materials

8 × 11in (20 × 28cm) piece of white evenweave linen with a thread count of 14 to 1in (2.5cm)

DMC stranded cottons as follows: 1 skein each of 3688 dusky pink, 948 pale pink, 958 turquoise

Preparation

1 Measure and mark the middle of the fabric with basting stitches (see Better Embroidery).

Working the embroidery

2 The centre of the chart is indicated by the arrows on the edges. This coincides with the basted stitches. Following the chart and the colour key, begin by embroidering in the middle of the design, using 2 strands of thread together. Complete the design as shown on the chart.

Finishing

3 Press the finished embroidery lightly on the wrong side.

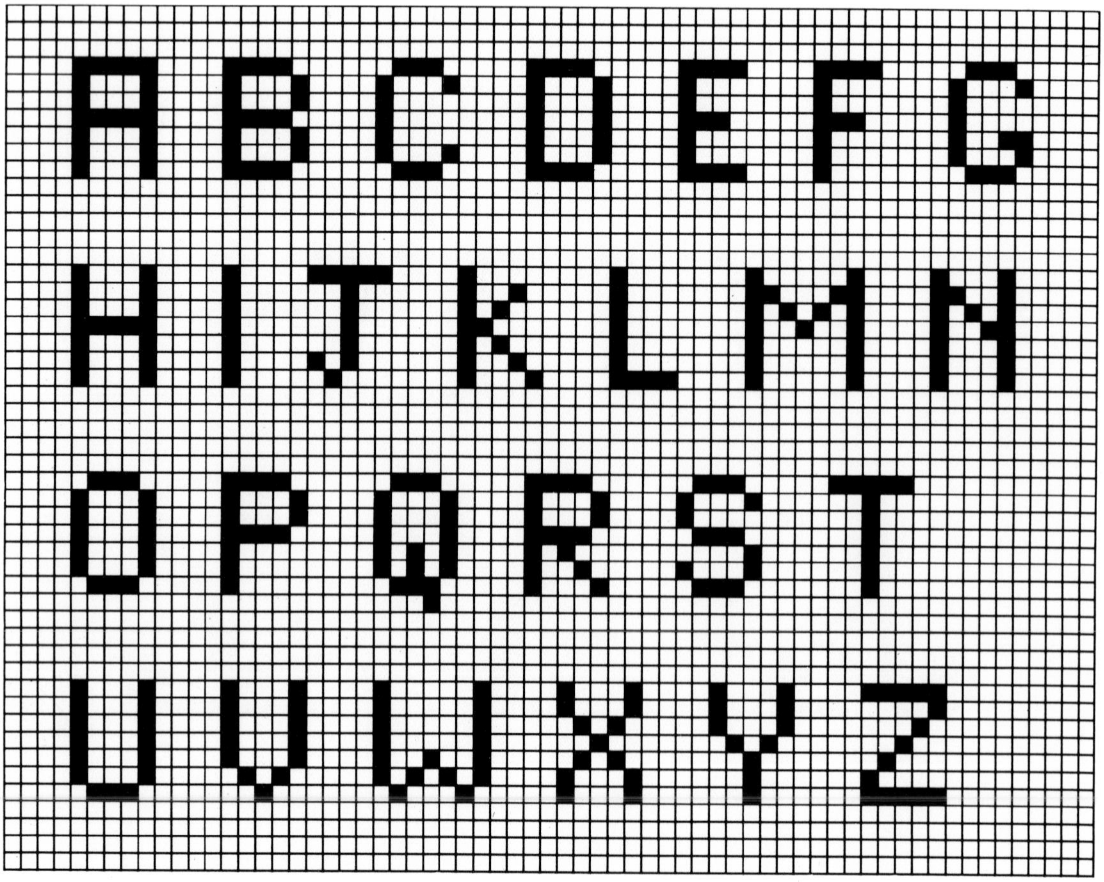

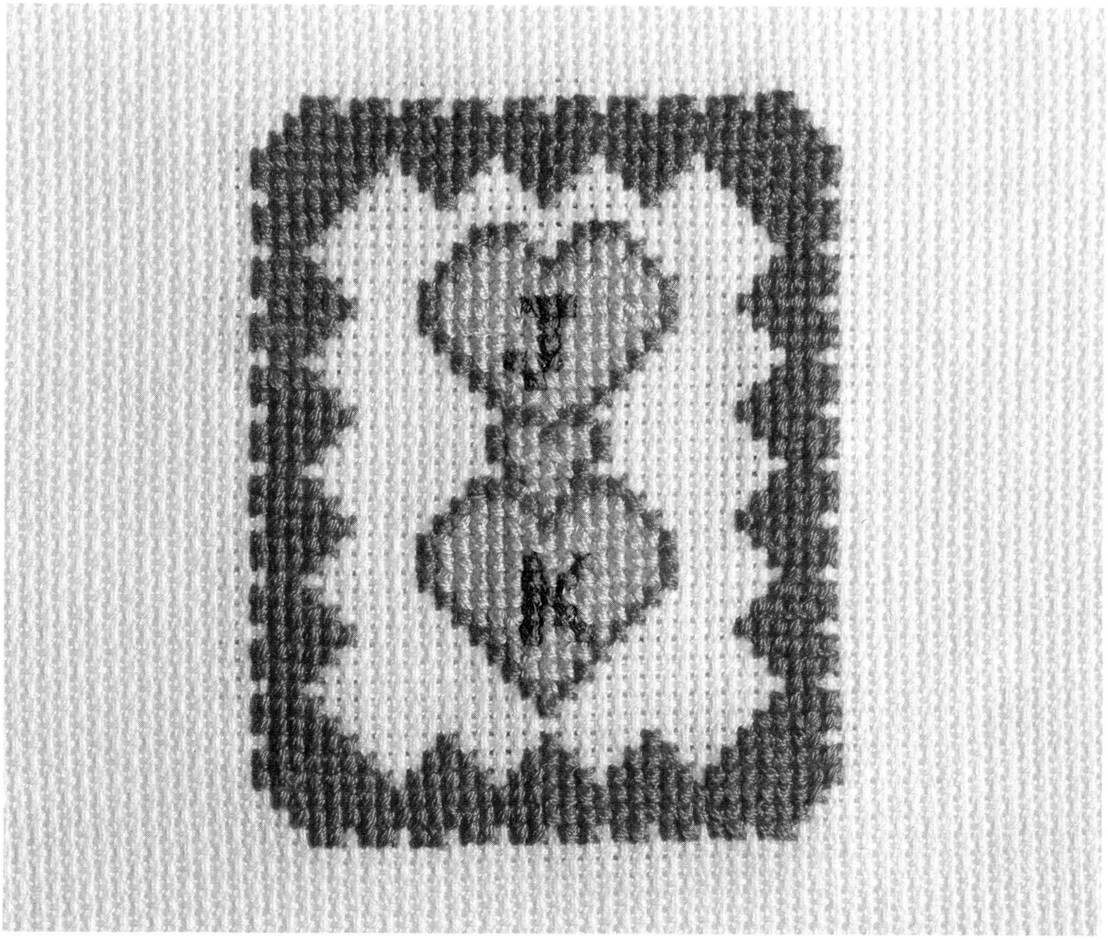

Size of finished embroidery: $2\frac{1}{2} \times 3$in (6 × 7.5cm)

Mounting

4 Mount the embroidery on cardboard for framing or insert it into a greetings card (see Better Embroidery).

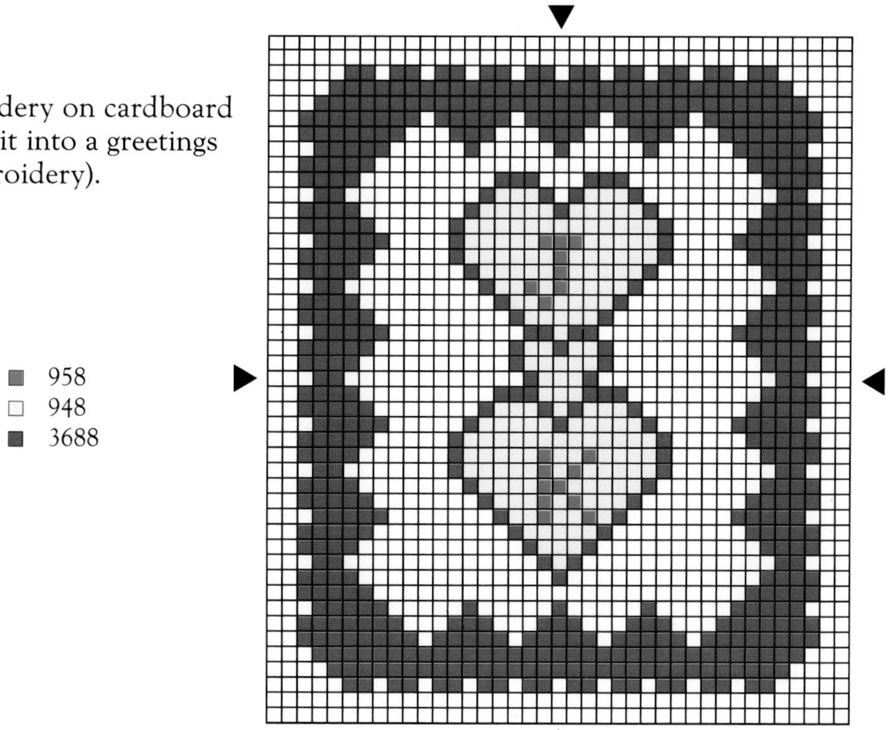

Hearts and roses

This romantic combination of hearts and roses speaks words of love. The dainty border could also be used to decorate a set of towels, the colours changed to match a room.

Materials

9 × 10in (23 × 25cm) piece of white evenweave linen with a thread count of 14 to 1in (2.5cm)

DMC stranded cottons as follows: 1 skein each of 906 leaf green, 210 mid-lavender, 48 shaded pink.

Preparation

1 Measure and mark the middle of the fabric with basting stitches (see Better Embroidery).

Size of finished embroidery: $3\frac{3}{4} \times 4\frac{1}{4}$in (9 × 10.5cm)

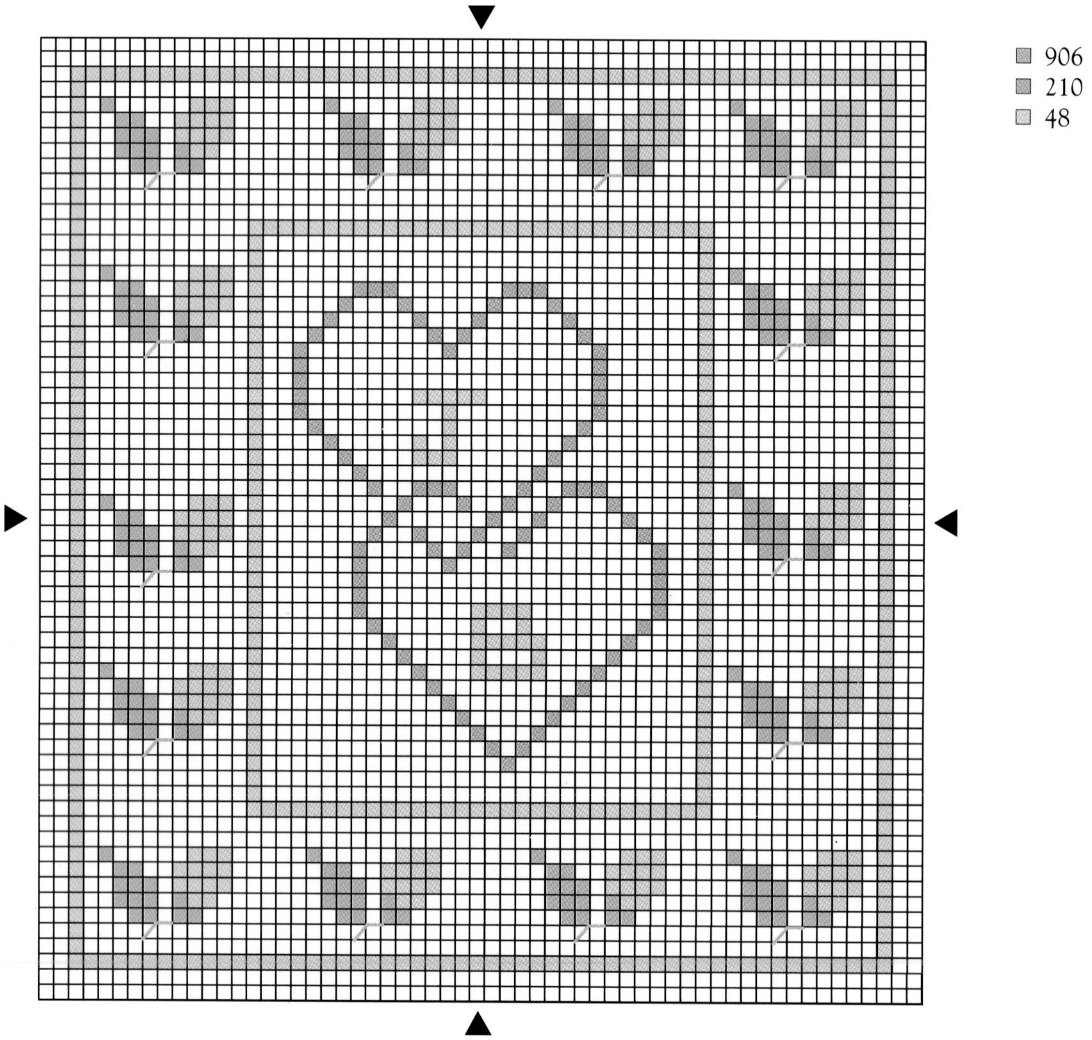

Working the embroidery
2 The centre of the chart is indicated by the arrows on the edges. This coincides with the basted stitches. Following the chart and the colour key, begin by embroidering the middle of the design, using 2 strands of thread together. Complete as shown on the chart.

Finishing
3 Remove the basting stitches. Press the finished embroidery lightly on the wrong side.

Mounting
4 Mount the embroidery on cardboard for framing (see Better Embroidery).

Loving thoughts

Here are two designs that would look equally effective as greetings cards, or mounted and framed as miniatures to express your thoughts in a very special way.

BROKEN HEART

Materials

8in (20cm) square of white evenweave linen with a thread count of 14 to 1in (2.5cm)

DMC stranded cottons as follows: 1 skein each of 501 dark green, 666 mid-red, 815 maroon, 116 shaded strawberry

White, square-window card blank

TRUE LOVE

Materials

7in (17.5cm) square of ecru evenweave linen with a thread count of 14 to 1in (2.5cm)

DMC stranded cottons as follows: 1 skein of 321 red, Silver embroidery thread

Red, round-window card blank

Preparation

1 Measure and mark the middle of the pieces of fabric with basting stitches (see Better Embroidery).

Working the embroidery

2 The centre of the charts is indicated by arrows on the edges. This coincides with the basted stitches. Following the charts and the colour keys, begin by embroidering the middle block of colour, using 2 strands of thread together. Complete the design as shown on the chart. Work lines in back stitch.

Finishing both cards

3 Remove the basting stitches. Press the finished embroideries lightly on the wrong side.

4 Trim the embroidery edges to fit inside the card, behind the window, leaving as much allowance as possible.

Size of finished embroidery: $2\frac{1}{4} \times 2$in (5.5×5cm)

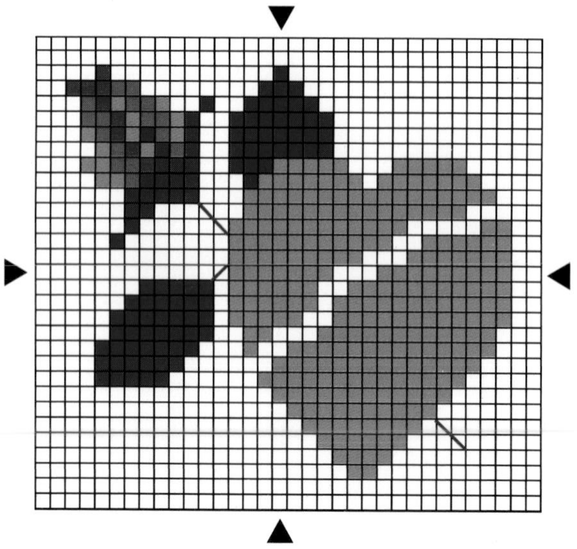

■ 501
■ 666
■ 815
■ 116

Size of finished embroidery: $1\frac{3}{8} \times 1\frac{1}{4}$in (3.5 × 3cm)

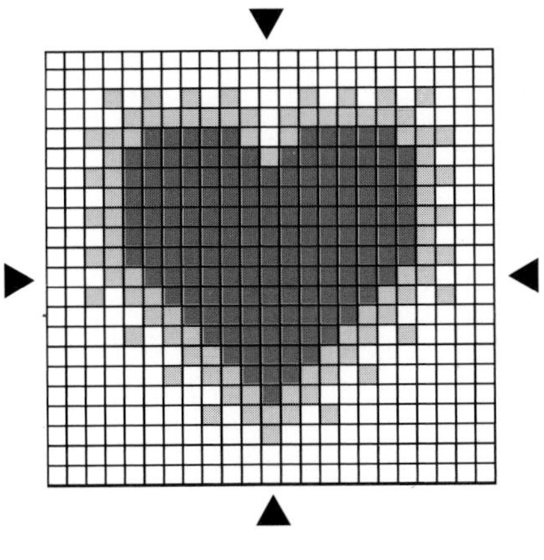

■ 321
□ Silver

5 Spread glue thinly around the edges of the window opening.

6 Stick the embroidery behind the window.

7 Spread a little glue round the edges of the left-hand panel and fold it over the embroidery. Press down firmly and leave until completely dry.

ABCDEFGHIJ
KLMNOPQRS
TUVWXYZ
abcdefghijklmnopq

PART VI

Samplers and Greetings

Alphabet sampler

The traditional sampler of alphabet letters and numbers has been a firm favourite for many years. This version will make a thoughtful gift to record a special occasion.

Materials

16 × 12in (40 × 31cm) piece of ecru evenweave linen with a thread count of 14 to 1in (2.5cm)

DMC stranded cottons as follows: 1 skein each of 353 beige, 347 russet, 3713 pale pink, 472 pale olive green, 3688 dusky pink, 776 light dusky pink, 342 lavender, 210 dark lavender, 3325 light cobalt blue, 310 black, 931 mid-petrol blue, 3675 dark petrol blue

Preparation

1 Measure and mark the middle of the fabric with basting stitches (see Better Embroidery).

Working the embroidery

2 The centre of the chart is indicated by the arrows on the edges. This coincides with the basted stitches. Following the chart and the colour key, begin by embroidering the middle block of colour, using 2 strands of thread together. Complete the design as shown on the chart.

Finishing

3 Remove the basting stitches. Press the finished embroidery lightly on the wrong side.

Mounting

4 Mount the embroidery on cardboard for framing (see Better Embroidery).

Samplers are very individual embroideries. Unless you are working from a purchased kit, you will probably have an idea of the motifs – and words – you want to include in your sampler. Perhaps the sampler is for a friend who is getting married, or a relative who is moving house. Perhaps someone is an enthusiastic tennis player, and you want to commemorate an important match. Samplers can become a permanent record of every happy occasion, or simply a chance for you to practise your stitchery for your own satisfaction.

Sources of motifs

A selection of motifs is given in Motif Medley which will help you in planning your sampler design. Various alphabets are given in this book, which you can adapt. Alternatively you can work out your own cross stitch motifs.

First, decide on the size of the sampler you wish to make. Choose your fabric, noting the thread count then calculate the number of threads horizontally and vertically to produce a sampler of the required size. Allow for a border and turnings. Having decided on the size of the fabric, mark the area on the graph paper, one square on the paper for every pair of threads on the fabric. Measure and mark the centre of the fabric with basting stitches. Mark the centre of the graph paper area. This gives you working guidelines.

ABCDEFGHIJ
KLMNOPQRS
TUVWXYZ
abcdefghijklmnopq
rstuvwxyz
1234567890

Ideas for the alphabet chart

The chart for an alphabet sampler given here is a simple design and ideal for a beginner. However, it has great potential for designing other more detailed samplers, incorporating motifs and a border. Decide the size of your original sampler first and then plan the border. This can be a single row of stitches or you can work two, or even three, borders, one inside the other. It might look effective to have a row of letters at the top of the sampler – work from this chart. Next, you might like to choose a row of simple flowers from the Motif Medley and work this across the fabric. Perhaps another border, worked across the sampler might come next and then a

Size of finished embroidery: 4¾ × 10in (12 × 25cm)

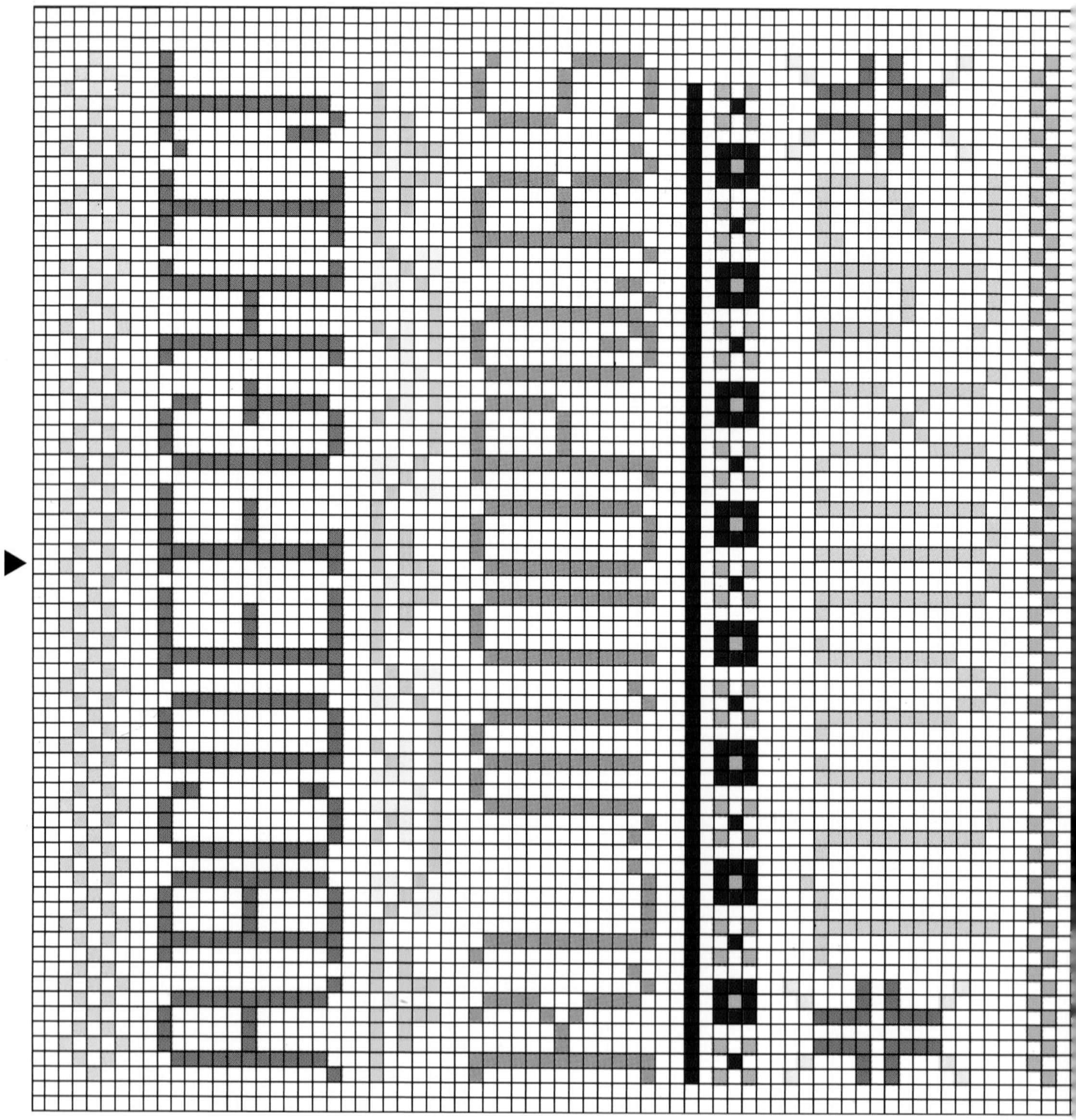

motif or two that particularly characterizes the recipient of your sampler. There are many motifs to choose from – or you might design your own. Refer to Better Embroidery for the technique. Another row of letters and a decorative border strip and your sampler may be complete.

If you want to add a message in small letters, you can use back stitch for this. Work out the words on squared paper first, so that you are sure of setting the words exactly in the centre – or you will find yourself involved in unnecessary unpicking. If you think it suitable, add your name and the date to the bottom area when you have completed the sampler.

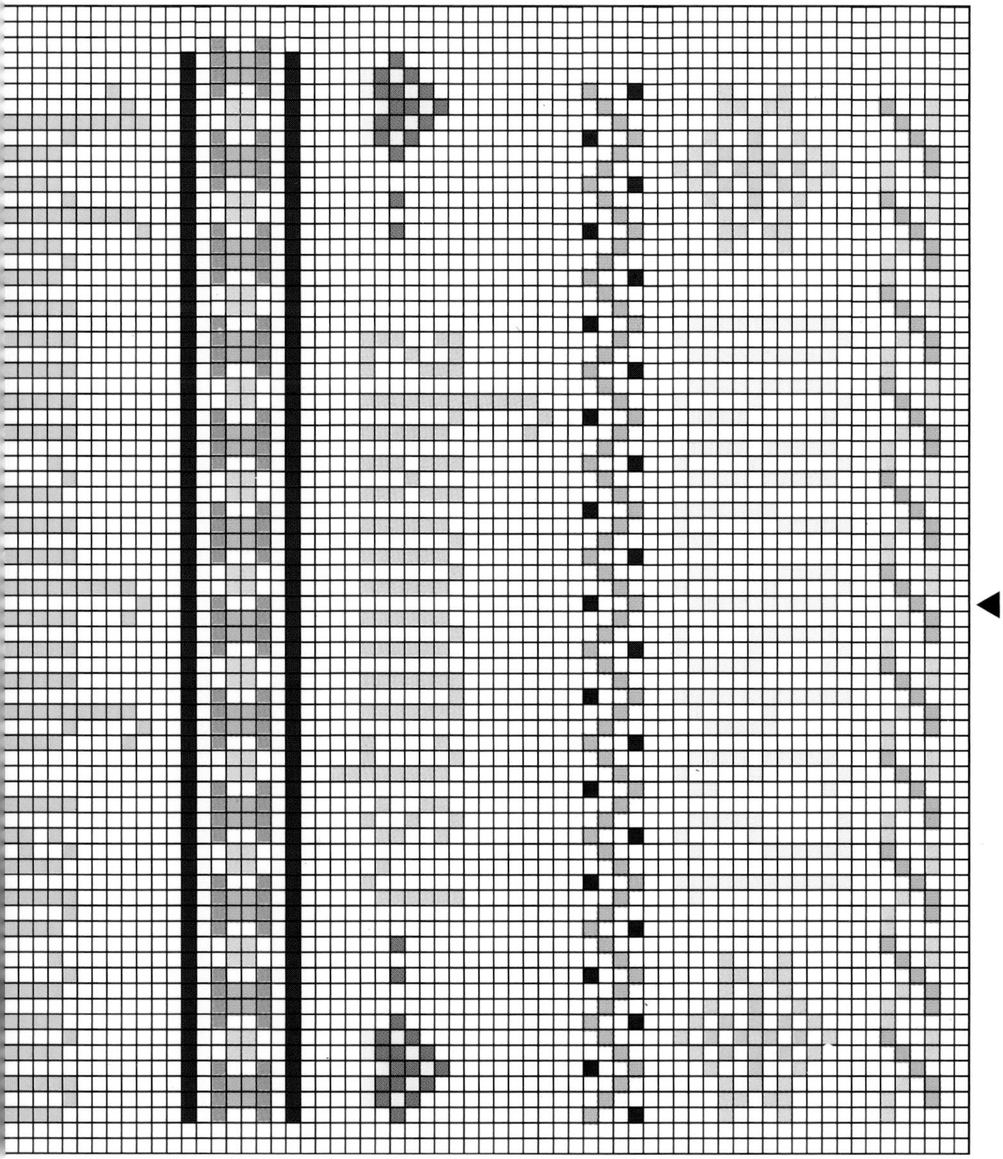

- 353
- 347
- 3713
- 472
- 3688
- 776
- 342
- 210
- 3325
- 3675
- 310
- 931

Decorative borders

A border can make all the difference to an embroidered picture – adopt the colours to match the picture's shades. You can also use these borders when planning a sampler.

Decorative borders
Use your own combination of colours and motifs to create a very personal and entirely unique border for your cross stitch designs.

If you are using a border pattern on a sampler, this should be carefully charted onto the graph paper first. Begin at the centre of one side of the graph paper shape, colouring in the squares, working towards one corner. To turn the corner, hold a mirror vertically on the graph paper at 45° to the line of the border pattern. This will reflect a symmetrical corner. Copy the corner area, then continue along the second side. Plot each corner in the same way.

When you are including letters or numbers, it is essential to count the number of squares each individual character takes, in depth and width. If suitable letters or numbers are not available as ready-made patterns, trace figures on squared paper, thus making charts of the letters, words or numerals you require. Allow at least one space (stitch) between each letter and four stitches between each word. Work out your letter or word spacing by practising various styles on spare sheets of graph paper, until you are satisfied with the results. They can then be charted onto your design sheet. Spaces between words can be lengthened or shortened to fit the space available and names can be worked in full or with initials and surname. Dates can be in words or numbers.

Small symbols or sections of border pattern can be worked at the ends of short rows of lettering to fill spaces. In old samplers, crowns and hearts were often used for this purpose. A tiny symbol can also be used instead of spacing between words and simple lines of border patterns can be used to divide lines of text.

Decide on the number of squares that each chosen motif will take, allowing one or more squares for spacing between motifs. Count the number of repeats that can be worked across the fabric. Once you have decided on the number and spacing of your motifs, draw them onto your chart.

A traditional sampler would have included a decorative border, an alphabet, numbers and a suitably uplifting moral or cautionary verse. The initials and name of the needlewoman and either her date of birth or the date on which the sampler was completed might also be added. For a truly authentic effect, remember that an old sampler would not have a mount card within the frame.

Hold the mirror vertically at 45° to the border.

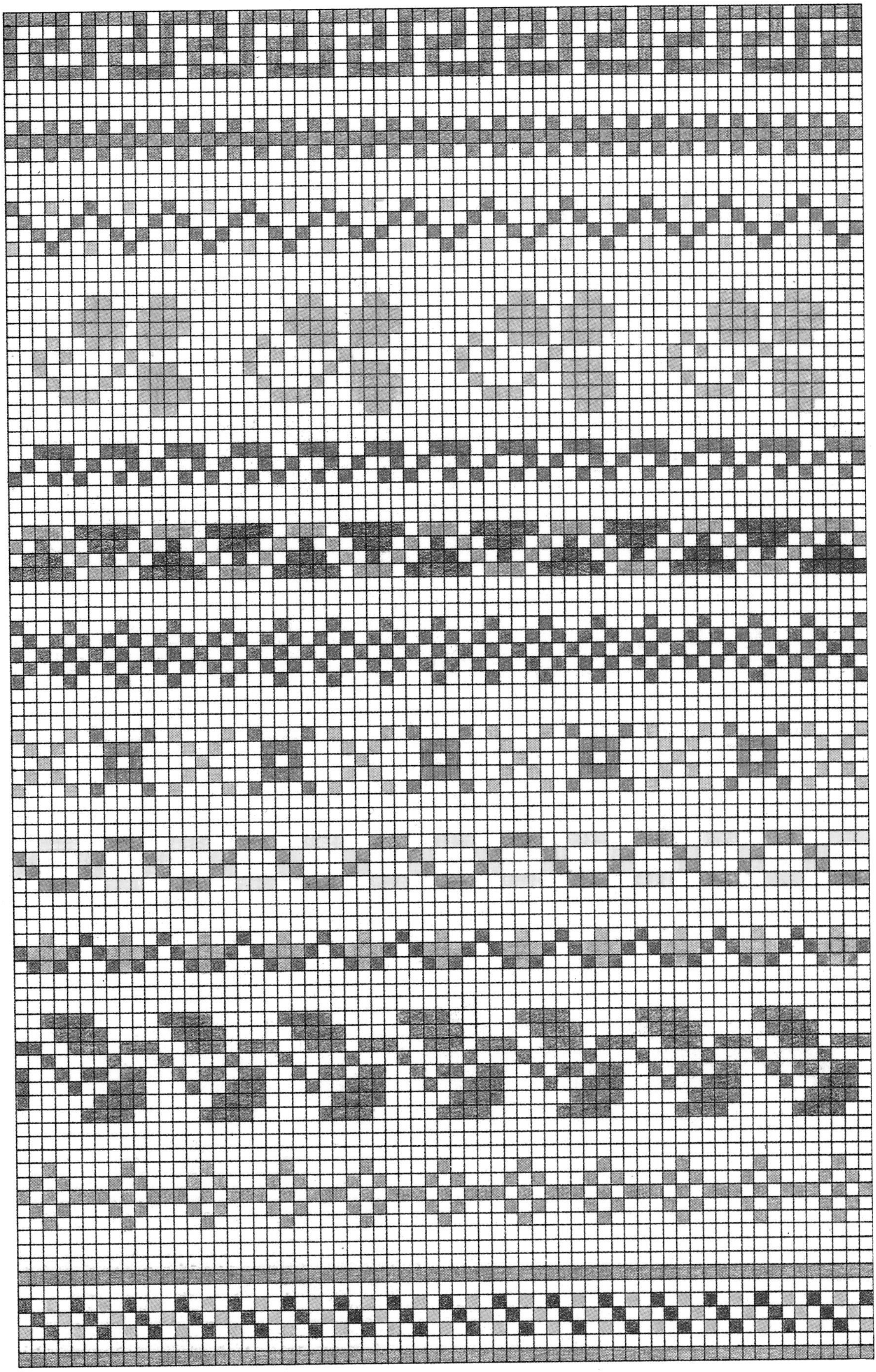

Horseshoes and roses

What better way to mark the happy occasion, than with a personalized wedding sampler of roses and horseshoes? Add the names of the couple and the wedding date.

Materials

16 × 11in (40 × 28cm) piece of white evenweave linen with a thread count of 14 to 1in (2.5cm)

DMC stranded cottons as follows: 1 skein each of 905 mid-leaf green, 471 mid-olive green, 776 light dusky pink, 948 pale pink, 894 dark pink, 3072 light grey, 414 charcoal grey

Preparation

1 Measure and mark the middle of the fabric with basting stitches (see Better Embroidery).

Working the embroidery

2 The centre of the chart is indicated by the arrows on the edges. This coincides with the basted stitches. Following the chart and the colour key, begin by embroidering the middle block of colour, using 2 strands of thread together. Complete the design as shown on the chart.

Finishing

3 Remove the basting stitches. Press the finished embroidery lightly on the wrong side.

Mounting

4 Mount the embroidery on cardboard for framing (see Better Embroidery).

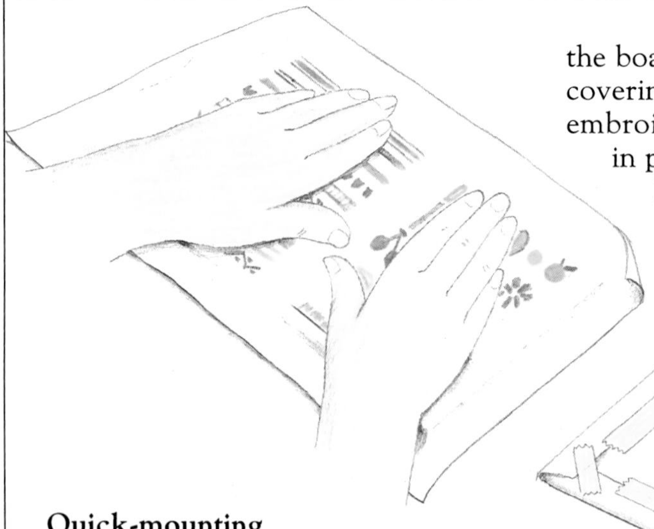

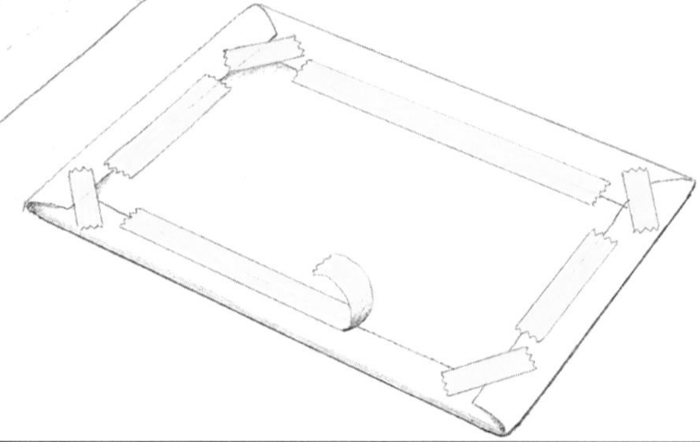

Quick-mounting

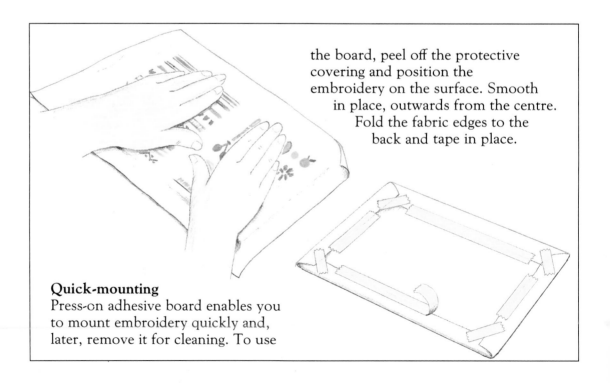

Press-on adhesive board enables you to mount embroidery quickly and, later, remove it for cleaning. To use the board, peel off the protective covering and position the embroidery on the surface. Smooth in place, outwards from the centre. Fold the fabric edges to the back and tape in place.

Size of finished embroidery: 5 × 9in (13 × 22.5cm)

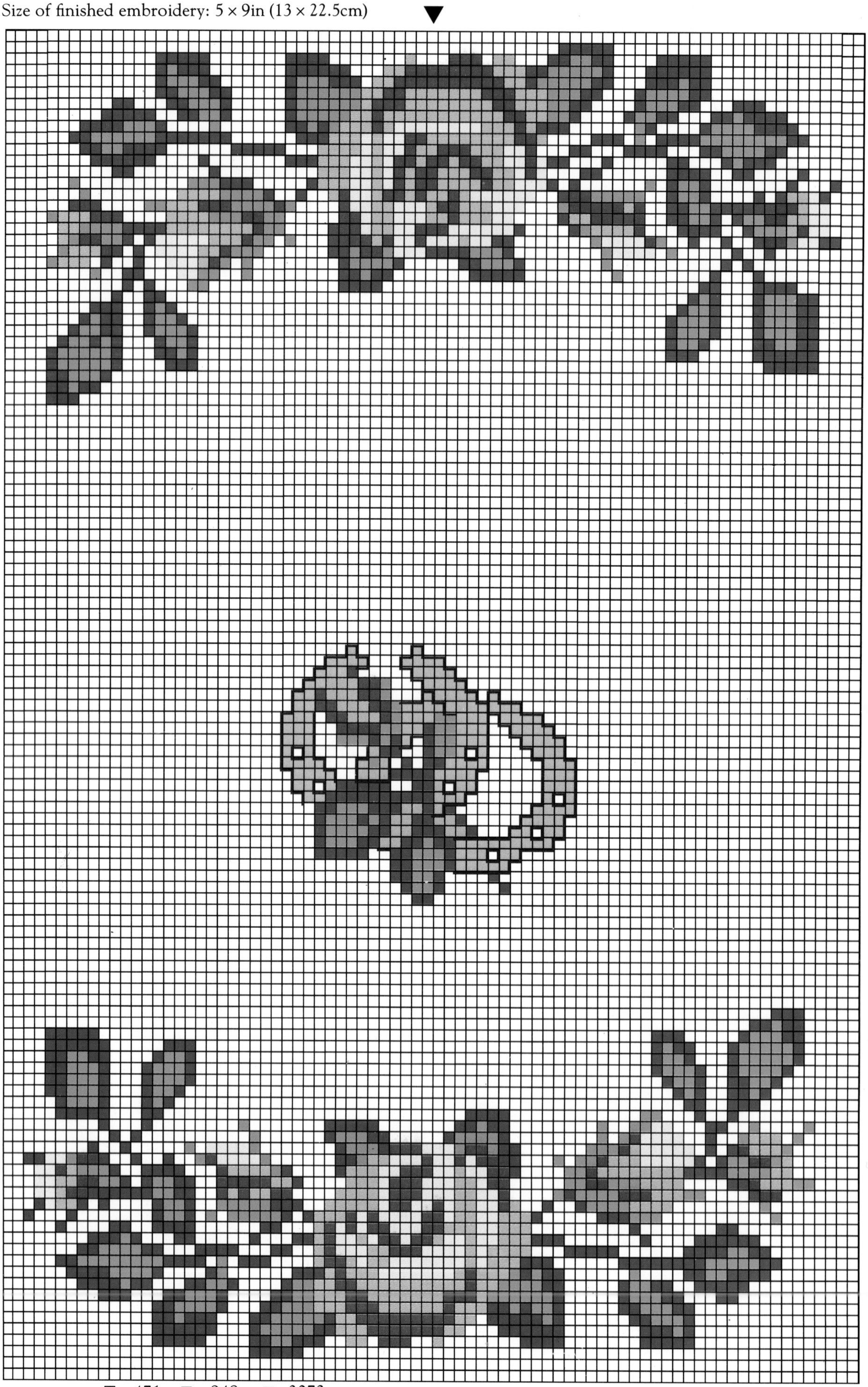

471 948 3072
905 776 894 414

Christmas sampler

Make this festive sampler to become part of your Christmas traditions. You could also abstract a motif for a bright border of Christmas trees on a seasonal tablecloth and table napkins.

Size of finished embroidery: $6\frac{3}{4} \times 3\frac{3}{4}$in (17 × 9.5cm)

•	White
■	433
■	774
■	905
■	561
■	606
■	957
■	209
■	3755
■	791
■	3072
■	310
■	727

Materials

12 × 14in (30 × 35cm) piece of ecru evenweave linen with a thread count of 14 to 1in (2.5cm)

DMC stranded cottons as follows: 1 skein each of white, 433 dark oak, 774 dark orange, 905 mid-leaf green, 561 dark hooker green, 606 crimson, 957 light pink, 209 mid-mauve, 3755 wedgwood blue, 791 French navy, 3072 light grey, 310 black, 727 yellow

Preparation

1 Measure and mark the middle of the fabric with basting stitches (see Better Embroidery).

Working the embroidery

2 The centre of the chart is indicated by the arrows on the edges. This coincides with the basted stitches. Following the chart and the colour key, begin by embroidering the middle block of colour, using 2 strands of thread together. Complete the design as shown on the chart.

Finishing

3 Remove the basting stitches. Press the embroidery lightly on the wrong side.

Mounting

4 Mount the embroidery on cardboard for framing (see Better Embroidery).

Waste canvas

When cross stitch is to be worked on a plain weave fabric – such as when decorating handkerchiefs, bedlinens, lingerie or children's clothes etc – waste canvas is used over the ground fabric to provide a guide for the stitches. Waste canvas can be purchased at most needlework counters but ordinary embroidery canvas can be used as long as the threads are not interlocked.

Baste the waste canvas into position on the fabric to be embroidered. Work the design, taking the cross stitches through the waste canvas and onto the fabric beneath, using the canvas threads to position the cross stitches.

When the embroidery is completed, dampen the embroidery with water until the canvas threads begin to soften and part. Gently withdraw the canvas threads, first the vertical then the horizontal. Remove the basting threads. It is important to match the canvas mesh to the ground fabric. A fine fabric will need a canvas with 14 or 16 mesh while a coarser ground fabric will need a mesh of 12 to 1in (2.5cm) or less.

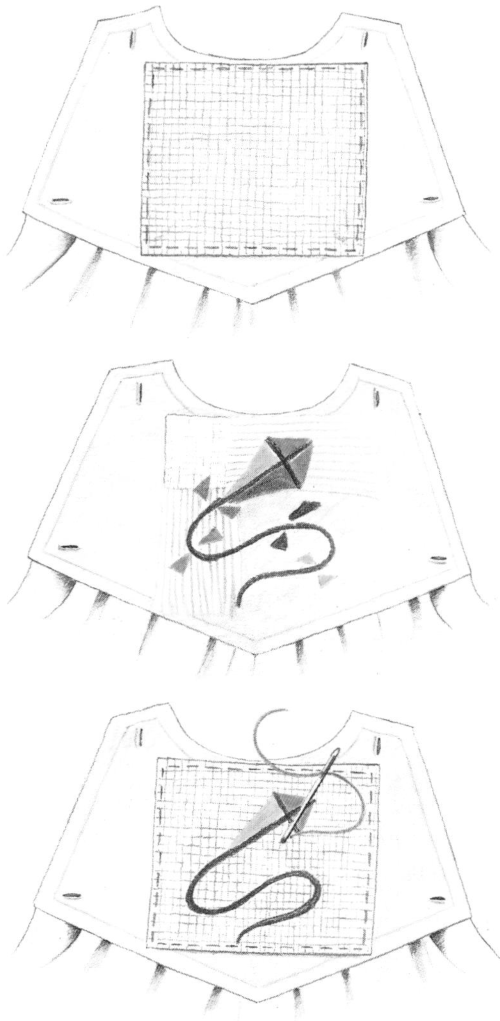

Christmas cards

Embroidered greetings cards are fun to make, taking only a few hours to complete – but they'll be treasured by friends and family for years to come.

CHRISTMAS STOCKING
Materials

4 × 6in (10 × 15cm) piece of white evenweave linen with a thread count of 14 to 1in (2.5cm)

DMC stranded cottons as follows: 1 skein each of 954 dark lime green, 666 red, 208 mid-purple, 604 pink, 3325 light cobalt blue, 310 black, 746 off-white

White greetings card blank with a rectangular window

Note: Define the stocking and parcels in back stitch, using a single strand of 310 black.

CHRISTMAS CANDLE
Materials

4 × 5in (10 × 12.5cm) piece of white evenweave linen with a thread count of 14 to 1in (2.5cm)

DMC stranded cottons as follows: 1 skein each of 743 orange, 3078 yellow, 772 pear green, 905 mid-leaf green, 501 dark green, 954 dark lime green, 910 mid-crimson, 948 pale pink, 414 charcoal grey, 920 copper

White greetings card blank with an oval window

Note: Outline the candle flame in back stitch, using a single strand of 414 charcoal grey.

Preparation

1 Measure and mark the middle of the fabric with basting stitches (see Better Embroidery).

Working the embroidery

2 The centre of the chart is indicated by arrows on the edges. This coincides with the basted stitches. Following the chart and colour key, begin by embroidering the middle block of colour, using 2 strands of thread together. Complete the design as shown on the chart.

Finishing

3 Remove the basting stitches. Press the finished embroidery lightly on the wrong side.

4 Trim the edges of the fabric to fit the card, leaving as much allowance as possible around the actual embroidery.

5 Spread glue thinly around the edges of the window.

6 Stick the embroidery behind the window.

7 Spread glue round the edges of the left hand panel and fold over the embroidery. Press down firmly and leave to dry thoroughly.

Size of finished embroidery: $1\frac{1}{2} \times 2\frac{1}{2}$in (4 × 6cm)

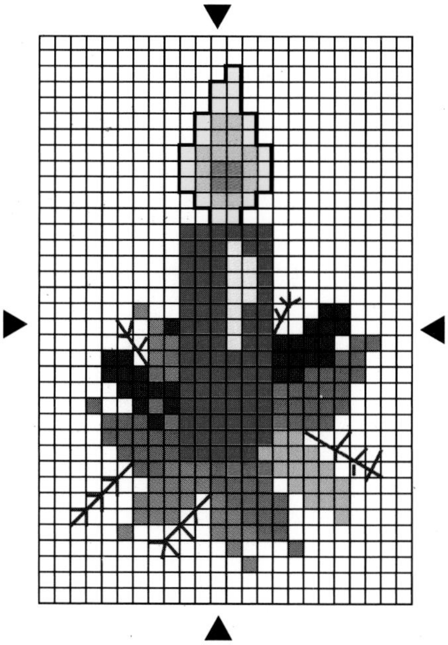

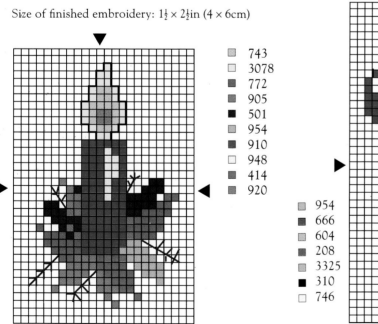

- 743
- 3078
- 772
- 905
- 501
- 954
- 910
- 948
- 414
- 920

Size of finished embroidery: $2 \times 2\frac{1}{2}$in (5 × 6cm)

- 954
- 666
- 604
- 208
- 3325
- 310
- 746

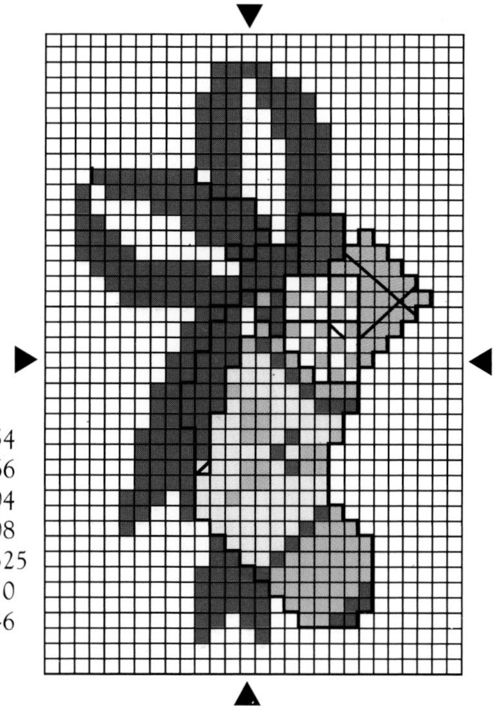

Welcome to baby

This charming baby sampler, can be worked with the alphabet or with the baby's name and date of birth. Use the motif to decorate a cot cover as well.

Materials
11in (28cm) square of white evenweave linen with a thread count of 14 to 1in (2.5cm)
DMC stranded cottons as follows: 1 skein each of white, 346 sienna brown, 504 light hooker green, 210 dark lavender, 310 black, 433 dark oak; you will also need 1 skein of 760 mid-salmon and 948 pale pink for a girl or 3746 wedgwood blue and 3753 light wedgwood blue for a boy

Preparation
1 Measure and mark the middle of the fabric with basting stitches (see Better Embroidery).

Working the embroidery
2 The centre of the chart is indicated by the arrows on the edge. This coincides with the basted stitches. Following the chart and the colour key, begin by embroidering the middle block of colour, using 2 strands of thread together. Complete the design as shown in the chart.

Finishing
3 Remove the basting stitches. Press the finished embroidery lightly on the wrong side.

4 Embroider trimmings on the crib in either 760 mid-salmon and 948 pale pink (for a girl) or 3746 wedgwood blue and 3753 light wedgwood blue (for a boy). Outline the crib, teddy and cushion in a single strand of 414 charcoal grey in back stitch.

Mounting
5 Mount the embroidery on cardboard for framing (see Better Embroidery).

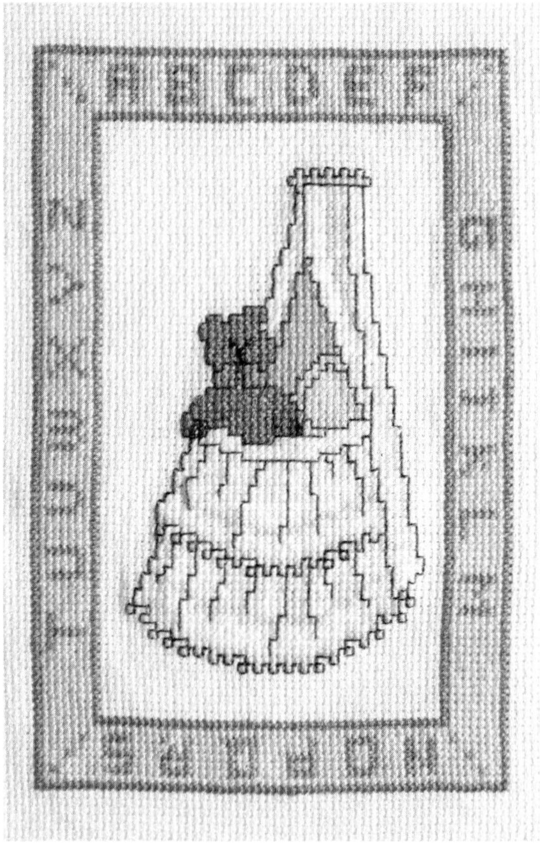

The crib motif could also be used on a variety of nursery accessories, using the waste canvas method

Size of finished embroidery: 6 × 7¼in (15 × 18cm)

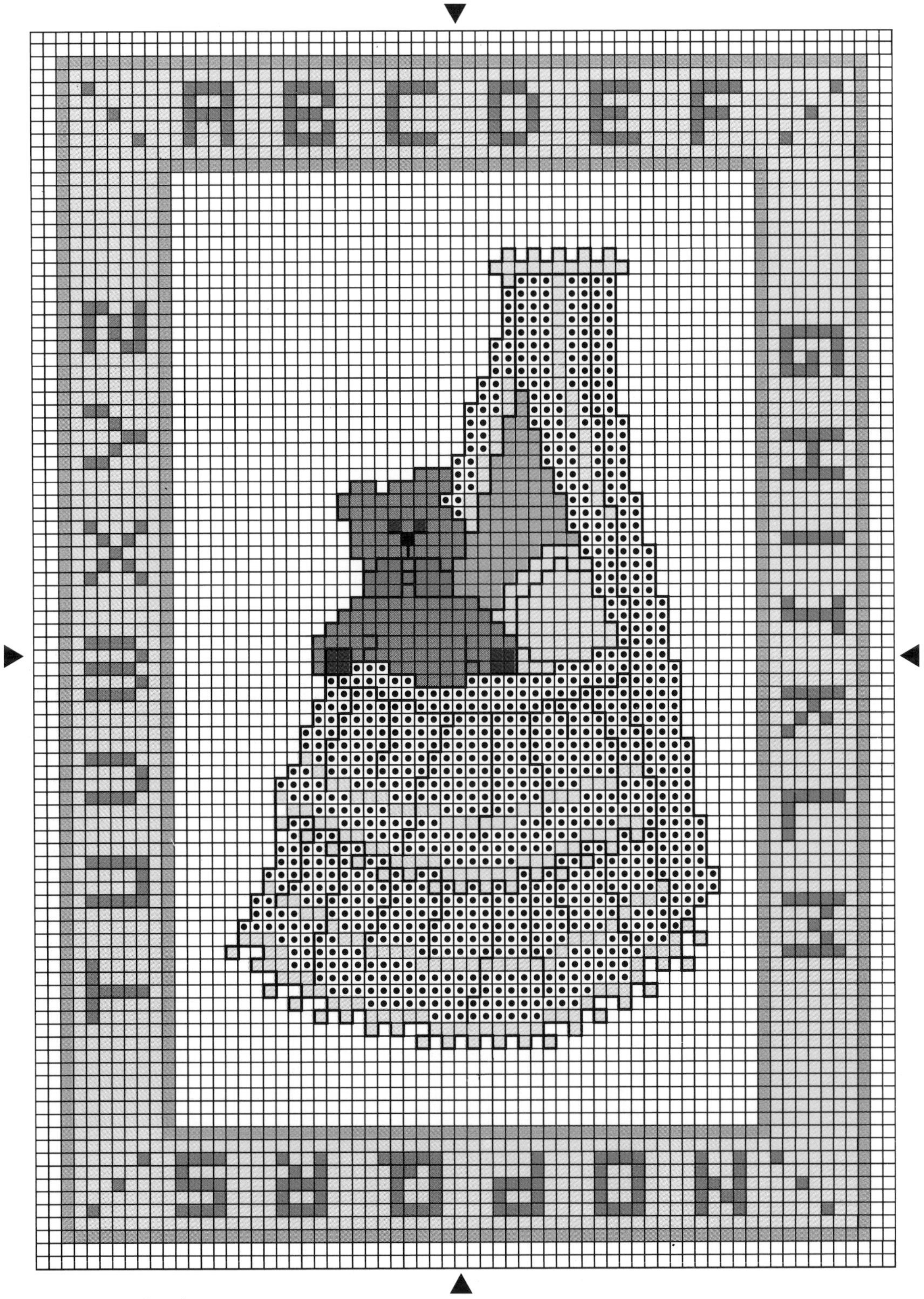

- White
- 433
- 504
- 346
- 210
- 310
- 760
- 948

Gardener's sampler

Here is a colourful picture that makes a perfect gift for a gardening friend. The border could also be embroidered on the pocket or along the hem of a gardening apron.

Materials

12½ × 10½in (31 × 26cm) piece of white evenweave linen with a thread count of 14 to 1in (2.5cm)

DMC stranded cottons as follows: 1 skein each of white, 3774 mid-beige, 680 chestnut, 778 light chestnut, 801 mid-brown, 433 dark oak, 774 dark orange, 444 light orange, 905 mid-leaf green, 910 light olive green, 501 dark green, 3348 mid-crimson, 740 pillar box red, 210 dark lavender, 552 dark purple, 3072 light grey, 414 charcoal grey

3774	774	740
680	444	210
778	905	552
801	3348	3072
433	501	414
	910	

Size of finished embroidery: 6 × 4¼ (15 × 10.5cm)

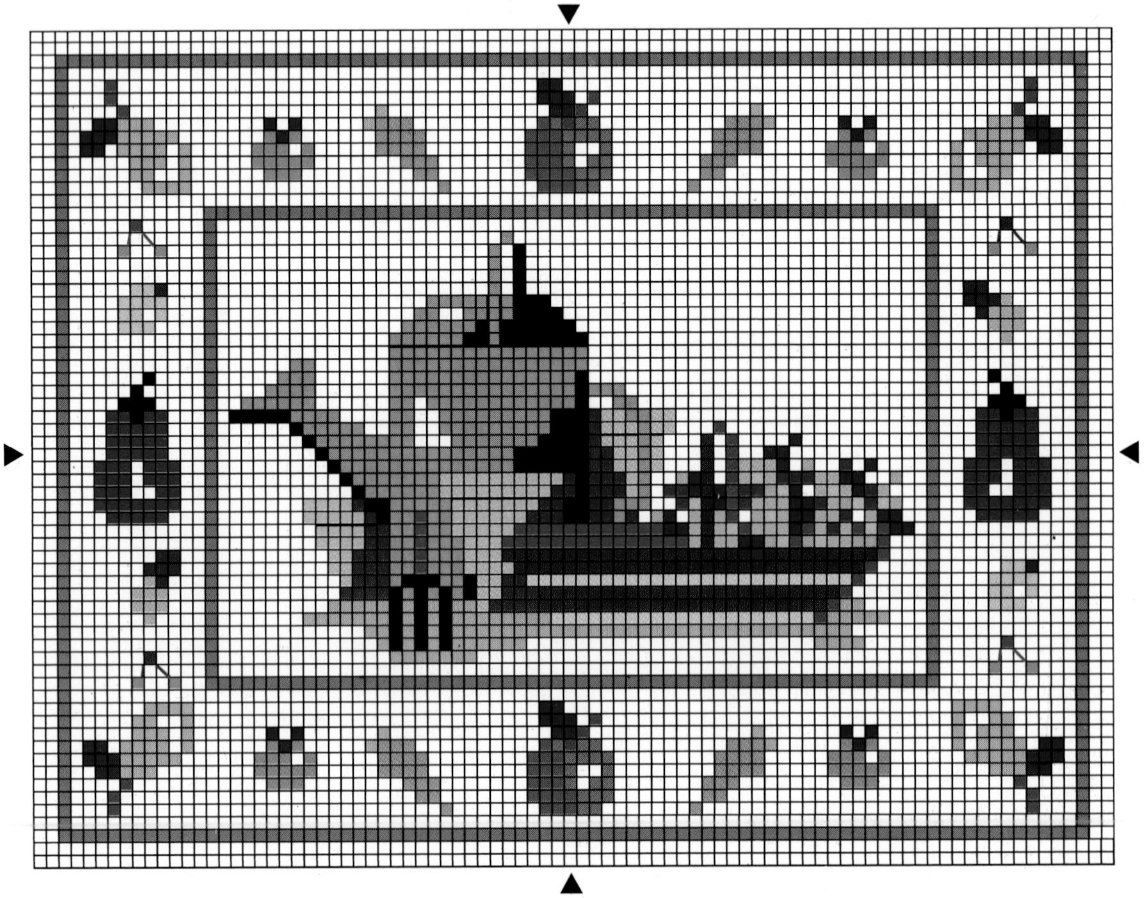

Preparation

1 Measure and mark the middle of the fabric with basting stitches (see Better Embroidery).

Working the embroidery

2 The centre of the chart is indicated by the arrows on the edges. This coincides with the basted stitches. Following the chart and the colour key, begin by embroidering the middle block of colour, using 2 strands of thread together. Complete the design as shown.

3 Define the watering can with 414 charcoal back stitch. Work the highlights on the fruits and vegetables in the border and the watering can in white.

Finishing

4 Remove the basting stitches. Press the finished embroidery lightly on the wrong side.

Mounting

5 Mount the embroidery on cardboard for framing (see Better Embroidery).

Home, sweet home

This picture of a little country cottage would make a treasured addition to any home. Names and a date could be substituted for the alphabet to provide a unique house-warming gift.

Materials

12 × 10in (30 × 25cm) piece of white evenweave linen with a thread count of 14 to 1in (2.5cm)

DMC stranded cottons as follows: 1 skein each of 739 beige, 725 rust, 839 dark brown, 433 dark oak, 905 mid-leaf green, 700 hooker green, 954 dark lime green, 606 crimson, 3072 light grey, 310 black, 561 bottle green, white

Size of finished embroidery: 6 × 5in (15 × 12.5cm)

Preparation

1 Measure and mark the middle of the fabric with basting stitches (see Better Embroidery).

Working the embroidery

2 The centre of the chart is indicated by the arrows on the edges. This coincides with the basted stitches. Following the chart and the colour key, begin by embroidering the middle block of colour, using 2 strands of thread together. Complete the design as shown in the chart.

▫ 739	▫ 954
▪ 725	▪ 606
▪ 839	▫ 3072
▪ 433	▪ 310
▪ 905	▪ 561
▪ 700	⊡ White

Finishing

3 Remove the basting stitches. Press the finished embroidery lightly on the wrong side.

Mounting

4 Mount the embroidery on cardboard for framing (see Better Embroidery).

USING FLEXI-FRAMES

Flexi-frames consist of two rings, an inner of rigid plastic and an outer of flexible plastic. Fabric is fitted between the two rings and afterwards, the flexi-frame can be used as a picture frame. Remove the finished embroidery from the frame. Place the rigid frame on the wrong side and trace round. Gather the edges, pull up the stitches and replace the embroidery in the flexi-hoop. Trim the excess fabric on the wrong side.

Greeting for a special friend

This pretty frame could contain a friend's initials, a date to mark a special occasion or, as here, simply a nosegay of blossoms.

Materials

11in (28cm) square of white evenweave linen with a thread count of 14 to 1in (2.5cm)

DMC stranded cottons as follows: 1 skein each of 472 pale olive green, 948 pale pink, 604 pink, 210 dark lavender, 3753 light wedgwood blue

Size of finished embroidery: 4¼ (10.25cm) square

Preparation

1 Measure and mark the middle of the fabric with basting stitches (see Better Embroidery).

- 472
- 948
- 604
- 210
- 3753

Working the embroidery
2 The centre of the chart is indicated by the arrows on the edges. This coincides with the basted stitches. Following the chart and the colour key, begin by embroidering the middle block of colour, using 2 strands of thread together. Complete as shown in the chart.

Finishing
3 Remove the basting stitches. Press the finished embroidery lightly on the wrong side.

Mounting
4 Mount the embroidery on cardboard for framing (see Better Embroidery).

Clown picture

This happy clown picture would make the perfect birthday present. Worked on canvas, the design is also suitable for a needlepoint cushion or a needlemade rug, using tapisserie wools or rug wool.

Materials

12in (30cm) square of white evenweave linen with a thread count of 12 to 1in (2.5cm)

DMC stranded cottons as follows: 1 skein each of 740 pillar box red, 902 leaf green, 774 orange, 726 yellow, white, 310 black, 791 French navy

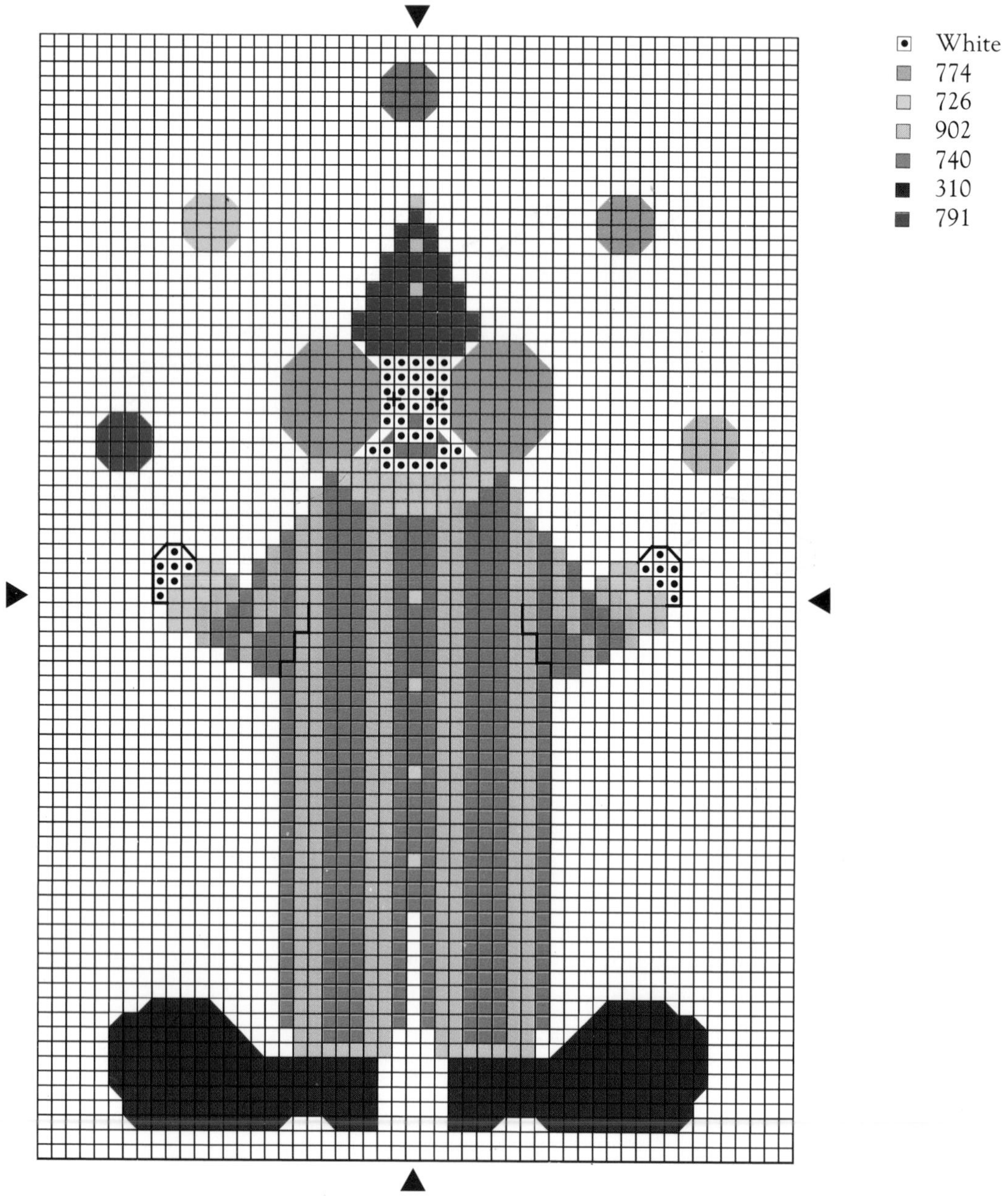

Preparation

1 Measure and mark the middle of the fabric with basting stitches (see Better Embroidery).

Working the embroidery

2 The centre of the chart is indicated by the arrows on the edges. This coincides with the basted stitches. Following the chart and the colour key, begin by embroidering the middle block of colour, using 2 strands of thread together. Complete the design as shown on the chart.

3 Using back stitch and a single strand of the relevant colour, embroider the definition lines as shown on the chart.

Finishing

4 Remove the basting stitches. Press the finished embroidery lightly on the wrong side.

Mounting

5 Mount the embroidery on cardboard for framing (see Better Embroidery). Size of finished embroidery $6\frac{5}{8} \times 4$in (17×10cm).

Motif medley

Use these motifs to create your own samplers or to personalize clothing, household linen and soft furnishings. They are also ideal for making special greetings cards.

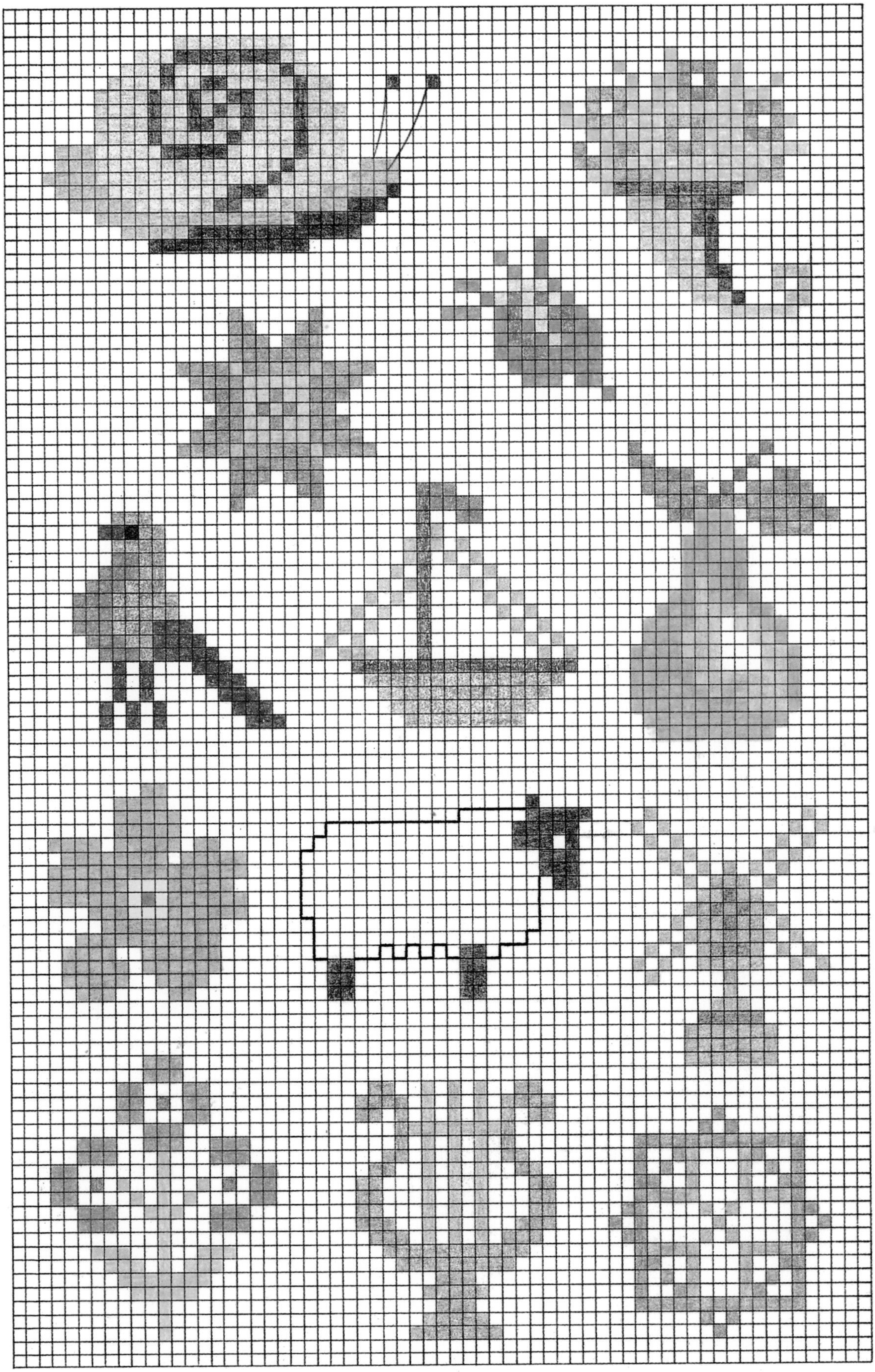

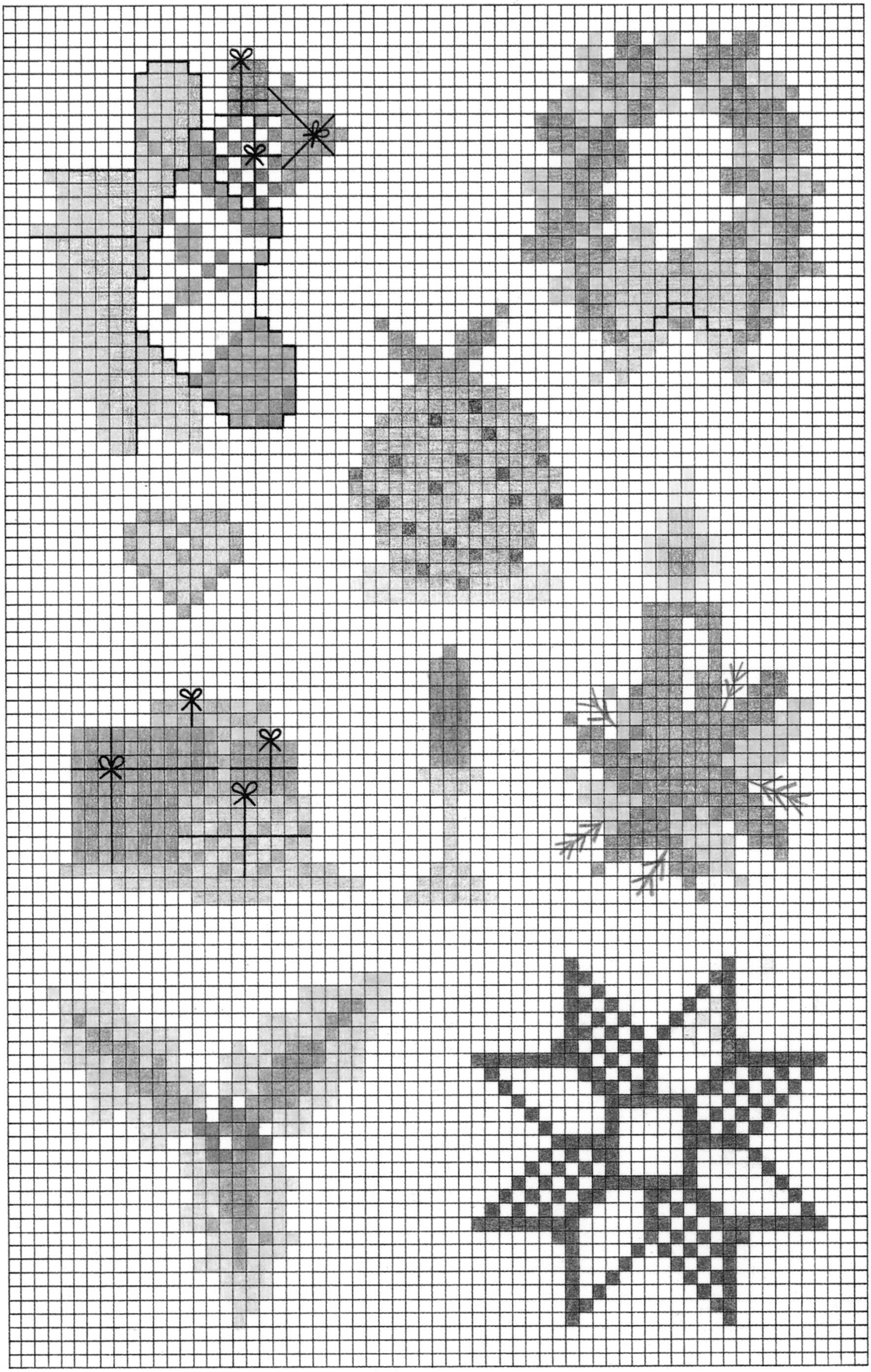

ABCDEFGHIJKLMN
OPQRSTUVWXYZ...

Better Embroidery

In this chapter you will find advice and tips on all aspects of embroidery – from choosing threads and fabrics and setting up your frame to charting your own cross stitch designs.

BASIC TOOLS AND EQUIPMENT

Very little basic equipment is required to enable you to produce stunning cross stitch designs. This chapter will give advice on choosing the right tools for the projects shown in this book.

Scissors

For cutting fabric to the correct size, sharp dressmaker's scissors will be required, while for general embroidery a pair of fine, pointed and very sharp embroidery scissors is essential.

Always keep your scissors for the purpose for which they were designed. Cutting paper will quickly blunt the blades. Never use unpicking tools for embroidery work as these can accidentally rip the ground threads of the fabric.

Needles

Round-ended tapestry needles are most suitable for working on evenweave fabrics. These will pass easily through the holes in the fabric, without snagging or splitting the threads. Split threads will result in distorted stitches, which will not lie correctly. Tapestry needles are available in sizes from 13 to 26. Chenille needles (sizes 13–24) are sharp-pointed with large eyes. Use these for general embroidery using heavier threads. Crewel needles (sizes 1–10) are also sharp with large eyes. Choose these for general, surface embroidery.

For basting and finishing projects, a range of sharps sewing needles will be required.

Needles should never be left in the fabric. They can cause the threads to distort and may leave a permanent stain.

Pins

Always use stainless steel pins for your work. Discard any that are bent or rusty and never leave pins in fabric for too long, as this can leave marks which will be difficult to remove. Glass-headed pins (which are manufactured from broken needles) are recommended. They are both strong and sharp.

Measuring aids

An accurate tape measure or ruler is essential for measuring and cutting fabric. When buying a new measure, make sure it shows both inches and centimetres and remember that cloth measuring tapes stretch with use. Check your tape measure against a ruler to ensure that the measurements are still accurate and replace it if necessary.

Thimbles

Many people find it helpful to work with a thimble. However, if you are not one of these, a piece of sticking plaster over the middle finger can help to prevent soreness that can be caused by the end of the needle.

THREADS AND YARNS

Most needlework shops stock a wide range of colours and types of thread. Choose the type suited to the kind of embroidery you are working and the effect you wish to achieve.

Stranded cotton

This is formed from six strands loosely twisted together. These strands can be separated and used individually for finer work or used in different combinations. As a general guide, on 10 to 16 count fabric use 2 or 3 strands; on 16 to 24 count use 2 strands and on 24 to 36 count use 1 strand. Stranded cotton works well in most types of embroidery.

Danish flower thread

This is a matte-finish thread made of combed cotton. On counts of 14 to 20 use 2 threads, on counts of 20 or more use 1 thread.

Soft embroidery cotton (coton à broder)

This is a dull-surfaced 5-ply thread, usually used on heavier fabrics.

Perlé (pearl) cotton

This is a glossy, twisted 2-ply thread which comes in three thicknesses. It is ideal for embroidery on coarse (low count) fabrics.

Pure silk

These four-strand threads have a high gloss sheen and come in a wonderful range of jewel-bright colours. Silk threads are colour-fast up to 60° and should be pressed with a cool iron. Silk threads are suitable for most kinds of fine embroidery.

Crewel wool

A fine, 2-ply, wool, this is used both in fine canvas embroidery and for surface stitchery on fabric.

Tapestry wool

This is a tightly twisted 4-ply yarn. It is available in a wide range of colours and is colour-fast. Usually used for canvaswork, tapestry wool can be divided into single strands for other types of embroidery.

FABRICS

Evenweave fabrics

This is the most popular fabric for cross stitch. It is so named because the number of warp and weft threads in a measured inch (2.5cm) is exactly the same. It can be obtained in a variety of sizes (thread counts) types and a range of pale colours. The highest number thread count denotes the finest weave and will, therefore, produce the smallest stitches. Fabrics range from 10 threads to the inch (2.5cm) to 36 threads to the inch (2.5cm).

Hardanger is a type of evenweave fabric in which the pairs of threads are woven together. This fabric is ideal for counted thread techniques, including cross stitch and blackwork embroidery, as the threads are easily counted and the embroidery remains firm during use.

Aida is an evenweave fabric in which the warp and weft threads have been grouped together. This creates clearly defined holes through which the needle can pass.

Binca or Bincarette is the name given to evenweave fabric with a count of 10 threads to 1in (2.5cm). Cross stitch worked on this is large and bold and is, therefore, suitable for children who are learning embroidery.

Plain weave fabrics

These do not have the characteristics of evenweave, but some types can be used for counted thread embroidery. Generally, plain weave fabrics have a smooth, tightly woven surface and the number of threads in the warp and weft are not always the same. This category includes cotton, cotton and polyester mixes, muslin, organdie, fine embroidery linen and speciality fabrics such as hessian (burlap) and hopsacking. Plain weave is most suitable for surface, free-style embroidery.

PREPARING FABRIC

If the fabric is creased in any way, particularly along the centre fold line, it is advisable to steam-iron thoroughly before cutting or beginning to embroider. Evenweave fabric tends to fray on cut edges, so either turn and baste a hem or bind the fabric edges with masking tape.

Before starting to embroider, the exact middle of the fabric must be located by carefully counting the threads along one side, then along the adjacent side to find the centres. Mark the half-way points with pins then with lines of coloured basting thread running from top to bottom and then across.

Where the two lines of threads cross is the centre point. When working with a very fine fabric, measure and mark the middle of the sides with pins then work lines of basting stitches between the pins.

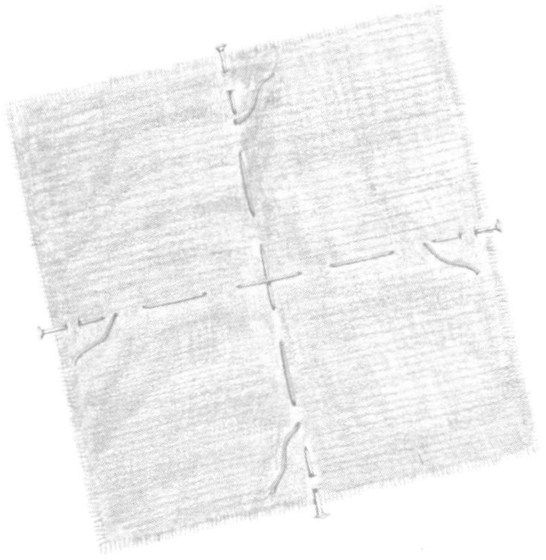

Work basting stitches top to bottom, then across.

Some embroidery fabrics are given a finishing dressing before they leave the manufacturer. This can make them feel fairly stiff to handle. You may want to wash this away before beginning to embroider, although the stiffness of the fabric can help to give your work an even tension.

Thread and fabric guide

The following will help you to choose the correct thickness of thread for the different thread count of fabrics available:-

For a thread count of 18 to 22 holes to 1in (2.5cm) choose coton perlé (pearl cotton). For a thread count of 20 to 40 holes to 1in (2.5cm) choose stranded cotton.
For a thread count of 24 to 28 holes to 1in (2.5cm) choose coton à broder (soft embroidery cotton).

EMBROIDERY FRAMES

In order to produce even, high quality cross stitch, it is essential to work with a frame. A correctly framed evenweave fabric enables the needleworker to work neatly and smoothly and the finished results will more than justify the time and initial effort required.

Experience will show which frame is best suited to a particular piece of work, but, in general, small motifs are most quickly and easily worked in a round, tambour frame, while larger, more elaborate pieces are better in rectangular or slate frames.

Stretcher frames are simply four pieces of wood joined at the corners. To attach the fabric, mark the middle of each side of the frame. Mark the centre of the fabric with basting stitches. Line up the marks and fix the fabric with staples or drawing pins. Old picture frames can also be used as a kind of stretcher frame.

Tambour or ring frames

A tambour frame consists of two rings, the outer of which has a screw fitting. This is tightened to enable the ring to hold the fabric firmly in place. Frames can be made of wood or plastic.

Tambour frames are available in several sizes from tiny, 4in (10cm) diameter embroidery rings to large quilting hoops of 15in (38cm) diameter.

Framing up tambour frames
1 Separate the two rings of the frame. Place the fabric to be embroidered over the smaller ring and fit the larger ring over this, making sure that the marked centre is in the middle of the frame.
2 Smooth the fabric out evenly and straighten the grain as you tighten the tension screw. As you continue to tighten the outer ring, pull the fabric gently from time to time to obtain an even and firm surface.

Pull the fabric edges gently for an even surface.

When working with slippery or delicate fabrics, it is advisable to bind the smaller ring with thin, cotton tape before assembling. This will help to hold the fabric more firmly and prevents damage to fine fabric.

At the end of each session, loosen the screw and remove the larger ring. Cover the worked embroidery with tissue to protect it. Replace the ring without screwing down tightly. At the next session, tighten the screw then tear the paper away over the embroidery.

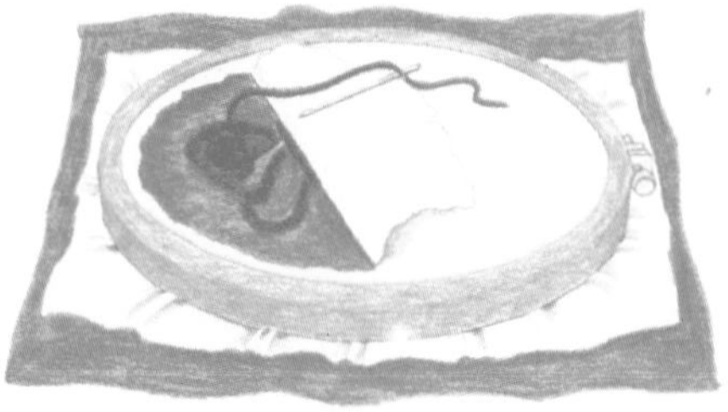

Protect partly-worked embroidery with tissue.

Working tip
The working thread can become tangled and twisted through the needle action. Let the needle drop and hang freely – the thread will untwist itself.

Rotating frames
These frames are composed of two top rollers or bars, with tapes attached, and two side sections. The rollers slot into the side pieces and are held securely by pegs or butterfly screw attachments. The tape length regulates the size of these frames and they vary from 12in (30cm) to 27in (68cm).

Framing up rotating frames
It is essential to allow at least an extra 1in (2.5cm) on all sides when buying or cutting the fabric. Baste a single hem on the top and bottom edges of the fabric. Oversew 1in (2.5cm)-wide strong tape down each side.

Working from the centre outwards, oversew the top and bottom hemmed edges to the roller tapes, using a strong thread and small stitches. Fit the rollers into the side pieces. Turn the rollers until the fabric is taut. Tighten the butterfly screws (or insert the pegs).

Thread a darning needle with strong thread and firmly lace the side edges to the side pieces. Oversew several times at each end to secure, wrapping the thread around the rollers before finishing. Tighten the lacings occasionally as you work. Slacken off the lacings between sessions.

Embroidery rings are useful when working small areas of embroidery, as a very tiny piece of fabric can be stitched onto a larger calico square before stretching it in the frame. Once the frame is set up, the calico behind the fabric area to be embroidered is cut away carefully, using fine, sharp scissors.

MAKING A START

If working cross stitch for the first time, choose a design that is not too complex. A small design with only a few colours is best. Work with good quality fabric and colour-fast threads.

It is advisable to work in a comfortable chair in a good light. This is particularly important when using higher count fabrics and several shades of colour. An overhead lamp is useful, particularly if it is fitted with a daylight simulation bulb. This will reduce eye strain and allow the correct colour matching of threads.

The best cross stitch embroidery has clearly defined stitches that cover the ground fabric well and look crisp and sharp. If the thread begins to fray while working, do not continue. Finish the thread off neatly and begin again.

To begin, cut a length of stranded yarn approximately 12in (30cm) and divide this into separate strands. Smooth each strand between finger and thumb before regrouping and threading the needle. Do not tie a knot in the end, as this will make the finished work lumpy. Pull the needle through from the front of the fabric, leaving a tail of about 2in (5cm) on the right side. Hold this tail securely while the first stitch is worked. When several stitches are completed, the tail can be threaded onto a needle and taken through to the back of the work and then woven through the back of worked stitches.

Working cross stitch

Cross stitch can be worked in rows from right to left or left to right, over any number of threads.

1 Bring the needle through at 1, insert diagonally at 2, bring out again above at 3. Insert again at 4 to make the next slanting stitch.

2 To complete the cross, work back in the opposite direction. From 3, go diagonally down to 4 and out at 5.

Working diagonally

1 Bring the needle through at 1, go diagonally down to 2, across to 3, insert at 4, come out at 5.

2 From 5, go diagonally down to 1 and out at 2.

3 Go diagonally up to 4 and out at 5. Continue.

Half cross stitches

Sometimes, single diagonal stitches are used on the edge of a design to achieve a rounded edge. Where this is required, diagonal lines, usually in the thread colour required, are printed across the pattern squares.

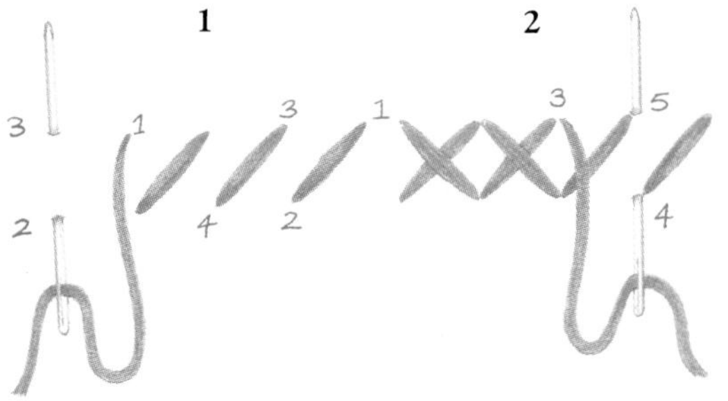

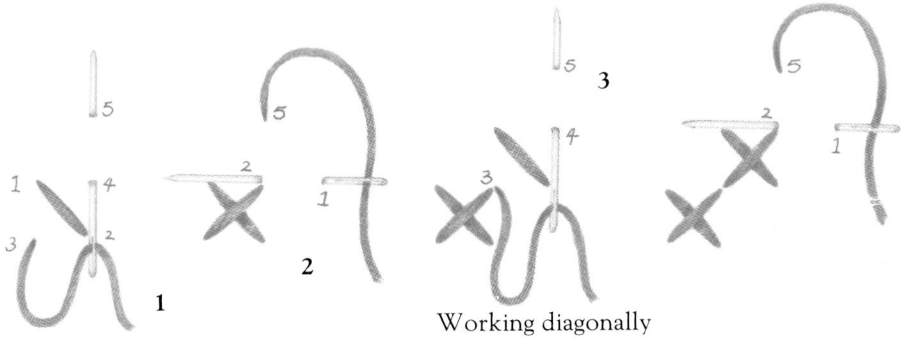

Working diagonally

When working surface embroidery, insert the needle on the right side a little way from the stitching, leaving a short tail. Work the embroidered area and finish off with a few small straight stitches. Draw the tail of thread through to the back of the work and darn in. Make sure that the finishing stitches are as flat as possible and not too close together. Snip away any excess threads.

Blocks of colour

To embroider a block of cross stitches in one colour, first work a row of half cross stitches, either horizontally or vertically. When the row is completed, work in the reverse direction completing the cross. Always work the top stitch of each cross stitch in the same direction on any piece of embroidery.

Scattered stitches

If stitches of one colour are scattered in small groups on the chart, do not fasten the thread off after each block, but take the thread through to the reverse of the fabric and secure, with the needle, away from the area being worked. Using another needle, continue to follow the chart until the first colour is required again. This method should only be used when working in a small area, otherwise the fabric may become puckered.

Large areas

When covering a large area, it is advisable to work in horizontal rows. The first diagonal of each stitch should be completed from right to left. Then, by working back along this row from left to right, the cross stitches will be formed. Continue to build the colour block by working each successive row in this way.

Working diagonally

To work diagonal lines of cross stitches work downwards or upwards and completing each complete cross before beginning the next.

Filling shapes

When filling a shape with colour, begin to embroider across its widest point. Try to bring the needle up through unworked fabric and down through holes where stitches have already been worked.

FOLLOWING A CHART

The cross stitch designs in this book are all worked from squared charts, in which each coloured square represents one cross stitch. A colour key is given with each chart for identifying the embroidery thread numbers.

The centre of the chart is indicated by the arrows at its edges. This coincides with the basting stitches worked to mark the middle of the fabric. The instructions given with each project tell you to begin working the embroidery from the middle of the design.

Check list

Here is your check list for working cross stitch projects.

Evenweave fabrics
Crewel needles
Sewing needles
Stranded embroidery cotton
Basting thread
Embroidery scissors
Dressmakers' scissors
Tape measure
Tambour hoop
Tissue paper
Embroidery pencils
Soft drawing pencils
Squared paper
Coloured pencils
Clear acetate grids
Pins
Crafts knife
Metal rule
Self-adhesive mounting boards
Adhesive tape, masking tape
Mounting cardboard
Button thread
Lacing needle

EMBROIDERY STITCHES

There are literally hundreds of embroidery stitches to choose from when you are decorating fabric. Here are some of the most popular.

Satin stitch

This is used for filling shapes. Work stitches evenly and laid so that they touch. Bring the needle through at A, insert it at B and bring it through again at C.

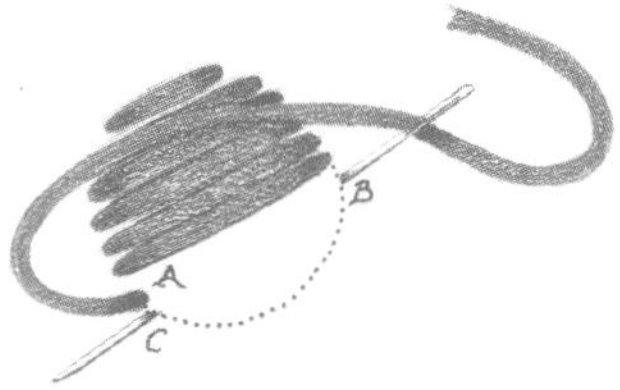

Straight stitch

Straight stitches are one of the simplest stitches and used individually or to build up designs, like this eight-point star. Bring the needle through at A, insert it at B and bring it through again at C.

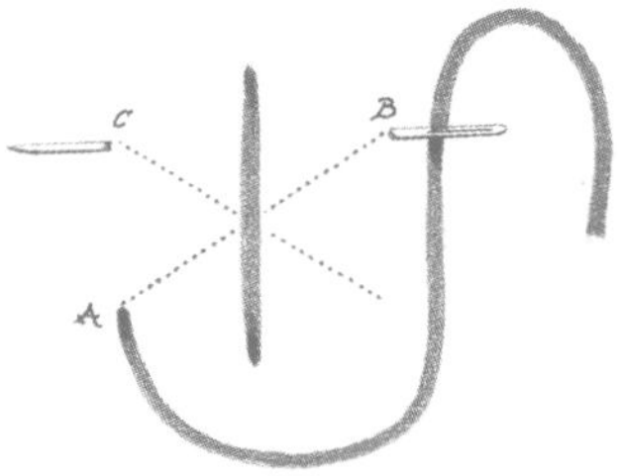

Back stitch

This stitch is used often in this book, usually to define a design line. It can be worked in straight lines or in curves. Bring the needle through at A, insert it at B and bring it out at C in front of A.

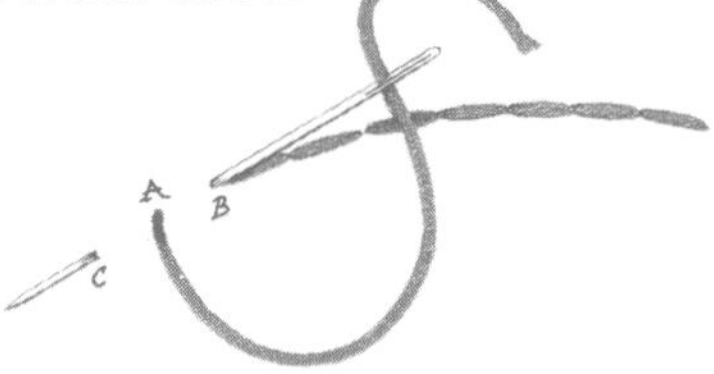

Stem stitch

As the name suggests this stitch is often used to indicate stems. Bring the needle through at A, the thread below the needle. Insert it at B and bring it through again at C.

Chain stitch

To work this stitch, bring the needle through at A and, with the thread below the needle, insert it beside A at B. The thread forms a loop. Bring the needle through at C, pull through gently, ready to start the next chain stitch.

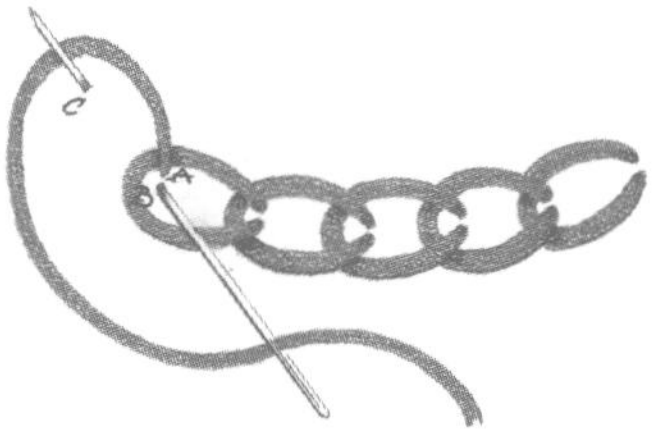

French knot

French knots are used single or massed in groups. Bring the needle through at A, wind the thread round the needle twice and then insert the point at B, close by A. Pull the thread through so that the knot tightens on the fabric surface.

Working tip
If a design is quite complex, gently pencil around the last completed stitches on the chart, before leaving the work for any length of time. The pencil marks can then be erased when the project is restarted.

FINISHING

Remove the embroidery from its frame. Snip and pull out any basting stitches. Snip off any stray threads from the back of the work wherever possible, but be careful not to cut too close to your stitching. Remove masking tape from the fabric edges if it has been used.

Press the work lightly on the wrong side, using a steam iron to smooth the fabric and 'emboss' the stitches.

If you are storing the finished embroidery, do not fold it. Store it flat in white, acid-free tissue paper.

FRAMING EMBROIDERY PICTURES

Consideration should be given to whether to frame the embroidery yourself or to take it to a professional. It should be delivered for framing ready mounted on cardboard. The type of frame should be carefully chosen and any framer familiar with framing textiles should be able to advise on this. Very fine work should be mounted behind glass to protect from dust and atmospheric pollution, but raised embroidery will be flattened and should be left unglazed. The most important consideration is that the glass should not touch the embroidery. A special spray can be used to give some protection to work framed without glass. Unglazed pictures can be given a slightly padded look, by inserting a layer of wadding between the embroidery and the cardboard mount.

It is possible to purchase non-reflective glass for framing, but this tends to alter the colours in the work very slightly, as it has a grey tinge.

MOUNTING EMBROIDERY

To prepare embroidery for framing, cut a sheet of white mounting card to the size of the frame rebate. Trim the embroidery fabric back to 2in (5cm) all round. Centre the embroidery on the card, right side up. Fold the top and bottom edges over to the back, then fold the side edges over. Push pins into the edges of the card to hold the fabric in place. Gently pull the fabric taut as you pin, so that the embroidery lies smooth and taut.

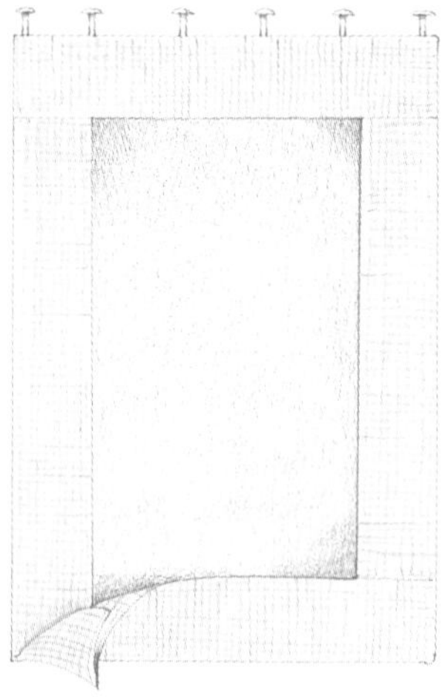

Fold the edges to the back and pin.

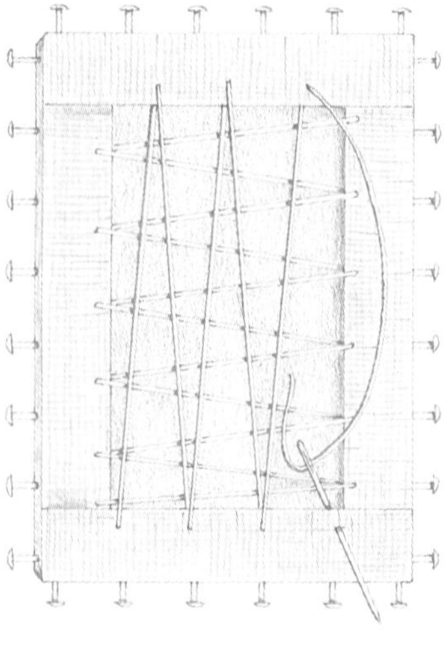

Lace from side to side then top to bottom.

Using a strong needle and a long length of thread, doubled and knotted, lace from side to side across the back of the work, starting in the middle of one side and pulling the fabric firmly with each stitch. Work the long sides first and then the short, keeping the embroidery centred on the cardboard. Continue until the embroidery is completely stretched and securely held. Secure the fabric edges to the cardboard with strips of masking tape.

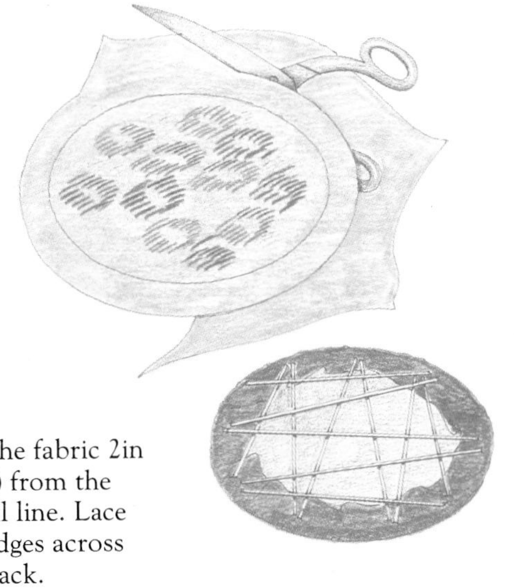

Cut the fabric 2in (5cm) from the pencil line. Lace the edges across the back.

Oval or round frames

When mounting an embroidery in an oval or round frame, do not remove the centre-marking basting stitches. Using a soft pencil, mark the mounting cardboard (usually supplied with the frame) horizontally and vertically through the centre point. Lay the embroidery face down on a clean surface and match up the marks on the cardboard with the basting stitches. When the mount is accurately placed, lightly pencil around it on the fabric. Now remove the basting threads and cut out the embroidery along the pencilled line. Back the embroidery with lightweight iron-on fusible interfacing and then fuse to the cardboard mount. The embroidery is then ready to frame.

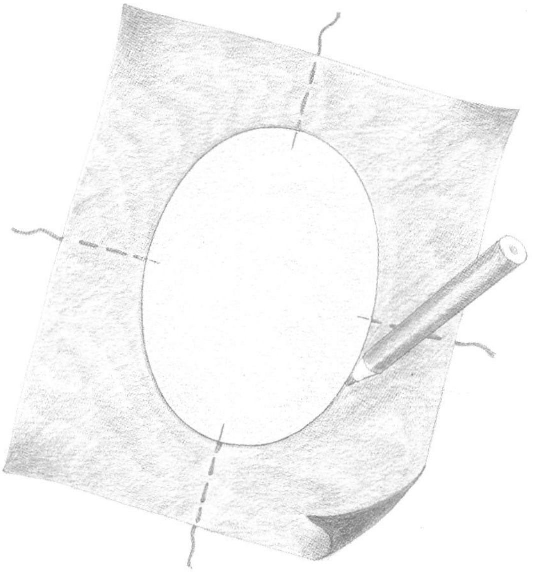

Line up the basting threads and pencil around.

An alternative method

Using the oval or round cardboard mount as a template, trace the shape on to the wrong side of the embroidery. Trim the excess fabric away, leaving a 2in (5cm) turning allowance from the pencil line. Run a gathering thread ½in (12mm) inside the pencilled line. Put the cardboard mount in position and draw up the fabric evenly, adjusting the gathers. Finish with a double back stitch to secure the gathers. To finish, either lace across the back of the work with strong thread or secure the fabric edges to the cardboard mount with masking tape.

Cross stitch is also a popular canvaswork stitch and is used for making needlework rugs, cushion covers, curtain tie-backs and other furnishings. Worked with tapestry wool on canvas with 12, 14 or 18 threads to 1in (2.5cm), the work can be fine and detailed. On coarser canvas, 10, 8 and 6 threads to 1in (2.5cm), doubled tapestry wool or rug wool is used. Most cross stitch motifs can be interpreted from evenweave fabric to canvas.

GREETING CARDS

Small cross stitch motifs are ideal for personalized greeting cards. A small design can usually be worked in just a few hours and, with a little thought, provides a distinctive message that will be treasured by the recipient. Ready-made greeting card blanks with cut-out windows can be purchased in a wide range of sizes and styles. Cards can also be made at home, using thin card or construction paper. Draw the shape of the envelope about ⅛in (3mm) smaller round. Draw shapes to the right and left. Draw and cut a window in the middle shape. Score and fold along the division lines.

Mounting the embroidery

When the embroidery is finished, press it lightly on the wrong side with a warm iron. Trim the fabric so that the motif is displayed centrally in the window.

Spread clear, all-purpose glue thinly around the edges of the window, on the inside of the card. Press the embroidery on to the glue, checking to see that its position is correct before finally pressing down. Fold and stick the left-hand panel over the embroidery. Leave to dry.

Glossary of embroidery terms

Aida a type of evenweave fabric.
Aida band a narrow band of evenweave fabric.
Binca a coarser weave evenweave fabric.
Coton à broder a fine cotton embroidery thread with a high twist.
Count the number of holes per inch (2.5cm) on an evenweave fabric.
Evenweave fabric a fabric woven with warp and weft threads of the same thickness and with the same number of threads in 1in (2.5cm).
Oversewing (overcasting) a stitch used to bind or hem an edge.
Perlé cotton (pearl cotton) a twisted embroidery thread with a high sheen.
Stranded cotton (embroidery floss) a loosely twisted, six-stranded embroidery cotton, which can be separated into individual threads for fine work.
Basting (tacking) large, temporary running stitches.
Wadding (batting) a padding fabric made from either cotton or synthetic material.

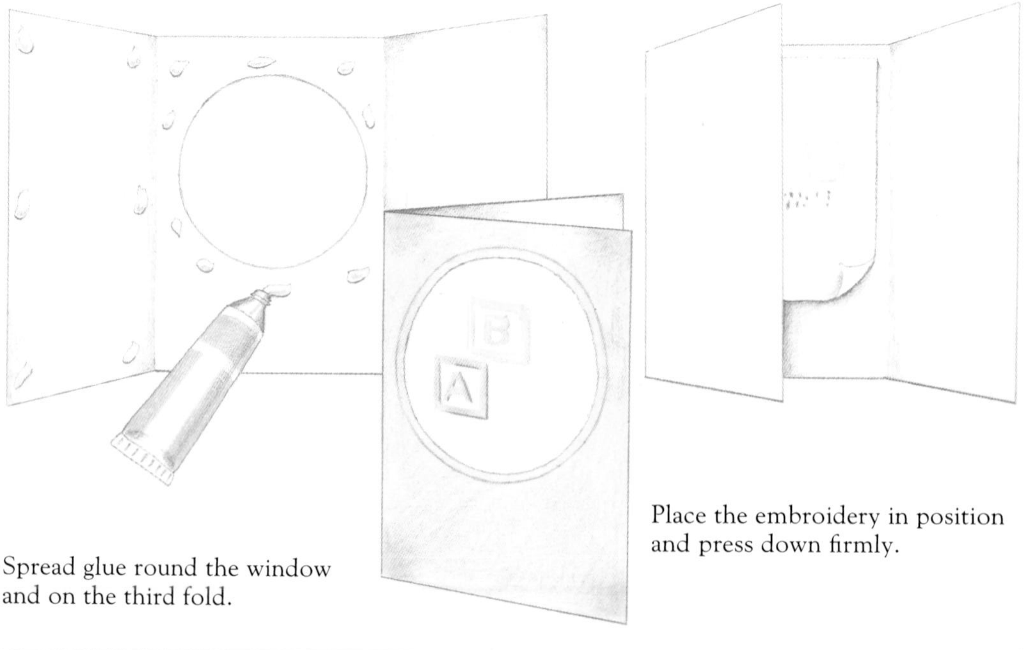

Spread glue round the window and on the third fold.

Place the embroidery in position and press down firmly.

EMBROIDERY STITCHES

Buttonhole or blanket stitch

Working from left to right, bring the needle through from the back of the work on the line where the loop is to be formed. Insert the needle a stitch length away and then back into the line. Do not pull the needle completely through the fabric. Place the thread around the needle tip and pull the needle through, to produce the loop.

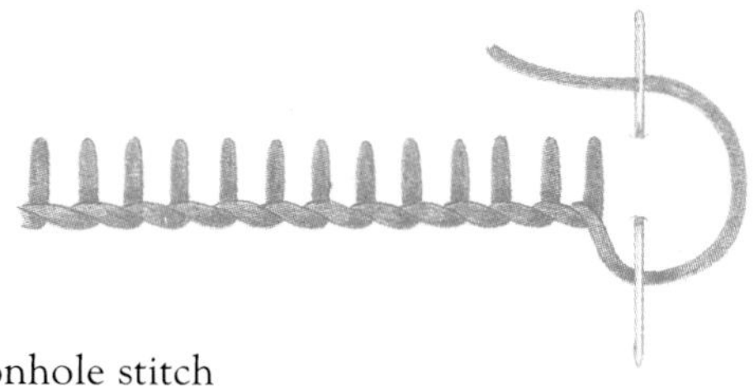

Buttonhole stitch

Fly stitch

Bring the needle through from the back of the work and insert again a stitch length away. Pull the thread through leaving a loop between the two points. Bring needle through mid-way between the points but a little lower. Loop the first stitch over the needle, pull down gently and secure with a tiny straight stitch, forming a 'V' shape.

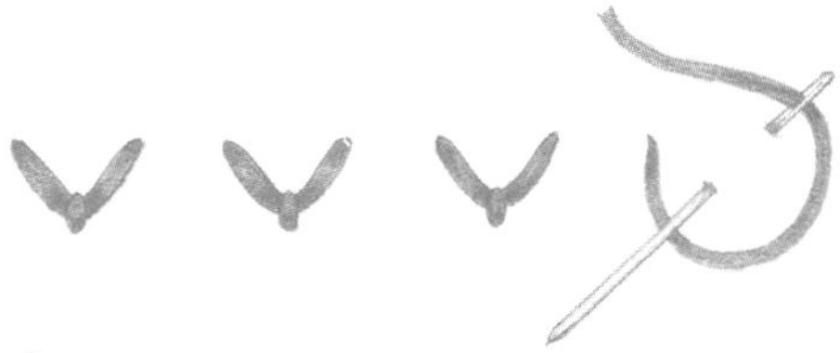

Fly stitch

Long and short (or encroaching satin) stitch

Work the outline first, using even long and short satin stitches. On curves and at the edge of the shape it may be necessary to alter the stitch length. When the outline is completed, work alternate rows of long and short stitches to build up the design.

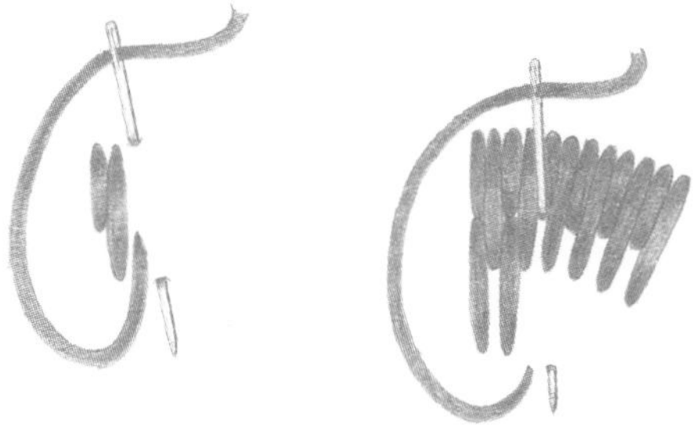

Long and short stitch

Double cross stitch

This is worked as a single cross stitch, which is then covered with a vertical and a horizontal stitch. Sometimes a small straight central binding stitch is made to hold the threads in position. A double cross stitch worked with a central tiny cross is sometimes called star stitch.

Double cross stitch

Long-legged cross stitch

The long arm of the stitch should be twice the length of the short arm. The first longer diagonal of the cross is made upwards from left to right, before completing the second arm of the cross. Unlike cross stitch it is impossible to work the first half of this stitch along the row first. Each cross should be completed before the next is started.

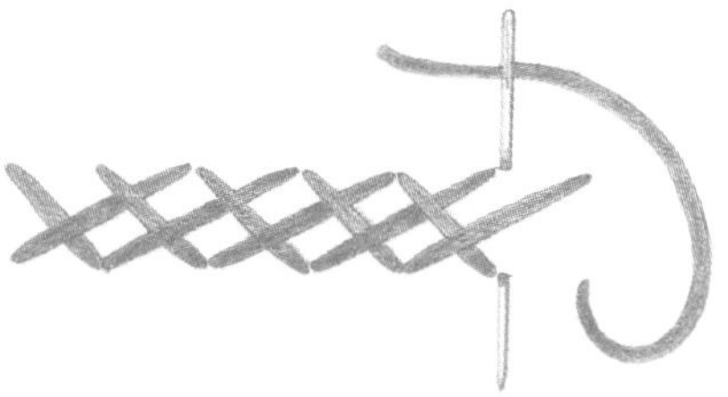

Long-legged cross stitch

MAKING CHARTS

Once you have learned how to work from a chart of coloured squares or symbols, you are ready to begin making your own charts. Do not be discouraged if you want a special design for a picture or sampler. Once your friends and family know that you do cross stitch they will be asking you for all kinds of designs – racing cars, aeroplanes, golfers, tennis players, footballers, swimmers – as well as certain flowers and shrubs and, sometimes, pictures of their houses. None of this should deter you. Making cross stitch charts is simplicity itself.

You need a picture or a design to work from. Pin this to a board and place a sheet of squared tracing paper on top. Usually, this has a scale of 10 squares to 1in (2.5cm). Draw round the main outlines of the picture. Now, using coloured pencils, colour in the squares of the paper, following the design lines underneath. Sometimes, a line will go through a square. This does not matter as long as you keep to the general design outline.

When you have finished, you will have produced a simplified version of the design, the shape converted into squares of colour. Draw a series of coloured-in squares down the side of your graph pattern, one square for each colour.

Now comes the creative part; go through your stock of stranded embroidery cottons and allocate a colour to each coloured square. Snip a small piece off and tape it alongside the square so that you can quickly identify the thread you are going to use.

The next stage is a little more difficult. You have to decide what size you want your motif to be. Each coloured square is going to be a cross stitch. Supposing your motif is 56 squares deep and 84 squares wide. On fabric with a count of 14 threads to 1in (2.5cm), your motif is going to be about 4 × 5in (10 × 12.5cm). Using a coarser fabric, with a count of 10 threads to 1in (2.5cm), the motif enlarges to just over 5½in (13cm) deep by nearly 8½in (21cm) wide. Thus, you can work your motif to any size you like, just by choosing the right count of fabric.

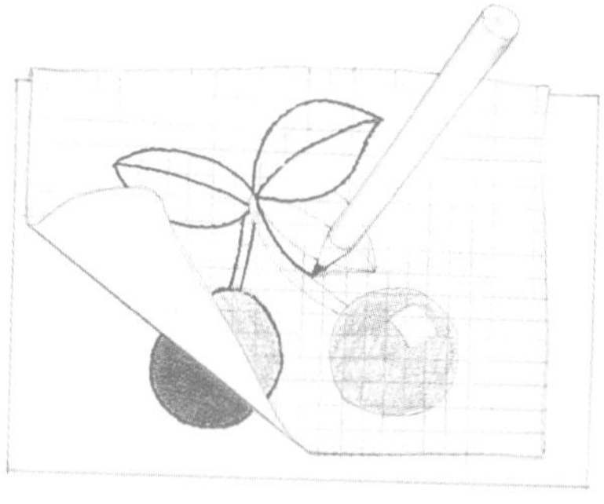

Trace the motif on to graph paper.

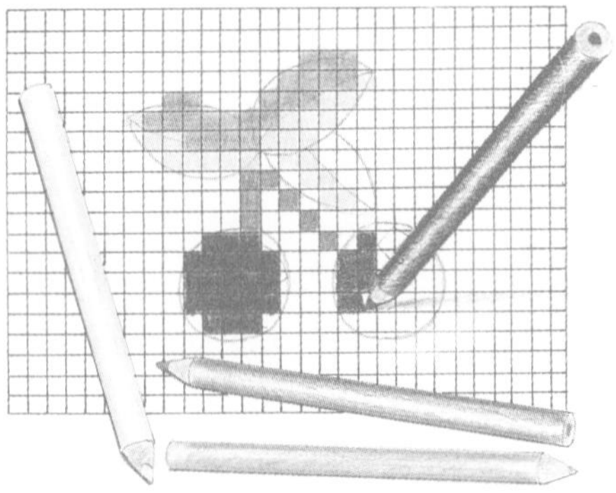

Colour in the squares, following the lines.

Symbol charts

Some cross stitch charts are given with symbols instead of coloured squares. You can make this type of chart, using clear sheets of acetate printed with squares. These are obtainable from some draughtsmen's suppliers and art materials shops.

Place the grid over the picture or drawing. Copy each square of the grid on to squared paper, using a symbol for each colour. Here are some symbols you might use, to represent colours.

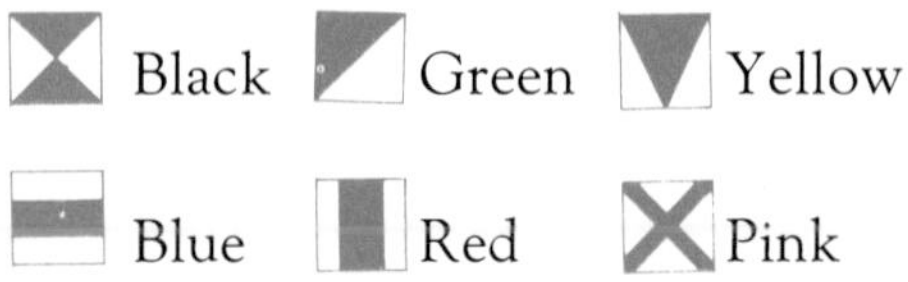

ASSISI EMBROIDERY

In this variation of cross stitch, a simple motif is left unworked while the surrounding fabric is covered with cross stitches. It is said to have been evolved in the 14th century by the nuns of the convent of St Francis of Assisi in central Italy. You may like to try this variation for yourself, working on a coloured Binca fabric using pearl cotton. A simple motif is given and, by working this in different colour combinations, a set of pretty Christmas tree decorations could be made.

Cut Binca fabric into 3in (7.5cm) squares, two for each decoration.

Work the design on one square in white or black thread on coloured fabric or in coloured thread on white fabric. Each square represents one cross stitch.

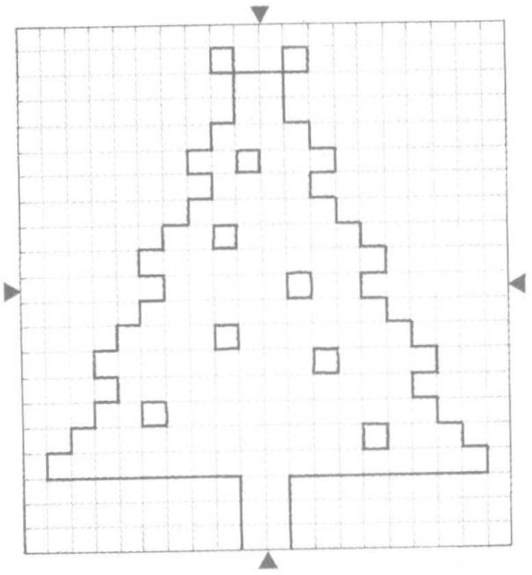

Join up the marks to make a squared chart. Each square is one cross stitch.

When the motif is completed, you can outline it with back stitches in a contrasting colour or metallic thread.

Make up the ornaments by sewing the embroidered square to an unworked square, right sides facing, leaving a gap in the seam. Turn right side out and stuff with toy filling.

Close the seam. Sew gold or silver lace round the ornament. Add glittering beads if you like. Sew a bow of narrow ribbon to one corner for a hanger.

Trim with lace and sew a ribbon bow to a corner for a hanger.

Assisi needlecase

Work yourself a needlecase with an initial in Assisi work. Cut Binca or Aida fabric to a rectangle and work from one of the letter charts given in this book, positioning the initial on the right hand end of the rectangle. Add a decorative border.

Back the embroidery with soft fabric and sew together, right sides facing, leaving a gap for turning. Turn right side out, press and close the seam with slip stitches. Cut two pieces of felt for the needlecase pages, fold and sew inside. Make a loop and button fastening on the edges of the needlecase.

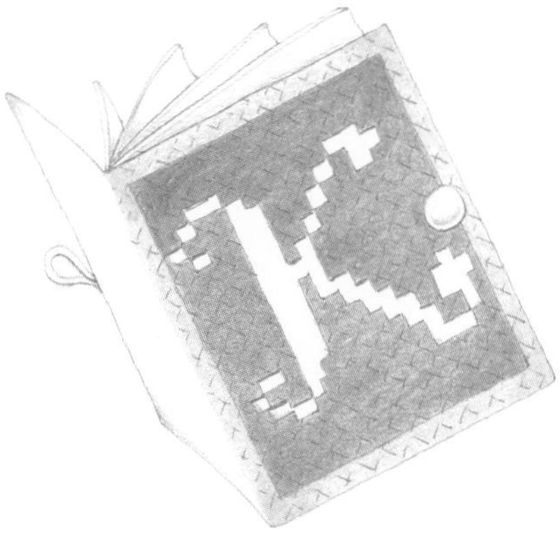

Work an initial on the cover.

NEEDLEPOINT

Needlepoint is another type of counted thread embroidery and most cross stitch designs can be interpreted on to canvas, using cross stitch or half cross stitch. Working on canvas is a way of enlarging a design.

If you are planning to enlarge one of the pictures in this book, for a cushion or a rug, it is good idea to copy the design on to squared paper first, deciding how many squares you will cover with each cross stitch. Not all designs enlarge successfully and, by working in this way, you might save yourself hours of wasted work and unpicking later.

Similarly, many of the smaller pictures can be interpreted on to very fine mesh canvas. For this type of embroidery, choose stranded crewel wool, separating and using single strands in the needle. Small, petit point motifs look exquisite on box tops, book covers, needle cases, pincushions and bookmarks.

BLOCKING CANVAS EMBROIDERY

Embroidery on fabric rarely distorts in working, especially if it has been worked in a frame. Usually all that is needed is a light pressing on the wrong side to return the work to shape. Canvas embroidery, on the other hand, often distorts and requires special treatment to return it to shape.

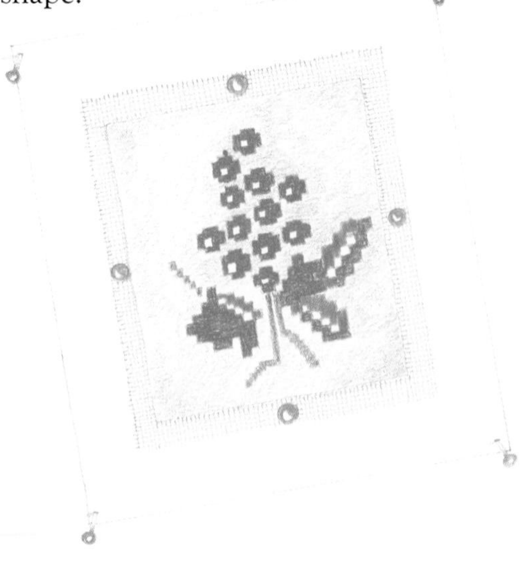

Pull and pin the dampened canvas into shape.

Trim the excess canvas from the embroidery leaving about 2in (5cm) all round. Pin a large sheet of white blotting paper to a board and draw out the finished size and shape of the worked canvas after trimming.

Take special care to get the sides straight and the corners square.

Dampen the finished embroidery on the wrong side (a laundry water spray is a good way to do this). Place the dampened embroidery face up on the blotting paper and gently pull on each of the sides in turn until the embroidery is square and fits the drawn shape exactly. If the canvas is badly distorted, you may have to pull quite firmly on opposite corners to remove the diagonal bias.

Using rustproof drawing pins, insert pins into the canvas in the middle of opposite sides. Working towards the corners, continue pinning until the canvas is stretched and taut and square on the board.

Leave the work to dry overnight.

Half cross stitch This stitch is exactly what it says – half a cross stitch and is the most used stitch in embroidery on canvas. You can use it instead of cross stitch to interpret cross stitch charts.

Work from right to left or left to right, but it is important that all the stitches slope in the same direction. Reverse the direction of working on the subsequent row.

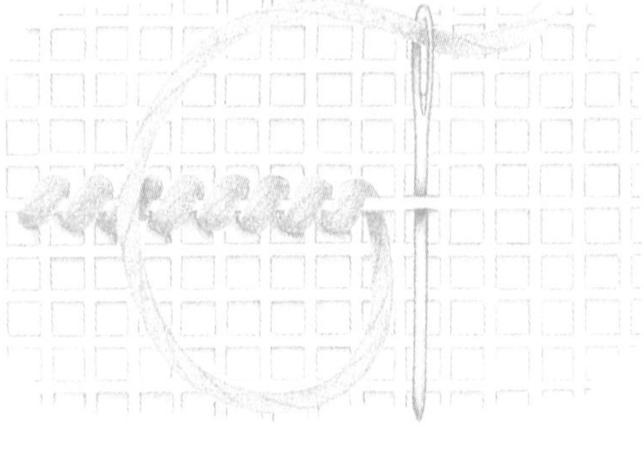

SEWING STITCHES

Sometimes you will need hand sewing stitches to make up pieces of embroidery. Here are the main stitches you will need.

When making up embroidered items, use all-purpose thread in a matching colour so that stitches do not show. A single strand of embroidery cotton can also be used, for oversewing or hemming.

Running stitch

This stitch is used to join pieces of fabric together. It is also used for gathering fabric. Begin with a small back stitch, pick up several small, even stitches on the needle and pull the needle through. If you are working a seam, work a back stitch occasionally to strengthen the seam.

Basting

This is used to hold two pieces of fabric together temporarily. Work it in the same way as running stitch but make the stitches $\frac{1}{4}$in (6mm) long with a $\frac{1}{4}$in (6mm) space between each stitch.

Oversewing

This simple stitch is useful for joining the edges of fabric together and can also be used to neaten seam edges to prevent them from fraying. Working from left to right, bring the needle through at A and insert the needle from the back of the work at B, bringing it through to the front at C, ready to start the next stitch. Keep stitches small and evenly spaced.

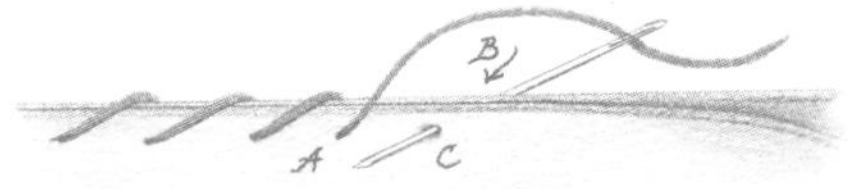

Gathering

Running stitch is used for gathering fabric. Work as running stitch and leave a length of thread at the end of the row for pulling up the gathers.

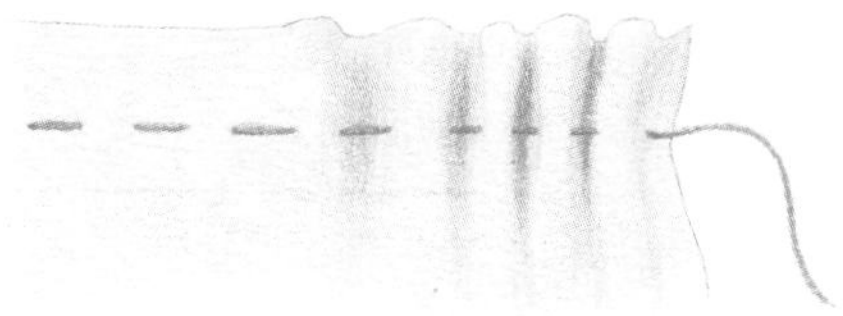

Hemming

Hemming is worked from right to left, taking up 2 threads of the fabric at the fold of the hem. Insert the needle obliquely on the edge of the fold.

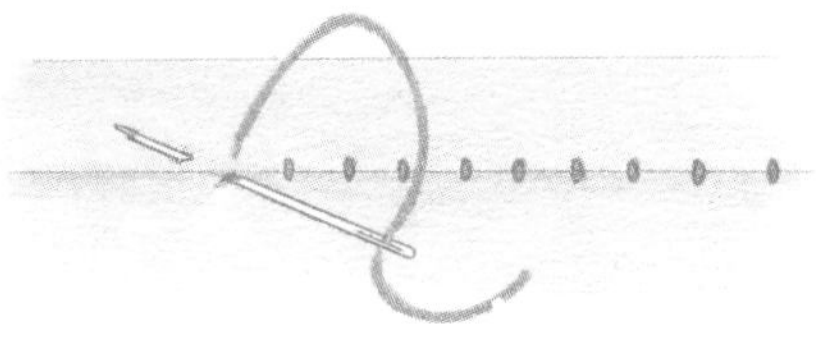

Slip stitch

Work from right to left and bring the needle up through the folded edge of the fabric. Pick up a thread or two on the opposite fabric then slip the needle through the folded edge for about $\frac{1}{8}$in (3mm). Bring the needle through and pull gently.

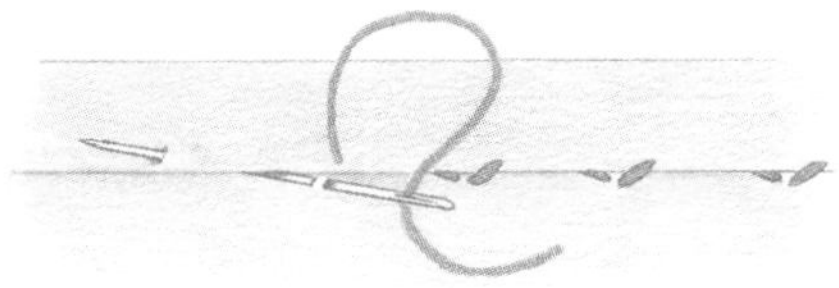

Useful Addresses

DMC Colbert
DMC Tapestry Wool
DMC Stranded
embroidery cottons
(embroidery floss)
DMC Pearl Cotton

United Kingdom
DMC Creative World
Pulman Road
Wigstone
Leicester
LE8 2DY

USA
The DMC Corporation
Port Kearny
Building 10
South Kearny
New Jersey 07032

Australia
DMC
51–66 Carrington Road
Marrickville
New South Wales 2204

Canada
Domcord Belding
660 Denison Street
Markham
Ontario L3R 1C1

South Africa
SATC
43 Somerset Road
P O Box 3868
Capetown 8000

New Zealand
Warnaar Trading Co Ltd
376 Ferry Road
P O Box 19567
Christchurch

Benelux
DMC
7/9 Rue du Pavillion
B-1210 Brussels
Belgium

Anchor Tapisserie Wool
Anchor Stranded
embroidery cottons
(embroidery floss)
Anchor Pearl Cotton

United Kingdom
Coats Patons Leisure
Crafts Group
McMullen Road
Darlington DL1 1YQ
Co. Durham

USA
Susan Bates Inc
30 Patewood Drive
Suite 351
Greenville
SC 29615

Australia
Coats-Patons Crafts
89–91 Peters Ave
Mulgrave
Victoria 3170

Canada
Coats Patons Canada
1001 Roselawn Avenue
Toronto
Ontario M6B 1B8

New Zealand
Coats Patons (NZ) Ltd
263 Ti Rakau Drive
Pakuranga
Auckland

Benelux
Coats FFR
9320 Erembodegem-Aalst
Belgium

Threads and yarns conversion chart

DMC	ANCHOR	DMC	ANCHOR	DMC	ANCHOR
48	1202	677	886	920	339
57	1203	680	901	921	338
92	1215	699	923	927	848
94	1216	700	230	931	921
104	1217	701	227	943	188
116	1207	702	244	948	933
208	111	718	89	950	4146
209	110	725	891	954	226
210	108	726	297	956	54
211	342	727	293	957	50
218	986	729	890	958	188
230	910	739	276	973	291
275	3078	740	316	975	352
310	403	742	303	993	204
320	215	743	305	996	443
321	47	744	295	3051	862
327	101	745	301	3072	397
341	120	746	02	3078	300
346	437	760	36	3325	130
347	13	761	24	3346	267
352	09	772	259	3347	266
353	06	774	304	3348	265
369	240	776	25	3607	87
400	351	778	968	3608	86
413	236	782	309	3609	96
414	399	783	308	3675	170
433	371	791	123	3688	895
434	370	792	837	3706	40
435	369	793	121	3713	73
436	363	797	139	3746	119
444	291	798	132	3753	128
445	289	799	130	3755	130
471	265	800	129	3771	382
472	842	801	359	3772	679
498	43	809	130	3774	376
501	217	813	161	3776	339
504	206	815	44	3793	76
552	100	825	147	7104	8436
553	98	827	160	7106	8214
561	210	832	907	7153	8488
562	216	838	381	7385	9006
563	208	839	380	7472	8132
564	203	890	683	7742	8136
603	76	892	35	7540	9006
604	51	894	26	7606	8196
606	46	905	257	7725	8132
648	399	906	256	7740	8166
666	9046	910	230	7942	8168

Acknowledgements

In the chapters Cross Stitch for the Home, Gift Ideas and Special Occasions, all designs are by Gail Lawther except the following: Welcome to the world cards (pages 30–33) Marianne Woodhouse. Cat card and picture (pages 64–67) Nicki Simmonds. Christmas cloth (pages 82–83) and Christmas cards (pages 86–89) Mary Hickmott Designs. Embroidery by Elizabeth Lance, Christopher Lawther, Gail Lawther, Nicky Simmons, Sue Slide, Ally Smith and Marianne Woodhouse. In Cross Stitch Pictures, all designs by Barbara Deer except: Blue Vase (pages 106–109) Julia Dixon; Tabby Cat (pages 126–127) Jenny Thorpe; An Abundance of Fruits (pages 130–131) Judi Lang; Home, Sweet Home (pages 164–165) Charlotte Dixon.